# Integrating Financial Markets in the European Union

# Integrating Financial Markets in the European Union

**Jan Lemmen**
*Financial Markets Group*
*London School of Economics, UK*

**Edward Elgar**
Cheltenham, UK • Northampton, MA, USA

Published by
Edward Elgar Publishing Limited
Glensanda House
Montpellier Parade
Cheltenham
Glos GL50 1UA
UK

Edward Elgar Publishing, Inc.
6 Market Street
Northampton
Massachusetts 01060
USA


A catalogue record for this book
is available from the British Library


**Library of Congress Cataloguing in Publication Data**

Lemmen, Jan, 1966–

JK      Integrating financial markets in the European Union / Jan Lemmen.
        Includes bibliographical references and indexes.
            1. Capital market—European Union countries.  2. Capital
        movements—European Union countries.  3. Finance—European Union
        countries.  I. Title.
        HG5422.L46   1998
        337.1'42—dc21                                               98–23715
                                                                        CIP


ISBN 1 85898 730 X


Printed and bound in Great Britain by
Biddles Ltd, Guildford and King's Lynn

# Contents

# List of Tables

# List of Figures

ix

# Acknowledgements

This book is the result of four years of academic research at the Department of Economics and the CentER for Economic Research of Tilburg University. I would like to take this opportunity to thank Sylvester Eijffinger for his friendship and unconditional support in supervising my thesis. From the very beginning he had faith in me. I was fortunate to work with him and his encouragement and enthusiasm are very much appreciated. Sylvester also co-authored the papers underlying Chapters 2–6. I also enjoyed working with Harry Huizinga, co-author of Chapter 6 and member of my PhD committee. Furthermore, I would like to thank the other members of the PhD committee: Jakob de Haan, Theo van de Klundert, Kees Koedijk and Theo Nijman.

Valuable comments were made by participants at the 1994 *Confederation of European Economic Associations Conference*, the 1995 *First International Stockholm Seminar on Risk Behaviour and Risk Management*, the 1996 *NBER Transatlantic Public Economics Seminar on Interjurisdictional Differences in Tax and Expenditure Policies*, and the 1994, 1995, 1996 and 1997 *Annual Congress of the European Economic Association*.

I am grateful to Eelke de Jong and Elmer Sterken for the evaluation of my PhD thesis proposal within the framework of the Netherlands Network of Economics (NAKE). In addition, I have benefited greatly from helpful comments on individual chapters by Julian Alworth, Jakob de Haan, Norbert Janssen, Alex Lammertsma, Theo Nijman, Frans de Roon and Harald Uhlig. I also benefited from comments made during the informal macro-seminars at Tilburg University and the Finance and International Financial Markets seminar at the Tinbergen Institute, Rotterdam. Needless to say all remaining errors are mine.

I thank my colleagues Bas van Aarle, Geert Almekinders, Erik Canton, Rudy Douven, Henri de Groot, Marco Hoeberichts, Zafar Iqbal, Frank de Jong, Francis Kumah, Theo Leers, Theodore Palivos, Eric Schaling, Willem Verhagen and all others, not least for their pleasant company. I thank the secretaries of the Department of Economics and the CentER for Economic Research for their assistance. I acknowledge the Financial Markets Group of the London School of Economics for creating the inspiring mix of monetary economics and finance which helped me considerably in the final preparations of this book. Finally, I thank my parents, brother, sister and family.

Several chapters in this book have already been published. The article in

*De Economist* laid the foundation of my book and has been used in various chapters. Chapter 2 is adapted from articles in the *Swiss Journal of Economics and Statistics* and *Kredit und Kapital*. Chapter 3 is an extended and updated version of the article in *Open Economies Review*. Chapter 4 appeared in the form of *CentER Discussion Paper* No. 9532. A shortened version of Chapter 5 is published in *Weltwirtschaftliches Archiv*. Chapter 6 is published in the *Journal of Public Economics*.


London, July 1998                                      Jan Lemmen

# 1. Integrating Financial Markets in the European Union: An Introduction

## 1.1  Introduction

The degree of financial integration achieved by capital flows remains a matter of debate. Despite rapid increases in the size of capital *flows*, the *stock* of cross-border holdings is still a small fraction of total financial assets and liabilities outstanding.[1] This is the conclusion of two recent studies of international diversification by French and Poterba (1991) and Tesar and Werner (1992).[2] Investors in each country have a 'home bias', which in most cases limits investment in foreign markets to less than 10 per cent of their financial assets. Despite the growth in cross-border capital flows, international diversification appears to be limited. Individual portfolios are more specialized in domestic securities. This is true even for institutional investors with long-term horizons such as life insurance companies and pension funds. Furthermore, when financial markets are deregulated and when restrictions on cross-border capital flows are liberalized, returns in domestic and foreign markets should be equalized. Yet, real returns on bonds and equities are hardly equalized. Also, studies of Feldstein and Horioka (1980) analyzing savings-investment correlations and Obstfeld (1986) analyzing consumption correlations find financial integration to be low. These stylized facts underline the importance of our study. So, it remains to be seen how well integrated financial markets have become.

Tables 1.1 and 1.2 provide own estimates of the growing internationalization of financial markets in the European Union (EU hereafter).[3] The *internationalization ratio* measured in terms of *flows* is the ratio of flows of external assets or liabilities to total flows of financial assets or liabilities. The *internationalization ratio* measured in terms of *stocks* is the ratio of outstanding external assets or liabilities to total outstanding financial assets or liabilities. Data on outstanding stocks and flows of assets or liabilities are limited. Therefore, we are not able to provide internationalization ratios for all EU countries. Table 1.1 shows that the external sector – when measured in terms of flows – has become increasingly important for the financing of the economy.[4] In the 1980s, capital *flows* have increased tremendously due to financial deregulation, modern communication technology and innovation of financial instruments. The degree

*Table 1.1 Financial internationalization ratio (flows, period averages in percentages)*

| Country | 1974–1978 | | 1979–1983 | | 1984–1988 | | 1989–1993 | |
|---|---|---|---|---|---|---|---|---|
| | Foreign | Domestic | Foreign | Domestic | Foreign | Domestic | Foreign | Domestic |
| Belgium | 15.5 | 15.4 | 25.1 | 19.6 | 27.6 | 28.8 | – | – |
| Finland | 12.0 | 6.0 | 12.5 | 8.6 | 14.7 | 11.2 | 24.5 | 11.5 |
| France | – | – | 9.6 | 8.2 | 8.8 | 9.1 | 16.9 | 16.5 |
| Germany | 8.4 | 12.8 | 9.7 | 8.5 | 11.8 | 23.7 | 16.9 | 20.1 |
| Italy | – | – | – | – | 7.0 | 5.3 | 15.9 | 13.3 |
| The Netherlands | – | – | – | – | 14.6 | 23.2 | 18.5 | 25.7 |
| Spain | 8.1 | 3.1 | 7.5 | 3.5 | 5.4 | 7.2 | 17.5 | 12.5 |
| Sweden | – | – | – | – | 9.0 | 6.9 | 17.1 | 21.1 |
| United Kingdom | – | – | – | – | 21.2 | 20.6 | 27.3 | 21.7 |

*Notes:*

Foreign   = foreign claims on domestic sectors.
Domestic = domestic claims on the rest of the world.
–            = no data available.

Data for other EU countries were not available.

*Source:* OECD, *Financial Accounts of OECD Countries*, Part II of OECD, Financial Statistics Monthly, Data Diskettes, Paris.

of internationalization is greatest in Belgium and the United Kingdom among the EU countries depicted. Cross-border acquisition of Belgium and British financial assets by nonresidents are 27.6 (1984–1988) and 27.3 (1989–1993) per cent of total financial flows, respectively. Cross-border acquisition of Belgium and Dutch residents of foreign liabilities are 28.8 (1984–1988) and 25.7 (1989–1993) per cent of total financial flows. The degree of internationalization is smallest in Italy and Spain.

As seen in Table 1.1, the internationalization of financial markets has been rapid – when measured in terms of flows. But Table 1.2 shows that the growth of the external sector – when measured in terms of stocks – is rather modest. Foreign asset and liability positions are about 10 per cent of total assets and liabilities.[5]

This book concentrates primarily on the progress made in integrating the financial markets in the EU. There are several reasons for employing European financial markets as the principal object of study. First, and most importantly, the EU financial markets are in the process of institutional integration. The institutional structures of financial markets in the EU have evolved around important directives of the European Commission. Most legal barriers to cross-

*Table 1.2 Financial internationalization ratio (stocks, period averages in percentages)*

| Finland | | 1974–1978 | 1979–1983 | 1984–1988 | 1989–1993 |
|---|---|---|---|---|---|
| Domestic financial sector | A | – | 65.1 | 58.2 | 57.3 |
| | L | – | 58.2 | 42.0 | 39.0 |
| Domestic non-financial sector | A | – | 22.1 | 29.1 | 31.8 |
| | L | – | 16.6 | 40.5 | 43.6 |
| Foreign sector | A | – | 12.8 | 12.7 | 10.9 |
| | L | – | 25.2 | 17.5 | 17.4 |
| France | | 1974–1978 | 1979–1983 | 1984–1988 | 1989–1993 |
| Domestic financial sector | A | – | 44.3 | 42.7 | 38.4 |
| | L | – | 40.7 | 43.5 | 40.1 |
| Domestic non-financial sector | A | – | 44.9 | 47.4 | 51.9 |
| | L | – | 41.6 | 46.8 | 49.5 |
| Foreign sector | A | – | 10.8 | 9.8 | 9.7 |
| | L | – | 17.7 | 9.7 | 10.4 |
| Germany | | 1974–1978 | 1979–1983 | 1984–1988 | 1989–1993 |
| Domestic financial sector | A | 43.9 | 45.3 | 44.3 | 44.7 |
| | L | 40.7 | 42.3 | 48.8 | 50.8 |
| Domestic non-financial sector | A | 47.0 | 45.3 | 44.6 | 42.3 |
| | L | 53.1 | 50.0 | 41.3 | 37.9 |
| Foreign sector | A | 9.1 | 9.3 | 11.1 | 13.1 |
| | L | 6.2 | 7.7 | 9.9 | 11.2 |
| Italy | | 1974–1978 | 1979–1983 | 1984–1988 | 1989–1993 |
| Domestic financial sector | A | – | 43.0 | 37.0 | 36.7 |
| | L | – | 40.6 | 34.8 | 35.7 |
| Domestic non-financial sector | A | – | 48.2 | 55.6 | 55.1 |
| | L | – | 51.7 | 57.6 | 54.7 |
| Foreign sector | A | – | 8.8 | 7.4 | 8.2 |
| | L | – | 7.7 | 7.6 | 9.6 |
| Spain | | 1974–1978 | 1979–1983 | 1984–1988 | 1989–1993 |
| Domestic financial sector | A | 52.9 | 44.9 | 44.9 | 45.8 |
| | L | 49.4 | 33.6 | 42.6 | 42.3 |
| Domestic non-financial sector | A | 42.6 | 49.5 | 49.3 | 47.1 |
| | L | 42.9 | 59.8 | 50.1 | 47.9 |
| Foreign sector | A | 4.6 | 5.6 | 5.8 | 7.2 |
| | L | 7.6 | 6.6 | 7.4 | 9.7 |
| Sweden | | 1974–1978 | 1979–1983 | 1984–1988 | 1989–1993 |
| Domestic financial sector | A | – | 43.1 | 44.9 | 47.2 |
| | L | – | 34.7 | 36.3 | 37.0 |
| Domestic non-financial sector | A | – | 35.5 | 37.1 | 35.4 |
| | L | – | 56.1 | 53.9 | 50.1 |
| Foreign sector | A | – | 5.3 | 5.3 | 6.2 |
| | L | – | 9.2 | 9.8 | 12.8 |

*Notes:*

A = assets
L = liabilities
– = no data available

Figures may not add up to 100 per cent due to rounding. Data for other EU countries were not available.

*Source*: OECD, *Financial Accounts of OECD Countries*, Part II of OECD, Financial Statistics Monthly, Data Diskettes, Paris.

border capital flows either have been removed or are scheduled to be removed. The process of legal integration is nearly complete. Furthermore, the EU has adopted a stronger form of harmonization for its financial services, a policy of mutual recognition whereby member states within the EU have agreed to allow financial intermediaries from other states to operate under home country rules and supervision. Second, the EU financial markets are fairly well established compared to the financial markets of developing countries. Third, whether the EU financial markets are integrated is still unclear from an empirical standpoint, despite the institutional process being almost complete. As will be demonstrated in subsequent chapters, integration across national borders is still uneven. Fourth, data on many European financial markets are readily available. Finally, we hold that integration attempts across the world are more of a geographical nature. This book restricts the set of countries to those belonging to the EU. This decision acknowledges the recent intuition provided by Krugman (1991) that international trade and geography are deeply related. Although the liberalization of capital movements in industrial countries has been the goal of the OECD's Code of Liberalization of Capital Movements since 1961, the most important among the geographical integration attempts have been the EU, the European Free Trade Association (EFTA) and the North American Free Trade Association (NAFTA). Alongside the free movement of goods, persons and services, the free movement of capital within the European Community (EC) is one of the basic freedoms laid down by the Treaty establishing the European Economic Community (EEC). Hence, the EU financial markets can serve as an excellent sample to test for financial integration.

We shall briefly highlight the important steps taken to liberalize capital flows in the EU. There was relatively little capital mobility between the EC member states at the start of the 1980s compared to the considerable progress which had been made on intra-EC trade and the spectacular development of international financial relations through the Euro markets. Many European countries continued to maintain controls on capital flows. In fact, some European countries even strengthened their controls.[6] It was only in the middle of the 1980s that the liberalization of European capital movements became a major goal. The 1985 White Paper sought complete liberalization of capital movements, including those of a purely monetary nature not linked to commercial transactions.[7] Subsequently, the Single European Act adopted in February 1986, amending the Treaties establishing the EEC, set a target date of 31 December 1992 for the EC to create an area without internal frontiers in which free movement of goods, persons, services and capital would be guaranteed. The Single European Act sets in motion a programme for the creation of a unified European financial market. In June 1988, the European Commission adopted a directive to liberalize all intra-EC capital flows as from 1 July 1990 (with a brief delay for Greece, Ireland, Portugal and Spain until 31 December 1992). This directive has been instrumental in promoting the liberalization of capital controls by EC member states. By 1 July 1990, cross-border capital transactions were virtually free.

Building on this decision to liberalize capital movements in the EC, the Delors Report (1989) put forward a three-stage plan to prepare for an Economic and Monetary Union (EMU) in Europe. The first stage should accomplish the liberalization of financial markets, the enlargement of the membership in the Exchange Rate Mechanism (ERM) of the European Monetary System (EMS), and a change in the mandate of the Committee of Central Bank Governors of the EC central banks to promote the co-ordination of monetary policies. The second stage should establish the European Monetary Institute (EMI), which would initially operate alongside the national monetary authorities. One of the main tasks of the central banks will be the harmonization of the monetary instruments and targets. In addition, steps will be taken to ensure full central bank independence from other national authorities. The third stage should accomplish the irrevocable fixing of exchange rates among national currencies eligible to join the third stage. Eligibility is based upon the Maastricht convergence criteria that EC countries have to meet. Convergence criteria have been formulated with respect to inflation differentials, exchange rate stability, long-term interest rate differentials, fiscal deficits and government debt. The European Central Bank (ECB) and the European System of Central Banks (ESCB) will be responsible for the monetary policy in the participating member states (see Committee of Governors of the Central Banks of the Member States of the European Economic Community, 1993).[8]

This book is divided into three parts. The first part consists of a review of the literature on measuring capital mobility and carries out various tests to assess the degree of financial integration in the EU, covering the period 1979 to 1993 in particular.[9] We apply the three principal methods of measuring the degree of capital mobility: (1) interest rate parity conditions, (2) savings-investment correlations and (3) consumption correlations. The second part will be primarily concerned with the determination of financial integration. First, we document the fundamental determinants of financial integration in the EU. Second, we analyze remaining factors which influence the movement of capital within the EU. Particularly, we analyze the incidence of nonresident interest withholding taxation in the government debt markets. The third part summarizes and concludes.

The rest of the introductory chapter is organized as follows. In Section 1.2, we define the concept of financial integration. We discuss two aspects of financial integration which are of central importance: capital mobility and asset substitutability. Section 1.3 presents a framework for analysis where the various measures of capital mobility are introduced. Section 1.4 deals with six distinct factors which determine the degree of capital mobility and asset substitutability. Finally, Section 1.5 further elaborates on the plan and organization of the book.

## 1.2    The Definition of Financial Integration

There is no unambiguous definition of financial integration in the literature. We should therefore stress that in this book, *perfect financial integration* means that there are *no barriers* (that is, no capital controls and other institutional barriers) that prevent investors from changing their portfolios instantaneously. Financial integration, when defined as a *state*, refers to the extreme cases of perfect (absence of barriers) and no integration (presence of barriers). Financial integration, when defined as a *process*, refers to the gradual dismantling of capital controls and other institutional barriers effecting the degree of financial integration (see Balassa, 1962).[10] In our view, financial integration is a matter of *degree*, and the extreme cases (perfect and no integration) are only of theoretical interest. The best approach is to measure the degree of financial integration.

In the context of a definition of financial integration, the terms *capital mobility* and *asset substitutability* are of central importance. Therefore, a brief discussion of these terms is useful (see Boothe, Clinton, Côté and Longworth, 1985, Caramazza, Clinton, Côté and Longworth, 1986, Akhtar and Weiller, 1987 and Reinhart and Weiller, 1987). Table 1.3 shows how the two terms are related (Gärtner, 1993, p. 12). Contrary to Gärtner (1993), we also indicate possible factors which determine the degree of capital mobility and asset substitutability. Section 1.4 will examine these determinants in more detail. The rows of Table 1.3 distinguish between perfect and imperfect capital mobility. The columns of Table 1.3 distinguish between perfect and imperfect asset substitutability among assets denominated in different currencies. The links between financial assets are described by the well-known interest rate parity conditions. Table 1.3 shows how capital mobility and asset substitutability bear on two important interest parity conditions: covered interest parity (CIP) and *ex ante* uncovered interest parity (UIP). Of the four alternatives which are logically possible, alternative III has to be excluded since perfect capital mobility is a necessary condition for perfect asset substitutability. A foreign asset can

*Table 1.3 Different degrees of capital mobility and asset substitutability*

| CIP | | Asset substituta-bility | |
| --- | --- | --- | --- |
| | | Perfect | Imperfect |
| | Perfect | I: $i = i^* + (f-s)$ | II: $i = i^* + (f-s) + AR + PR$ |
| Capital mobility | | | |
| | Imperfect | III: *Impossible* | IV: $i = i^* + (f-s) + AR + CC + PR$ |

| Ex ante UIP | | Asset substituta-bility | |
| --- | --- | --- | --- |
| | | Perfect | Imperfect |
| | Perfect | I: $i = i^* + (Es-s)$ | II: $i = i^* + (Es-s) + AR + PR + ER$ |
| Capital mobility | | | |
| | Imperfect | III: *Impossible* | IV: $i = i^* + (Es-s) + AR + CC + PR + ER$ |

*Notes:* Here $i$ is the nominal return in the home country, $i^* + (f-s)$ is the expected and realized nominal return in the foreign country denominated in the currency of the home country, $i^* + (Es-s)$ is the expected nominal return in the foreign country denominated in the currency of the home country, $AR$ indicates asset specific types of risks, $CC$ indicates capital controls and other institutional barriers, $PR$ indicates political risks and $ER$ indicates exchange risks. Table 1.3 abstracts from the role of transaction costs (see Section 1.4).

*Sources:* Gärtner (1993, p. 12) and own extension.

never be a perfect substitute for some domestic asset unless tied-up funds can be repatriated. Capital can only be considered *perfectly mobile* if it can be moved into the preferred form of investment any time without delay and in the desired amount. In alternatives I and II, portfolio adjustments are *instantaneous*. Finally, alternative IV arises if portfolio adjustments are slow and assets are imperfect substitutes. Dornbusch (1980, p. 176) defines perfect capital mobility as the combination of perfect substitutability of domestic and foreign bonds and the instantaneous adjustment of actual to desired portfolio holdings (alternative I). However, it is certainly possible that capital is perfectly mobile, while foreign and domestic assets are *imperfect substitutes* (alternative II). Thus, alternatives I and II conform to our definition of perfect financial integration in the sense that there are no capital controls and other institutional barriers ($CC$) that prevent investors from changing their portfolios instantaneously. Financial assets denominated in domestic currency may not be perfect substitutes for financial assets denominated in foreign currency because of exchange risks ($ER$). In addition, asset-specific types of risks ($AR$) and political risks ($PR$) make domestic and foreign assets less substitutable. Risk-averse market participants are only *willing* to hold foreign currency denominated assets if they receive compensation for $AR$, $PR$ and $ER$ in the form of a risk premium. Whether asset stocks actually change depends on the *ability* of investors to adjust their portfolios.[11] To test for the degree of financial integration, it is normally assumed that asset-specific types of risks are minimal. Assets are alike in all respects except for their currency of denomination. Thus, financial integration is associated with the equalization of returns of similar financial assets across markets so that the *law of one price* holds. Next, Section 1.3 discusses some measurement issues. We argue that financial integration need not be measured solely in terms of interest returns.

## 1.3   The Measurement of Financial Integration

One of the difficulties with the measurement of financial integration lies in the fact that no single approach to the measurement of financial integration has become widely accepted. The operational framework in this book is drawn from the three most influential methods to measure the degree of financial integration: (1) interest parity conditions, (2) savings-investment correlations and (3) consumption correlations. Consequently, an eclectic approach to the topic of financial integration is made. The purpose of this section is to examine the different criteria for measuring the degree of capital mobility. To this end, we use a slightly modified version of a model presented in Dooley, Frankel and Mathieson (1987). Dooley et al. (1987) examine the financial and real links between and within two countries' financial markets. Vikøren (1994) extends the model of Dooley et al. (1987) by assuming that there exists a Euro market for bonds denominated in the currency of the home country ($E$). We further increase the relevance of the model by assuming that there also exists a Euro market for bonds denominated in the currency of the foreign country ($E^*$). The financial assets in both countries consist of money, bonds and claims on physical capital (equity claims). So, the assets available to the residents of the home country are domestic base money ($M$), domestic bonds ($B$), bonds denominated in the currency of the home country but traded abroad ($E$), bonds denominated in the currency of the foreign country but traded abroad ($E^*$), foreign bonds ($B^*$) and domestic equity claims, that is, claims on physical capital ($C$).[12] We assume that (Euro) bonds are internationally traded securities while money and equity claims are non-traded securities.[13] Money and (Euro) bonds are imperfect substitutes for equity claims. We neglect the distinction between nominal and real balances, since for the moment prices are assumed to be given and constant.

Now, we write down a standard six-assets portfolio-balance model.[14] The demand for each asset is assumed to be a function of output $Y$, total financial wealth $W$ and relative asset returns $i$, $i^{Euro}$, $i^*+(f-s)$, $i^*+(Es-s)$, $i^{*Euro}+(f-s)$, $i^{*Euro}+(Es-s)$ and $i^c$. The home demand for these assets can be specified as follows:

$$M^d = M^d[\,i, i^{Euro}, i^*+(f-s), i^*+(Es-s), i^{*Euro}+(f-s),\ldots,$$
$$i^{*Euro}+(Es-s), i^c, Y, W\,] \tag{1.1}$$
$$M_i<0, M_{i^{Euro}}<0, M_{i^*+(f-s)}<0, M_{i^*+(Es-s)}<0, M_{i^{*Euro}+(f-s)}<0,\ldots,$$
$$M_{i^{*Euro}+(Es-s)}<0, M_{i^c}<0, M_Y>0, M_W>0$$

$$B^d = B^d[\,i, i^{Euro}, i^*+(f-s), i^*+(Es-s), i^{*Euro}+(f-s),\ldots,$$
$$i^{*Euro}+(Es-s), i^c, Y, W\,] \tag{1.2}$$
$$B_i>0, B_{i^{Euro}}<0, B_{i^*+(f-s)}<0, B_{i^*+(Es-s)}<0, B_{i^{*Euro}+(f-s)}<0,\ldots,$$
$$B_{i^{*Euro}+(Es-s)}<0, B_{i^c}<0, B_Y<0, B_W>0$$

$$E^d = E^d[\,i, i^{Euro}, i^*+(f-s), i^*+(Es-s), i^{*Euro}+(f-s),\ldots,$$
$$i^{*Euro}+(Es-s), i^c, Y, W\,] \tag{1.3}$$
$$E_i<0, E_{i^{Euro}}>0, E_{i^*+(f-s)}<0, E_{i^*+(Es-s)}<0, E_{i^{*Euro}+(f-s)}<0,\ldots,$$
$$E_{i^{*Euro}+(Es-s)}<0, E_{i^c}<0, E_Y<0, E_W>0$$

$$SB^{*d} = B^{*d}[\,i, i^{Euro}, i^*+(f-s), i^*+(Es-s), i^{*Euro}+(f-s),\ldots,$$
$$i^{*Euro}+(Es-s), i^c, Y, W\,] \tag{1.4}$$
$$B_i^*<0, B_{i^{Euro}}^*<0, B_{i^*+(f-s)}^*>0, B_{i^*+(Es-s)}^*>0, B_{i^{*Euro}+(f-s)}^*<0,\ldots,$$
$$B_{i^{*Euro}+(Es-s)}^*<0, B_{i^c}^*<0, B_Y^*<0, B_W^*>0$$

$$SE^{*d} = E^{*d}[\,i, i^{Euro}, i^*+(f-s), i^*+(Es-s), i^{*Euro}+(f-s),\ldots,$$
$$i^{*Euro}+(Es-s), i^c, Y, W\,] \tag{1.5}$$
$$E_i^*<0, E_{i^{Euro}}^*<0, E_{i^*+(f-s)}^*<0, E_{i^*+(Es-s)}^*<0, E_{i^{*Euro}+(f-s)}^*>0,\ldots,$$
$$E_{i^{*Euro}+(Es-s)}^*>0, E_{i^c}^*<0, E_Y^*<0, E_W^*>0$$

$$C^d = C^d[\,i, i^{Euro}, i^*+(f-s), i^*+(Es-s), i^{*Euro}+(f-s),\ldots,$$
$$i^{*Euro}+(Es-s), i^c, Y, W\,] \tag{1.6}$$
$$C_i<0, C_{i^{Euro}}<0, C_{i^*+(f-s)}<0, C_{i^*+(Es-s)}<0, C_{i^{*Euro}+(f-s)}<0,\ldots,$$
$$C_{i^{*Euro}+(Es-s)}<0, C_{i^c}>0, C_Y<0, C_W>0$$

where $i$ is the interest rate on domestic bonds, $i^{Euro}$ is the interest rate on bonds denominated in the currency of the home country but traded abroad, $i^{*Euro}$ is the interest rate on bonds denominated in the currency of the foreign country but not traded in the foreign country, $i^*$ is the interest rate on foreign bonds, $i^c$

is the yield on domestic equity claims equal to the marginal product of the capital stock, $f$ is the forward exchange rate in logarithm, $s$ is the spot exchange rate in logarithm, $f-s$ is the forward premium (discount) on the foreign currency in logarithm and $Es-s$ is the expected change in the log of the spot exchange rate. Exchange rates are defined according to the continental definition of the exchange rate (that is, domestic currency units per unit of foreign currency). The signs of the partial derivatives are given below the demand equations. Domestic wealth will be allocated among the six assets:

$$W = M^d + B^d + E^d + C^d + SB^{*d} + SE^{*d} \qquad (1.7)$$

Equations (1.1)–(1.7) are generally used to represent financial markets in a portfolio-balance model. These equations assume that as output increases the demand for domestic bonds, Euro bonds, foreign bonds and domestic equity claims decreases and the demand for domestic money increases. If financial wealth increases, the increase is allocated among the six assets in fixed proportion. If the domestic interest rate increase the demand for domestic bonds increases at the expense of domestic money, Euro bonds denominated in the currency of the home and foreign country and domestic equity claims. If domestic and foreign (Euro) bonds are imperfect substitutes internationally, the partial derivatives

$$B_i, \, B_{i\,Euro}, \, B_{i^*+(f-s)}, \, B_{i^*+(Es-s)}, \, B_{i\,Euro+(f-s)}, \, B_{i\,Euro+(Es-s)}$$

$$E_i, \, E_{i\,Euro}, \, E_{i^*+(f-s)}, \, E_{i^*+(Es-s)}, \, E_{i\,Euro+(f-s)}, \, E_{i\,Euro+(Es-s)}$$

$$B_i^*, \, B_{i\,Euro}^*, \, B_{i^*+(f-s)}^*, \, B_{i^*+(Es-s)}^*, \, B_{i\,Euro+(f-s)}^*, \, B_{i\,Euro+(Es-s)}^*$$

$$E_i^*, \, E_{i\,Euro}^*, \, E_{i^*+(f-s)}^*, \, E_{i^*+(Es-s)}^*, \, E_{i\,Euro+(f-s)}^*, \, E_{i\,Euro+(Es-s)}^*$$

are finite. That is, the returns on domestic and foreign (Euro) bonds differ by a risk premium. If domestic and foreign (Euro) bonds are *perfect substitutes* all partial derivatives are infinite. This implies that all expected returns across financial markets are equalized.

The links between the financial and real sector *within* each country are as follows (Dooley et al., 1987, p. 525). Real investment is defined as transforming current output into a capital good that has an 'own' rate of return in terms of future output (Dooley et al., 1987, p. 525 and Vikøren, 1994, p. 5). The return on equity claims is equal to the marginal revenue product of the capital stock. Note that the cost of capital ($i^c$) need not be equal to the domestic interest rate ($i$) as savers may demand an interest rate different from the cost of capital to willingly hold bonds and claims on the capital stock. Investment ($I$) will be positive when the present value of expected future output exceeds the cost of capital

$$I = I(i^c, \psi) \qquad (1.8)$$

where $\psi$ is a shift parameter. Savings $(S)$ in each country are assumed to be a function of the different rates of return and a shift parameter $\Phi$:

$$S = S[\, i, i^{Euro}, i^* + (f - s), i^* + (Es - s), i^{*Euro} + (f - s), \ldots, \\ i^{*Euro} + (Es - s), i^c, \Phi\, ] \qquad (1.9)$$

Note that (1.9) is a non-standard savings function, since it is more common to assume that savings depend only on $i$ and $\Phi$. The real sector links *between* countries are derived from the above conditions and the balance of payments constraint. That is, the net excess demand for the traded securities (domestic and foreign bonds and Euro bonds denominated in the currency of the home and foreign country) should be equal to the difference between savings and investment.

Within the framework above, we are able to examine and compare the different measures of capital mobility that are applied in this book: (1) interest rate parity conditions, (2) savings-investment correlations and (3) consumption correlations. Traditionally, interest rate parity has been used to describe the financial and real linkages between countries. Equations (1.1)–(1.7) and Table 1.4 summarize the financial and real linkages between countries.[15] When financial markets are deregulated and when restrictions on cross-border capital

*Table 1.4 The pyramid of financial and real linkages*

| | Domestic market | Euro markets | Foreign market |
|---|---|---|---|
| 1 | | $i^{Euro} = i^{*Euro} + (f - s)$ | |
| 2 | | $i^{Euro} = i^{*Euro} + (Es - s)$ | |
| 3 | $i = \quad i^{Euro}$ | | $i^{*Euro} \quad = i^*$ |
| 4 | $i = \quad i^{*Euro} + (f - s)$ <br> $i - (f - s) = i^{*Euro}$ | $i^{Euro} - (f - s)$ <br> $i^{Euro} =$ | $= i^*$ <br> $i^* + (f - s)$ |
| 5 | $i = \quad i^{*Euro} + (Es - s)$ <br> $i - (Es - s) = i^{*Euro}$ | $i^{Euro} - (Es - s)$ <br> $i^{Euro} =$ | $= i^*$ <br> $i^* + (Es - s)$ |
| 6 | $i =$ <br> $i - (f - s)$ | | $i^* + (f - s)$ <br> $= i^*$ |
| 7 | $i =$ <br> $i - (Es - s)$ | | $i^* + (Es - s)$ <br> $= i^*$ |
| 8 | $Er =$ <br> $Er - (Es - s)$ | | $Er^* + (Es - s)$ <br> $= Er^*$ |
| 9 | $Er = [i - (Ep - p)] =$ | | $Er^* = [i^* - (Ep^* - p^*)]$ |

*Sources:* Herring and Litan (1995, pp. 30–31) and author's own summary of the literature.

flows are eliminated, interest rate returns in national and international markets in the same currency are equalized. In the model above, this corresponds to examining the relationship between the interest rate on domestic bonds $i$ and the interest rate on bonds denominated in domestic currency but traded abroad $i^{Euro}$, that is, closed interest parity. The closed interest parity condition can be written as $i = i^{Euro}$ for the home country (see row 3 of Table 1.4). The returns are denominated in the currency of the home country. A similar condition can be derived for the foreign country $i^{*Euro} = i^{*}$ (row 3). Now, returns are denominated in the currency of the foreign country. Chapter 5 will address closed interest parity for short-term bonds while Chapter 6 will, among others, address closed interest parity for long-term bonds. Alternatively, in rows 4 and 5 we calculate synthetic approximations of closed interest differentials. For the home country we arrive at the following condition $i = i^{*Euro} + (f - s)$ or $i = i^{*Euro} + (Es - s)$. Chapter 5 will use this result to measure the intensity of capital controls.

Chapter 2 also examines the degree of financial integration in terms of interest rate returns. In the model above, this corresponds to examining the relationship between the return on domestic bonds $i$ and the returns on foreign bonds $i^{*} + (f - s)$ and $i^{*} + (Es - s)$. CIP can be written as $i = i^{*} + (f - s)$ (row 6), while *ex ante* UIP can be written as $i = i^{*} + (Es - s)$ (row 7). Note that only domestic distortions impair closed interest parity, while domestic and foreign distortions impair CIP and *ex ante* UIP. If CIP does not hold, this suggests there are unexploited profit opportunities from interest arbitrage. If *ex ante* UIP does not hold this suggests that either CIP does not hold and/or that exchange risks exist. Subsequently, if we relax the assumption of constant prices in our model above and assume that the expected change in the exchange rate $Es - s$ just offsets the expected inflation differential $(Ep - p) - (Ep^{*} - p^{*})$, we arrive at the *ex ante* real interest parity condition (RIP) $r = r^{*}$ (row 9).[16] Chapter 2 also examines the *ex ante* RIP condition. If the expected change in the exchange rate differs from the expected inflation differential, then, *ex ante* real UIP emerges $r = r^{*} + (Es - s)$ (row 8). Finally, CIP and *ex ante* UIP between Euro interest rates (rows 1 and 2) do not really constitute a test of financial integration in the sense of *cross-border* capital flows between countries (see Lemmen and Eijffinger, 1993, p. 189). Therefore, the integration of Euro markets is not discussed any further.

Chapter 3 is devoted to the study of the correlation of savings and investment in the EU. Savings-investment correlations were first examined by Feldstein and Horioka (1980). The motivation for examining the correlation between savings and investment is that only *short-run* savings-investment correlations may be used as an indication of the degree of capital mobility. We formulate an error-correction model of savings-investment correlations to distinguish between *short-* and *long-run* savings-investment correlations. Theoretically, long-run savings-investment correlations should be close to one (as was found by Feldstein and Horioka), while short-run correlations may differ from one. A country may run a current account deficit for a short period of time but current account imbalances must accumulate to zero over a long period of time unless the country defaults on its foreign debt.

Chapter 4 is devoted to the study of consumption correlations in the EU. The motivation for examining consumption correlations is that cross-border capital flows can increase welfare by enabling countries to smooth out consumption over time (referring to the Euler equation test of financial integration by Obstfeld, 1986). A high correlation between domestic and foreign consumption might indicate a high degree of cross-border capital mobility. Financial integration probably has reduced constraints on consumption expenditure.

## 1.4 The Determination of Financial Integration

Next, we comment on six distinct factors which influence capital mobility and asset substitutability (see Kasman and Pigott, 1988). Capital mobility essentially depends on transaction costs (b) and capital controls (c). Asset substitutability essentially depends on asset-specific types of risks (a), political risks (d), exchange risks (e) and purchasing power risks (f).

### (a) Asset-specific types of risks

The assets being considered may differ in default risks, market liquidity, acceptability, and so on. Government assets, for example, are generally regarded to be less subject to default risks than private assets.[17] Assets may also differ in tax status, eligibility for discounting at the central bank, compulsory reserve requirement ratios as well as other characteristics.[18] Moreover, in many of the national financial markets, there were often large differentials between bank loan rates charged to firms $(i_l)$ and unregulated money market rates (either inter-bank domestic deposit or Euro deposit rates) $(i_d)$. Without distortions, one would normally expect bank lending rates to be slightly higher than unregulated money market rates, reflecting higher risks, fees and commissions for financial services. By contrast, a low or negative difference between the two interest rates gives an indication of distortions from interest rate controls and market conventions maintained within each banking system.[19] Thus a low or negative difference gives an indication of the extent to which projects with a low market rate of return, but with preferred access to credit, can obtain financing because of regulation (Edey and Hviding, 1995, p. 19). Edey and Hviding document the impact of these distortions. They calculate average loan/deposit rate spreads in national financial markets denominated in the same currency. Table 1.5 reports their results. By the end of 1990, direct interest rate regulation and regulation-driven credit rationing had virtually disappeared from the EU countries. Remaining loan/deposit rate spreads can be explained by fees and commissions for financial services which, unlike interest rates, have usually not been subject to the intervention by governments but are determined by market forces.

In the analysis of interest parity conditions in Chapters 2, 5 and 6, we shall attempt to confine comparisons to assets with equal asset-specific types of risks, although this is not entirely possible due to lack of data. The estimated degree of capital mobility may be highly sensitive to which series of domestic interest rates is used to depict 'the' domestic interest rate. This problem is circumvented by choosing interest rates of *representative* segments of the money market that are most freely determined and are least subject to domestic regulation and other distortions. That is, the deregulation of the national financial markets (the freeing of markets from either direct interest rate regulation and regulation-driven

*Table 1.5 National loan/deposit rate spreads*

$$i_l - i_d$$

|  | 1960–1969 | 1970–1974 | 1975–1979 | 1980–1984 | 1985–1989 | 1990–1994 |
|---|---|---|---|---|---|---|
| Belgium | 1.8 | 2.1 | 1.7 | 2.8 | 2.4 | 3.6 |
| Germany | 3.6 | 4.6 | 4.0 | 3.8 | 4.0 | 4.3 |
| Finland | – | –0.9 | –1.6 | –3.6 | –2.1 | –0.1 |
| France | – | –3.0 | –1.0 | –3.0 | 0.8 | 0.6 |
| Italy | – | 2.1 | 4.1 | 1.7 | 2.3 | 2.2 |
| The Netherlands | 2.0 | 2.7 | 2.7 | 2.2 | 1.7 | 1.0 |
| Spain | – | – | –1.7 | 0.7 | 2.6 | 2.8 |
| United Kingdom | –2.1 | –1.3 | –0.9 | 0.1 | 0.8 | 1.2 |

*Notes:*

Belgium:            Overdrafts with commercial banks less three-month tender rate on Treasury certificates.
Germany:            Interest rate on short-term bank credit less three-month Euro deposit rate.
Finland:            Commercial banks' lending rate less three-month interbank rate.
France:             Prime rate less three-month interbank rate.
Italy:              Overdrafts with commercial banks less three-month interbank rate.
The Netherlands:    Mortgage loan rate less three-month interbank rate.
Spain:              Credit rate less three-month interbank rate.
United Kingdom:     Building society mortgage rate less three-month interbank rate.

*Sources:* © OECD (1995), Reproduced by permission of the OECD from Edey and Hviding (1995, p. 19), 'An Assessment of Financial Reform in OECD Countries', *OECD Economic Studies*, No. 25, Paris.

credit rationing) is assumed to be completed. Furthermore, we usually confine our comparisons to *short-term* assets (bonds and deposits). It would also be interesting to compare yields on long-term bonds and equities in the same currency. However, it is difficult to find long-term bonds with equivalent maturities and levels of asset-specific types of risks. Furthermore, unavailability and thinness of forward exchange markets for longer maturities also complicates comparisons. Therefore, Chapters 2 and 5 will compare yields on representative short-term securities. Chapter 6, however, will be concerned with closed interest parity of *long-term* government bonds calculated with the help of *interest rate swaps*. It is also rather difficult to comply with the comparability assumption with respect to the integration of equity markets. Cross-country differences in asset-specific risks of equities are considerable. The diverse share price indices are less comparable.[20] By providing a setting in which the assumption of similar risk instruments is satisfied, the Euro markets have given us the cleanest test of financial integration. Because the Euro market is so competitive, the Euro loan rates are only slightly above the Euro deposit rate for prime customers. Asset-specific types of risks in Euro markets are minimal.

## (b) Transaction costs

Transaction costs depend on the differential costs of trading across different currencies and include not only brokerage costs but also information and time costs. Brokerage costs are expected to vary with the volume of transactions, while information costs depend on the number of outlets searched and the marginal benefit from searching (Otani and Tiwari, 1981, p. 797). The time costs will vary with the wage/shadow wage rate or the marginal disutility of work. Investors may simply have less information about foreign markets. Language barriers and financial reporting differences may hinder foreign investment. Using bid/ask spreads to measure transaction costs associated with covered interest rate transactions, Clinton (1988) estimated that Euro market transaction costs ranged from 0.025 per cent per annum for the German mark to 0.039 per cent per annum for the French franc over the period November 1985 to May 1986.[21] Transaction costs create specific bands around closed and covered interest parity. It is reasonable to assume that these bands are narrow and that movements within the bands are random. Hence, significant and systematic divergences between two interest rate returns can only be interpreted as the result of capital controls, not by transaction costs.

## (c) Capital controls

Existing capital controls reduce the mobility of capital between two financial markets leading to closed interest differentials.[22] This differential may be positive or negative, depending on how the controls were designed.[23] Capital controls basically come in two varieties. Closed interest differentials are negative (positive) when capital export (import) restrictions exist. Governments may restrict resident purchases of foreign assets (and sometimes nonresident outflows as well). Such *outward* controls, which are usually designed to support a weak currency, lead to a closed interest rate differential favouring the foreign market.

Alternatively, governments may restrict nonresident purchases of domestic assets to reduce pressures towards an appreciation of the domestic currency. Such *inward* controls may lead to an interest differential favouring the domestic market. Only a few countries like Germany, Switzerland and Japan have resorted to such inward controls. Capital controls can also take the form of a tax on interest earnings. Then, arbitrage keeps the after-tax interest on the taxed security tied to the tax-free interest on the untaxed security (see Chapter 6).

### (d) Political risks

Even if no capital controls separate the markets, investors may perceive political or sovereign risks involving future restrictions (Aliber, 1973). Political or sovereign risks arise because of concern that the national authorities of one country might impose capital controls, taxes, or other regulatory measures on foreign investments in their market or on their residents' investments in other markets. Political risks may also reflect the political costs of interest rate decisions designed to defend exchange rate parities. Political risks are perceived to be of negligible importance in the Euro market.

### (e) Exchange risks

Importantly, financial transactions involve uncertainty about the denomination of financial transactions. When forward rates are biased predictors of future spot rates and if market participants expect exchange rate variability to be high, uncovered holdings of foreign currency denominated assets become risky. Risk-averse investors will demand compensation for the exchange risks they take. *Ex ante* UIP is the hypothesis that the exchange risk premium is equal to zero. Of course, the characteristics of the ERM of the EMS where currencies are allowed to fluctuate within small margins are of crucial importance for the size of the exchange risk premium. Expectations of exchange rate stability increases substitutability between assets denominated in different currencies. In principle, exchange risk of any given foreign currency may well be uncorrelated with other risks faced by investors. This nonsystematic risk can be diversified away, and therefore will not affect foreign investment decisions. However, the systematic risk of an appreciation of the home currency relative to all others would be a risk common to all foreign investors and cannot be diversified away. None the less, as long as risk-averse investors get a fair reward for the exchange risk they bear, they still may want to hold foreign assets in their portfolio.

### (f) Purchasing power risks

The final factor causing return differentials between two countries is expected differences between domestic and foreign inflation rates. Inflation differentials may also influence asset substitutability. Monetary policies were used intensively to fight inflation in most of the EU countries leading to lower purchasing power risks. To some extent, a *divergence* in short-term interest rates can help promote *convergence* in inflation and thus long-term interest rates. It makes it hard to distinguish the effect on short-term interest rates of financial integration from the effect of monetary policy convergence. High nominal short-term interest differentials may be explained by the use of the nominal short-term interest rate as a policy instrument to maintain the exchange rates in the allowed fluctuation margins of the ERM.

## 1.5 Plan and Organization of the Book

This book includes three main parts, all having the EU countries as their principal objects of study. Part I, entitled 'The Measurement of Financial Integration', is taken up in Chapters 2, 3 and 4. Part II, entitled 'The Determination of Financial Integration', is taken up in Chapters 5 and 6. Part III, entitled 'Conclusion', is taken up in Chapter 7. The chapters are self-contained, and the reader may, without reference to other chapters, follow the analysis presented.

The main objective of the first part of the book is to examine theoretically and empirically the degree of financial integration within the EU. This is pursued by applying and critically discussing the three most influential methods for measuring the degree of financial integration. Chapter 2 presents empirical evidence on the degree of financial integration as measured with interest parity conditions. We examine the effects of capital controls, exchange risks and deviations from purchasing power parity on interest parity between EU countries and Germany. Furthermore, we assess how far the integration of financial markets has progressed. Subsequently, Chapter 3 applies savings-investment correlations to assess the degree of financial integration in the EU, and Chapter 4 applies consumption correlations to assess the degree of financial integration in the EU.

The objective of the second part of the book is twofold. First, Chapter 5 documents the fundamental determinants of financial integration in the EU. As a starting point for considering the determinants of financial integration, we discuss relevant measures of the intensity of capital controls. Subsequently, Chapter 5 will go into the underlying determinants of the intensity of capital controls. Second, we analyze remaining factors which are likely to influence the movement of capital within the EU. Particularly, Chapter 6 is concerned with the incidence of nonresident interest withholding taxes in the international three-month Treasury bill market and the international five-year government debt market. Finally, the third part summarizes and concludes. Chapter 7 summarizes the evidence on the measurement and determination of financial integration in the EU and concludes with some suggestions for future research.

# Notes

1. Flow variables are measured over some time interval while stock variables are measured at a particular point in time.

2. See also the evidence in Bisignano (1994) and Marston (1995).

3. See the OECD (1996) for historical data on issues of international bonds (Euro and foreign bonds) and syndicated bank loans. See also the report of the Group of Ten (1993).

4. Of course, financial integration is not the only important structural change affecting European financial markets. Besides, internationalization, Lemmen and Eijffinger (1995b) also analyze other structural changes (disintermediation, securitization and so on). See also Sijben (1994, pp. 353–79) and the other chapters in Fair and Raymond (1994).

5. The 'OECD Financial Accounts of OECD Countries' have the following sectoring: (1) financial institutions, (2) general government, (3) non-financial enterprises, (4) households and (5) rest of the world. Domestic non-financial sectors are (2), (3) and (4).

6. Rogoff (1985) concludes that the presence of capital controls may explain why Italy and France were able to reduce fluctuations in their exchange rates against the DM without reducing fluctuations in real interest differentials.

7. The Commission of the European Communities (1989) summarizes the relevant extracts of the EEC Treaties and Community Directives which govern capital movements within the EC.

8. Eijffinger (1996) addresses the design of future European monetary policy.

9. Note that the existence of international financial markets can be traced back to the eighteenth and nineteenth centuries (Neal, 1987, 1991).

10. That is why the title of this book is 'Integrating Financial Markets in the European Union'.

11. Akhtar and Weiller (1987, p. 19) argue: 'In practice, components of rates of return, for example, exchange rates, may adjust quickly without actual movements of capital, that is capital mobility may just be incipient'.

12. Bonds are interest-earning assets and are distinguished from money by the fact that they do bear interest.

13. In terms of the literature, we are thus assuming 'perfect capital mobility' with respect to bonds but not with respect to equity claims. Furthermore, we abstract from currency substitution.

14. This model closely corresponds to a schematic overview of financial relationships in the EU that we have suggested elsewhere (Lemmen and Eijffinger, 1993).

15. See Kneeshaw and Van den Bergh (1985) for an early contribution.

16. Studies of *ex ante* RIP include Cumby and Obstfeld (1984), Mishkin (1984) and Frankel and MacArthur (1988). Other references are given in the following chapters.

17. Foreign asset positions also matter for default risk.

18. Chapter 6 will analyze the incidence of nonresident interest withholding taxes.

19. The OECD (1992) reviews the developments in several national banking systems.

20. Therefore, we only briefly address the integration of European equity markets in Chapter 4. We refer to Jorion and Schwartz (1986) and Akdogan (1995) who examine equity market integration with the help of asset-pricing models. In the framework of the Capital Asset Pricing Model (CAPM), integration imposes restrictions on the pricing of assets by ruling out relationships between expected returns and purely national factors. With complete segmentation only national factors should enter the pricing of assets.

21. See also Frenkel and Levich (1975, 1977).

22. Previous studies of capital controls include Otani and Tiwari (1981), Dooley and Isard (1980) and Ito (1986).

23. Note that the Euro markets operate free of any capital controls and other institutional barriers.

# PART I

# THE MEASUREMENT OF FINANCIAL INTEGRATION

# 2. The Price Approach to Financial Integration: Decomposing European Money Market Interest Differentials

## 2.1 Introduction

This chapter deals with a theoretical and empirical analysis of money market integration in the EC since the start of the EMS in March 1979.[1] The key question is whether the step-by-step liberalization of short-term capital movements in the EC, in preparing for the EMU, has brought about a higher degree of money market integration in the EC. The analysis intends to shed some light on the changes in the degree and speed of money market integration over time.[2] Although, short-term capital mobility between European countries may seriously hinder the process of monetary unification in Europe, the degree and speed of money market integration in Europe are seldomly estimated.[3] We examine money market integration by comparing covered, uncovered and real interest differentials.[4] This chapter is also relevant for international portfolio management and corporate treasury management. For example, for an investor who wants to invest in foreign assets, the question whether covered or uncovered interest parity hold has direct implications for the question whether or not he or she should hedge his or her foreign investment.

Chapter 2 is organized as follows. Section 2.2 specifies an ascending order of three alternative criteria for short-term capital mobility, that is, covered nominal interest parity (CIP), *ex ante* uncovered nominal interest parity (UIP) and *ex ante* real interest parity (RIP). Subsequently, we introduce the decomposition method of Frankel and MacArthur (1988) to identify the main components of above interest parity conditions. Section 2.3 describes the data and sets out the empirical methodology. Section 2.4 estimates the size and variability of mean (absolute) deviations from CIP, *ex post* UIP and *ex post* RIP of ten European countries *vis-à-vis* Germany to assess the *degree* of money market integration. The total sample period March 1979–August 1992 is split with the Basle–Nyborg agreement of September 1987. Section 2.5 estimates a time trend in mean absolute deviations from above interest parity conditions to asses the *speed* of money market integration. Subsequently, Section 2.6 documents the

21

trade-off between the degree and speed of money market integration in Europe.
Finally, Section 2.7 concludes.

## 2.2   Three Alternative Criteria for Short-term Capital Mobility

Quantifying the degree of money market integration implies measuring the
degree in which short-term capital flows equalize expected and realized returns
on comparable money market assets denominated in different currencies.
Essentially, the criteria for short-term capital mobility are nothing more than
a reinterpretation of the familiar interest parity conditions. Following Frankel
and MacArthur (1988), Table 2.1 summarizes an ascending order of three
alternative criteria for short-term capital mobility according to their cumulative
assumptions. The criteria for capital mobility rely on the dispersion of *prices*
(that is, short-term interest rates) of comparable European money market assets.
Hence, they fit into the price approach to financial integration (see Feldman,
1986).[5] According to Frankel (1989) and Lemmen and Eijffinger (1993) the
interest parity conditions in Table 2.1 measure three different types of perfect
capital mobility.

The first criterion – CIP – examines perfect capital mobility of type I. CIP
holds if the forward premium (discount) $f_t^{t+k} - s_t$ equals the difference between
the domestic and foreign nominal interest rate $i_{t,t+k} - i_{t,t+k}^*$ at the appropriate
maturity:

$$i_{t,t+k} - i_{t,t+k}^* = f_t^{t+k} - s_t \qquad (2.1)$$

A forward premium (discount) on foreign currency means that the forward price
of foreign currency delivered and paid for some time in the future expressed
in domestic currency is higher (lower) than the current spot price. If the domestic
nominal interest rate is higher (lower) than the foreign nominal interest, the
lower (higher) foreign nominal interest rate is compensated by a forward
premium (discount) on foreign currency. Investors will buy (sell) foreign
currency spot to sell (buy) it forward. A premium (discount) on the foreign
currency corresponds with an expected future rise (fall) in the spot exchange
rate. Perfect capital mobility of type I implies a zero covered nominal interest
differential or in other words a zero country premium $i_{t,t+k} - i_{t,t+k}^* - (f_t^{t+k} - s_t)$
$= 0$. Deviations from CIP reflect barriers to the integration of financial markets
across national boundaries such as transaction costs, capital controls, information
costs, tax laws that discriminate by country of residence, default risk and risk
of future capital controls (Frankel, 1992, pp. 200–1). The second criterion –
*ex ante* UIP – examines perfect capital mobility of type II. Replacement of
the forward exchange rate $f_t^{t+k}$ by the expected future spot exchange rate $E_t s_{t+k}$

yields UIP. This replacement is allowed if exchange rate expectations are held with certainty or if investors are risk-neutral.[6] Note, however, that certainty with respect to exchange rate expectations and risk neutrality are sufficient conditions but not necessary conditions for UIP. There are other conditions for having a zero risk premium, for example, if all exchange risk is nonsystematic risk in the world of the Capital Asset Pricing Model (that is, $\beta_{Currency} = 0$). UIP holds if the expected nominal exchange rate change $E_t(s_{t+k} - s_t)$ equals the nominal interest differential $i_{t,t+k} - i^*_{t,t+k}$ at the appropriate maturity:

$$i_{t,t+k} - i^*_{t,t+k} = E_t(s_{t+k} - s_t) \qquad (2.2)$$

Investors expect an exchange rate depreciation when the domestic nominal interest rate exceeds the foreign nominal interest rate. The second criterion can be framed in terms of the decomposition method of Frankel and MacArthur (1988). They decompose *ex ante* uncovered nominal interest differentials as follows:

$$i_{t,t+k} - i^*_{t,t+k} - E_t(s_{t+k} - s_t) = [i_{t,t+k} - i^*_{t,t+k} - (f_t^{t+k} - s_t)] + [(f_t^{t+k} - s_t) -$$
$$E_t(s_{t+k} - s_t)] \qquad (2.3)$$

*Ex ante* UIP requires a zero country premium $i_{t,t+k} - i^*_{t,t+k} - (f_t^{t+k} - s_t) = 0$ and a zero exchange risk premium $(f_t^{t+k} - s_t) - E_t(s_{t+k} - s_t) = 0$.

CIP and *ex ante* UIP measure two important aspects of financial integration: capital mobility and substitutability among assets denominated in different currencies. CIP is an *arbitrage* condition with covered positions and therefore a *riskless* operation with respect to exchange rate risk.[7] The degree of substitutability between domestic and foreign bonds based on exchange rate risk and the degree of risk aversion of the investors are therefore completely irrelevant. Since the absence of CIP suggests that there exist arbitrage opportunities, CIP indeed should hold in integrated markets. Frankel (1992, p. 197) argues that CIP is an unalloyed criterion for capital mobility in the sense of the degree of financial market integration across national boundaries. The absence of UIP, however, implies the existence of a risk premium in the exchange rate and as long as this is a fair reward for the risk that investors have to bear with respect to the currency, the absence of UIP does not necessarily imply a form of capital immobility.[8] Exchange risk which is not priced hampers capital mobility across national borders. The CIP condition is a more appropriate criterion for geographical money market segmentation across countries while the *ex ante* UIP condition is a more appropriate criterion for the overall analysis of integration between short-term financial markets, that is, money and foreign exchange markets (Haldane and Pradhan, 1992b, p. 5). Contrary to the CIP condition, the UIP condition can only give an *indirect* indi-

*Table 2.1 Interest parity conditions and their cumulative assumptions*

---

**I    Covered nominal interest parity (CIP)**

Assumption:

$$i_{i,t+k} - i_{i,t+k}^* = f_t^{t+k} - s_t$$

Yields:

$$i_{i,t+k} - i_{i,t+k}^* = f_t^{t+k} - s_t$$

---

**II    *Ex ante* uncovered nominal interest parity (UIP)**

Assumptions:

$$i_{i,t+k} - i_{i,t+k}^* = f_t^{t+k} - s_t$$

$$E_t s_{t+k} = f_t^{t+k}$$

Yield:

$$i_{i,t+k} - i_{i,t+k}^* = E_t(s_{t+k} - s_t)$$

---

**III    *Ex ante* real interest parity (RIP)**

Assumptions:

$$i_{i,t+k} - i_{i,t+k}^* = f_t^{t+k} - s_t$$

$$E_t s_{t+k} = f_t^{t+k}$$

$$E_t(s_{t+k} - s_t) = E_t(p_{t+k} - p_t) - E_t(p_{t+k}^* - p_t^*)$$

Yield:

$$E_t r_{i,t+k} = E_t r_{i,t+k}^*$$

---

**Symbols:**

$i_{t,t+k}$ = domestic nominal rate of interest at time $t$ on a $k$-period bond held between time $t$ and $t+k$

$f_t^{t+k}$ = forward exchange rate at time $t$ for the delivery of foreign currency at time $t+k$

$s_t$ = spot exchange rate at time $t$ (that is, domestic currency units per unit of foreign currency)

$p_t$ = domestic price level at time $t$

$r_{t,t+k}$ = domestic real rate of interest at time $t$ on a $k$-period bond held between time $t$ and $t+k$

$E_t$ = conditional expectations operator based upon the information available at time $t$, that is, $E(./I_t)$

$k$ = holding period of the underlying financial instrument

* = denotes a foreign variable

$t$ = denotes time $t$

*Notes:* Table 2.1 is framed according to the terminology introduced by Frankel and MacArthur (1988). All variables except the interest rates are expressed in natural logarithms. Lower-case variables represent natural logarithms. For example, the exact expression of CIP is: $(1 + i_{t,t+k})/(1 + i_{t,t+k}^*)$ $= F_t^{t+k}/S_t$. We obtain the logarithmic approximation, that is, $i_{t,t+k} - i_{t,t+k}^* = f_t^{t+k} - s_t$, by taking natural logarithms of both sides and applying the approximation that $ln(1+x) \approx x$ for small $x$ where $ln(S_t) = s_t$, $ln(F_t^{t+k}) = f_t^{t+k}$, $ln(1 + i_{t,t+k}) \approx i_{t,t+k}$ and $ln(1 + i_{t,t+k}^*) \approx i_{t,t+k}^*$.

*Sources:* Frankel and MacArthur (1988) and Frankel (1989).

cation of money market integration. In fact, perfect capital mobility of type I is compatible with both, zero and nonzero exchange risk premia. Booth, Clinton, Côté and Longworth (1985, p. 16) denote CIP with perfect capital mobility and *ex ante* UIP with perfect capital substitutability. We denote CIP with perfect capital mobility of type I and *ex ante* UIP with perfect capital mobility of type II.

The third criterion – *ex ante* RIP – examines perfect capital mobility of type III or in other words perfect financial and non-financial capital mobility (see, for example, Haldane and Pradhan, 1992b, p. 5). Non-financial capital mobility refers to the mobility of goods and services and the mobility of the production factors labour and physical capital (technology). Goods, services, labour and physical capital cannot be costlessly transferred from one country to another. Branson (1988, p. 1120), however, notes that perfect goods market integration may be a sufficient condition for *ex ante* RIP to hold because of factor price equalization. *Ex ante* RIP means that the expected domestic real interest rate $E_t r_{t,t+k}$ and the expected foreign real interest rate $E_t r_{t,t+k}^*$ are equal. In fact, *ex ante* RIP assumes that *ex ante* relative purchasing power parity (PPP) holds continuously. Substitution of *ex ante* relative PPP ( $s_{t+k} - s_t) = E_t(p_{t+k} - p_t) - E_t(p_{t+k}^* - p_t^*)$ for the expected exchange rate change in equation (2.2) leads to *ex ante* RIP:

$$E_t r_{t,t+k} = E_t r_{t,t+k}^* \qquad (2.4)$$

The third criterion can also be framed in terms of the decomposition method of Frankel and MacArthur. By adding and subtracting the forward premium (discount) and the expected depreciation (appreciation), we obtain an expression of the *ex ante* real interest differential:

$$E_t(r_{t,t+k} - r_{t,t+k}^*) = [i_{t,t+k} - i_{t,t+k}^* - (f_t^{t+k} - s_t)] + [(f_t^{t+k} - s_t) - E_t(s_{t+k} - s_t)] +$$

$$[E_t(s_{t+k} - s_t) - E_t(p_{t+k} - p_t) + E_t(p_{t+k}^* - p_t^*)] \qquad (2.5)$$

The last two components together constitute the currency premium, because they pertain to differences in assets according to the currency in which they are denominated (that is, currency factors), rather than the political jurisdiction in which they are issued (that is, country factors).[9] Consequently, the RIP condition can only give an *indirect* indication of money market integration. Perfect capital mobility of type III requires a zero country premium, a zero exchange risk premium *and* a zero expected real exchange rate change or in other words a zero deviation from *ex ante* relative PPP $[E_t(s_{t+k} - s_t) - E_t(p_{t+k} - p_t) + E_t(p_{t+k}^* - p_t^*) = 0$.

## 2.3 Data and Methodology

We calculate mean deviations and mean absolute deviations from CIP, *ex post* UIP and *ex post* RIP of ten European countries *vis-à-vis* Germany.[10] The European countries considered are Belgium, Denmark, France, Greece, Ireland, Italy, The Netherlands, Portugal, Spain and the United Kingdom.[11] The data used are monthly observations of three-month domestic money market interest rates, spot exchange rates *vis-à-vis* the Deutsche mark (DM), forward exchange rates *vis-à-vis* the DM of the same three-month maturity and consumer price indices (see Appendix 2A1 at the end of this chapter).[12] Of course, this does not rule out possible imperfections in the data. As is evident in the following analysis, it is difficult to obtain consistent interest rate, exchange rate and price level data.

Since direct DM forward and spot exchange rates are *not* available for all EC countries considered and/or over a sufficiently *long* period, we calculate cross-rate exchange rates. Concerning these cross-rate calculations, we already *presume* in the investigation design perfect capital mobility of type I. However, this is only possible on the basis of the assumption of perfect arbitrage between markets of foreign exchange. Due to transactions costs in triangular arbitrage cross-rate calculations may not exactly correspond to direct quotations (Frenkel and Levich, 1975). Therefore, all results in this chapter should be interpreted with caution. In constructing DM forward and spot exchange rates, US dollar cross-rate calculations are preferred because of the reserve currency status of the US dollar, the role of the US dollar as the world's major intervention currency and the scale and efficiency of the US financial markets. At least with US dollar cross-rate calculations, the transactions costs involved in triangular arbitrage are minimized.

Another difficulty with respect to the measurement of money market integration results from the fact that financial assets are heterogeneous. Measuring money market integration with parity conditions boils down to finding similar assets in terms of default risk, size, depth and term to maturity. We obtained *representative* three-month domestic money market interest rates from Eurostat (see Appendix 2A1). Furthermore, for tests of interest parity conditions it is important that the timing of the interest rate data corresponds with the timing of the exchange rate data.[13] We agree with Haldane and Pradhan (1992b, p. 8) that *domestic* money market interest rates are to be preferred to pick up the effect of capital controls between EC countries in a way potentially overlooked if Euro currency interest rates are used.[14]

An even more serious problem concerns the modelling of exchange rate and price expectations.[15] Because exchange rate and price expectations cannot be observed, one generally formulates an assumption on how expectations are formed. We proxy exchange rate and price expectations by their observed values on the basis of rational expectations. Of course, there are other methods to model exchange rate and price expectations, for example, from an ARIMA model (see Barro and Sala-I-Martin, 1990, p. 17), survey data (see Haldane and Pradhan, 1992b) or regression analysis.[16] However, these methods also do not rule out systematic forecast errors.[17] When exchange rate expectations are assumed to be rational, *ex ante* UIP changes into *ex post* UIP. Rational expectations imply that the realized exchange rate change is used as a proxy for the expected exchange rate change. The underlying assumption of rationality means that the forecast errors of exchange rates have mean zero $E(\eta_{t+k}/I_t) = E_t s_{t+k} - s_{t+k} = 0$ and are uncorrelated. Hence, the *ex ante* spot exchange rate at time $t+k$ conditional on available information at time $t$ equals the *ex post* spot exchange rate at time $t+k$, that is, $E_t s_{t+k} = s_{t+k}$. Deviations from *ex post* UIP may therefore be caused by the lack of capital mobility of type II and or expectational errors.[18] Similarly, *ex ante* RIP is difficult to calculate since expected inflation rates are not observable. The calculation of *ex post* real interest rate differentials implicitly assumes that expectations are rational. The *ex post* real interest rate is defined as the nominal interest rate minus the realized rate of inflation, $r_{t,t+k} = i_{t,t+k} - (p_{t+k} - p_t)$ for the domestic country and $r_{t,t+k}^* = i_{t,t+k}^* - (p_{t+k}^* - p_t^*)$ for the foreign country. The forecast errors of inflation equal the forecast errors of real interest rates: $\varepsilon_{t+k} = E_t r_{t,t+k} - r_{t,t+k}$ and $\varepsilon_{t+k}^* = E_t r_{t,t+k}^* - r_{t,t+k}^*$. The forecast errors of inflation and real interest rates $E(\varepsilon_{t+k}/I_t) = 0$ and $E(\varepsilon_{t+k}^*/I_t) = 0$ have mean zero and are uncorrelated. The equality of real interest rates across countries than implies (Mishkin, 1984, p. 1347): $E_t r_{t,t+k}^* = E_t r_{t,t+k}^* = r_{t,t+k}^* = r_{t,t-k}^*$.

Following Gaab, Granziol and Horner (1986, p. 693), we express deviations from CIP, *ex post* UIP and *ex post* RIP in *percentages per year*.[19] Deviations from CIP are defined as $[\ln(1+i_{t,t+3}) - \ln(1+i_{t,t+3}^*) - (12/3)(f_t^{t+3}-s_t)] \times 100$ where $i_{t,t+3}$ and $i_{t,t+3}^*$ are representative domestic and foreign money market interest rates over the three-month holding period expressed in percentages per year and $[(12/3)(f_t^{t+3}-s_t)] \times 100$ is the three-month forward premium (discount) *vis-à-vis* the DM expressed in percentages per year. Returns are measured in the domestic currency.[20] Similarly, deviations from *ex post* UIP are defined as $[\ln(1+i_{t,t+3}) - \ln(1+i_{t,t+3}^*) - (12/3)(s_{t+3}-s_t)] \times 100$ where $[(12/3)(s_{t+3}-s_t)] \times 100$ is the realized rate of depreciation (appreciation) *vis-à-vis* the DM over the three-month holding period expressed in percentages per year.[21] Deviations from *ex post* RIP are defined as $[[\ln(1+i_{t,t+3}) - (12/3)(p_{t+3}-p_t)] - [\ln(1+i_{t,t+3}^*) - (12/3)(p_{t+3}^*-p_t^*)]] \times 100$ where $[(12/3)(p_{t+3}-p_t)] \times 100$ is the change in natural logarithms of domestic consumer price indices over the three-month holding period in percentages per year. The *ex post* exchange risk premium is defined as the difference between the forward premium (discount) and the realized spot exchange rate change $[(12/3)(f_t^{t+3}-s_t) - (12/3)(s_{t+3}-s_t)] \times 100$ expressed in percentages per year. Deviations from *ex post* PPP are defined as $[(12/3)(s_{t+k}-s_t) - (12/3)(p_{t+k}-p_t) + (12/3)(p_{t+k}^*-p_t^*)] \times 100$. Finally, the *ex post* currency premium is defined as $[[(12/3)(f_t^{t+3}-s_t) - (12/3)(s_{t+3}-s_t)] + [(12/3)(s_{t+k}-s_t) - (12/3)(p_{t+k}-p_t) + (12/3)(p_{t+k}^*-p_t^*)]] \times 100$. We calculate consumer price index based real interest rates for three reasons. First, its monthly availability (except for Ireland whose consumer price indices are only quarterly available), second, the EMU-criterion for inflation is framed in terms of changes in the consumer price index and third, the basket of goods contains traded and non-traded goods and thus is a better measure of purchasing power than when the basket contained only traded goods (see Italianer, 1993, p. 24).

The sample period March 1979–August 1992 is split into two subperiods: March 1979–September 1987 and October 1987–August 1992. The break is formed by the Basle–Nyborg agreement of September 1987 when the Committee of Governors agreed on a number of measures to change the operating mechanisms of the EMS to promote exchange rate stability. Table 2.2 summarizes the Basle–Nyborg agreement and the four stages of the transmission mechanism of monetary policy, that is, monetary instruments, monetary indicators, monetary targets and policy goals. The Basle–Nyborg agreement opted for a more active and concerted use of available instruments (exchange rate movements within the band, interest rate changes and foreign exchange market interventions) to promote exchange rate stability in the ERM. Improved coordination of interest rate policies to keep the exchange rates within the band and a more flexible use of existing fluctuation margins helped to prevent specu-

*Table 2.2 The Basle–Nyborg agreement and the transmission mechanism of monetary policy*

| Transmission mechanism | Basle–Nyborg agreement |
|---|---|
| Monetary instruments | More coordinated management of official rates.<br><br>Improvement of practices and conditions for intervention at or within the margins:<br><br>a. Extension of the duration of very short-term financing to finance intervention in EMS currencies from two-and-a-half to three-and-a-half months. Doubling of the ceiling applied to automatic renewal for three months of these financing operations from 100 per cent to 200 per cent of the central banks' debtor quota in the short-term monetary support.<br>b. Availability of very short-term financing, on certain conditions, for intra-marginal interventions.<br>c. Change of the acceptance limit on official ECU settlements of outstanding claims in the very short-term financing in excess of their obligations (50 per cent) up to 100 per cent.<br><br>More flexible use of authorized fluctuation margins.<br><br>Realignments. |
| Monetary indicators | Interbank money market rates. |
| Monetary targets | Main target Germany: growth of M3.<br><br>Additional target Germany: real DM/US dollar exchange rate.<br><br>Main target other European countries: relative position own currency within the ERM band and/or the nominal exchange rate of own currency *vis-à-vis* the DM/US dollar.<br><br>Additional target other European countries: growth of M1, M2 or M3. |
| Policy goals | Domestic price level. |

*Sources:* Committee of Governors of the Central Banks of the Member States of the European Economic Community (1987) and Eijffinger (1993, p. 134).

lative attacks on the ERM central rates. Furthermore, the break coincides with a relatively calm period with less frequent and sizeable exchange rate realignments (devaluations). After January 1987 no major realignment occurred for more than five years until the EMS exchange crisis of September 1992. In addition, a number of EC countries entered the ERM of the EMS. Nevertheless, concerns arose about the 'asymmetry' in the EMS where Germany focuses on price stability and other ERM countries focus on maintaining their currency's exchange rates *vis-à-vis* the DM. We choose Germany as the reference country, because of its anchor function in the EMS.

Table 2.3 reports the developments in the frequency and magnitude of exchange rate realignments within the ERM of the EMS. In the first subperiod March 1979–September 1987 the exchange rate of high inflation countries usually devalued immediately during periods of exchange rate tensions to maintain

*Table 2.3 Dates and sizes of EMS realignments (per cent)*[a]

| Date | Bel | Den | Fra | Ger | Ire | Ita[d] | Net | Por | Spa | UK[d] |
|---|---|---|---|---|---|---|---|---|---|---|
| 24/09/79 | – | –3.00 | – | +2.00 | – | – | – | – | – | – |
| 30/11/79 | – | –5.00 | – | – | – | – | – | – | – | – |
| 23/03/81 | – | – | – | – | – | –6.00 | – | – | – | – |
| 05/10/81 | – | – | –3.00 | +5.50 | – | –3.00 | +5.50 | – | – | – |
| 22/02/82 | –8.50 | –3.00 | – | – | – | – | – | – | – | – |
| 14/06/82 | – | – | –5.75 | +4.25 | – | –2.75 | +4.25 | – | – | – |
| 21/03/83 | +1.50 | +2.50 | –2.50 | +5.50 | –3.50 | –2.50 | +3.50 | – | – | – |
| 18/05/83[b] | –1.90 | –1.90 | –1.90 | –1.90 | –1.90 | –1.90 | –1.90 | – | – | – |
| 22/07/85 | +2.00 | +2.00 | +2.00 | +2.00 | +2.00 | –6.00 | +2.00 | – | – | – |
| 07/04/86 | +1.00 | +1.00 | –3.00 | +3.00 | – | – | +3.00 | – | – | – |
| 04/08/86 | – | – | – | – | –8.00 | – | – | – | – | – |
| 12/01/87 | +2.00 | – | – | +3.00 | – | – | +3.00 | – | – | – |
| 08/01/90 | – | – | – | – | – | –3.68 | – | – | – | – |
| 14/09/92[c] | +3.50 | +3.50 | +3.50 | +3.50 | +3.50 | –3.50 | +3.50 | +3.50 | +3.50 | +3.50 |
| 17/09/92[c] | – | – | – | – | – | – | – | – | –5.00 | –5.00 |
| 23/11/92 | – | – | – | – | – | – | – | –6.00 | –6.00 | – |
| 01/02/93 | – | – | – | – | –10.0 | – | – | – | – | – |
| 14/05/93 | – | – | – | – | – | – | – | –6.50 | –8.00 | – |

*Symbols:*

| | | | | | | |
|---|---|---|---|---|---|---|
| Bel | = | Belgium/Luxemburg franc | | Ita | = | Italian lira |
| Den | = | Danish krona | | Net | = | Dutch guilder |
| Fra | = | French franc | | Por | = | Portuguese escudo |
| Ger | = | German mark | | Spa | = | Spanish peseta |
| Ire | = | Irish pound | | UK | = | British pound sterling |
| – | = | devaluation | | + | = | revaluation |

*Notes:*

[a]  Core-EMS countries which participate in the ERM of the EMS from 13 March 1979 onwards are: Belgium, Denmark, France, Germany, Ireland, Italy, The Netherlands and Luxemburg. Non-core-EMS countries are Spain which participates in the ERM as of 16 June 1989, the United Kingdom (as of 8 October 1990) and Portugal (as of 6 April 1992) and Greece which does not participate in the ERM at all. Belgium, Denmark, France, Germany, Ireland, The Netherlands and Luxemburg have a fluctuation margin of ± 2.25 per cent, Italy has a fluctuation margin of ± 6 per cent and as of 8 January 1990 ± 2.25 per cent, Portugal, Spain and the United Kingdom have a fluctuation margin of ± 6 per cent. On 1 August 1993, ERM bands were widened to ± 15 per cent except for the band between The Netherlands and Germany which remained unchanged at ± 2.25 per cent.

[b]  Adjustment of the theoretical central rates of the British pound sterling based on the market rates of 13 May 1983.

[c]  The realignment dates of 14 and 17 September 1992 reflect the first EMS exchange crisis.

[d]  The United Kingdom and Italy left the ERM on 17 September 1992.

*Source:* Eurostat (1993, p. 99).

competitiveness.[22] As a result the EMS behaved more or less as a 'crawling peg' system. The second subperiod October 1987–August 1992 was characterized by a widespread consensus to follow stability-oriented policies, an increasing convergence in inflation rates, and by long periods without realignments (Ungerer, 1990). The second subperiod also coincides with important capital liberalization directives. The sample period runs until the first

EMS exchange crisis of September 1992. Italy and the United Kingdom left the ERM and floated their currencies. Ireland, Portugal and Spain adjusted their central parity.

## 2.4 The Degree of Money Market Integration

This section examines the size and variability of mean deviations and mean absolute deviations from CIP, *ex post* UIP and *ex post* RIP to assess the degree of money market integration in Europe. First, we calculate monthly (absolute) deviations from CIP, *ex post* UIP and *ex post* RIP along the lines set out in Section 2.3. We regress those monthly (absolute) deviations ($y_t$ and $/y_t/$) against a constant term over the relevant period:

$$y_t = \beta_0 + e_t \qquad /y_t/ = \beta_0 + e_t \qquad (2.6)$$

If equation (2.6) is estimated with ordinary least squares (OLS) the coefficient $\beta_0$ is simply the mean (absolute) deviation:

$$\beta_0 = T^{-1} \sum_{t=1}^{T} y_t \qquad /\beta_0/ = T^{-1} \sum_{t=1}^{T} /y_t/ \qquad (2.7)$$

Table 2.4 reports mean (absolute) deviations from CIP, *ex post* UIP and *ex post* RIP of ten European countries *vis-à-vis* Germany over the periods March 1979–September 1987, October 1987–August 1992 and March 1979–August 1992. Moreover, Table 2.4 decomposes mean deviations from *ex post* UIP and *ex post* RIP into their components. Deviations from *ex post* UIP are decomposed into a country premium and an *ex post* exchange risk premium. Deviations from *ex post* RIP are decomposed into a country premium, an *ex post* exchange risk premium and a deviation from *ex post* PPP. Each of these components should be zero for a particular type of capital mobility to hold.[23] Of course, we cannot decompose mean *absolute* deviations into their components.

Although the calculations in Table 2.4 have been confined to the bilateral relationships between ten EC member states and Germany, Table 2.4 also determines those deviations between any two EC countries. For example, if mean deviations from *ex post* RIP between France and Germany and between the United Kingdom and Germany are known, we are able to calculate mean deviations from *ex post* RIP between France and the United Kingdom as follows: $r_{t,t+3}^{UK} - r_{t,t+3}^{FRA} = r_{t,t+3}^{UK} - r_{t,t+3}^{GER} - (r_{t,t+3}^{FRA} - r_{t,t+3}^{GER})$. The same holds of course for the building blocks of *ex post* RIP, that is, the country premium, the *ex post* exchange risk premium and the deviation from *ex post* PPP.

The use of mean deviations as a basis for the judgement of capital mobility may be misleading. Suppose all deviations are white noise. Under this condition

the expected deviation is zero but in any individual period large deviations may
occur. Large outliers may bias mean deviations while all other observations
are (close to) zero. Then, mean deviations signal perfect capital mobility despite
the fact that capital is immobile internationally. The analysis may suggest that
CIP holds *on average* over the period, while in fact it did not hold at *any instant*
during the period. Thus, the calculations in Table 2.4 are to be interpreted with
care. However, since in Figure 2A3.1 in Appendix 2A3 the underlying charts
are provided, this criticism is of limited importance. Furthermore, we also report
mean absolute deviations.

It is important to note that the error term $e_t$ in equation (2.6) will follow
a moving-average process of order two (MA(2)) because of what is known as
the *overlapping samples* problem (Hansen and Hodrick, 1980). The data
frequency (one month) exceeds the length of the holding period (three months).
With monthly data, any innovation occurring in month t will affect the value
of instruments maturing in months $t$, $t+1$ and $t+2$. This suggests correlation
between the error terms one and two months apart, but zero correlation between
error terms further apart (see Appendix 2A2). Therefore, Table 2.4 also reports
Newey–West (1987) standard errors to account for heteroscedasticity and
autocorrelation resulting from overlapping data.[24]

## (1) Deviations from CIP

The CIP condition is the least stringent criterion for money market integration.
Deviations from CIP, that is, country premia, measure the ability to move money
market assets across national borders. The country premium reflects the existence
of transaction costs, capital controls (existing or expected), information costs,
discriminatory tax laws, default risk and/or imperfections in the data.[25] A
negative country premium is indicative of capital export restrictions, the domestic
return is artificially low to the German return and capital export restrictions
exist. On the other hand, a positive country premium is indicative of capital
import restrictions (Commission of the European Communities, 1990, p. 160).

According to Table 2.4, the size and variability of country premia declined
significantly after the Basle–Nyborg agreement as indicated by the size and
variability of mean deviations and mean absolute deviations from CIP. Belgium,
Denmark, France, Ireland, Italy, The Netherlands, Spain and the United Kingdom
have average country premia in percentage per year of not more than 50 basis
points in absolute value over the period October 1987–August 1992, probably
only reflecting transaction costs.[26] Portugal and Greece are the only countries
with average country premia of more than 50 basis points in absolute value
over the period October 1987–August 1992. Investment in Portuguese escudo
gave an annual excess return of 0.55 per cent while investment in the Greek
drachma gave an annual loss of 3.41 per cent. An important explanation for
the above results was the directive of 24 June 1988, when the European

Commission stated that as from 1 July 1990 all short- and long-term capital movements in Europe are to be free of restrictions. However, Greece, Ireland, Portugal and Spain did not have to fulfil this directive until 31 December 1992. Moreover, Portugal and Greece had the possibility of postponing implementation of this directive until 31 December 1995. In practice this meant that restrictions on short-term capital movements had to disappear (many restrictions on long-term capital movements had already been lifted).

With respect to the size of *mean* CIP deviations [1] over the period March 1979–August 1992 – measured as the positive or negative difference from zero in absolute value – we may list the countries in ascending order of estimated degree of CIP integration as follows: Portugal, Greece (calculated over the period September 1984–August 1992), Spain, France, Italy, Denmark, Belgium, Ireland, the United Kingdom and The Netherlands. With respect to the size of *mean absolute* deviations from CIP [|1|] over the period March 1979–August 1992, we may list the countries in ascending order of estimated degree of CIP integration as follows: Portugal, Greece (calculated over the period September 1984–August 1992), Spain, France, Italy, Denmark, Ireland, Belgium, the United Kingdom and The Netherlands. The order of estimated degree of CIP integration as measured by mean deviations and mean absolute deviations appears to be almost equivalent. Thus, Portugal, Greece and Spain show the lowest degree of CIP integration *vis-à-vis* Germany and maintained many capital controls during the period March 1979–August 1992. The Netherlands and the United Kingdom show the highest degree of CIP integration. The results in Table 2.4 confirm the findings of a previous study of mean deviations from CIP relative to Germany over the period September 1982 to April 1988 (see Commission of the European Communities, 1990, pp. 160–1). The Commission of the European Communities basically transformed Frankel's (1989) calculations of money market interest rate differentials with respect to the United States in the following way: $r_{t,t+3}^{UK} - r_{t,t+3}^{FRA} = r_{t,t+3}^{UK} - r_{t,t+3}^{GER} - (r_{t,t+3}^{FRA} - r_{t,t+3}^{GER})$.[27]

## (2) *Ex post* exchange risk premia

Table 2.4 also reports the *ex post* exchange risk premium. The *ex post* exchange risk premium is the difference between the forward premium (discount) and the realized spot exchange rate change. It is difficult to know the exact sign and magnitude of the exchange risk premium because the expected exchange rate is not directly observable, so *ex post* devaluation in stead of *ex ante* devaluation has to be used. A positive (negative) *ex post* exchange risk premium arises when the *ex post* devaluation is lower (higher) than the forward premium.

With respect to the size of *mean ex post* exchange risk premia [2] over the period March 1979–August 1992 – measured as the positive or negative difference from zero in absolute value – we may list the countries in ascending order as follows: The Netherlands, Greece (calculated over the period Septem-

Table 2.4  Mean (absolute) deviations from CIP, ex post UIP and ex post RIP and their components (percentages per year)

$$y_t = \beta_0 + e_t \quad \text{and} \quad |y_t| = \beta_0 + e_t$$

| March 1979–September 1987 | CIP | | Exchange risk premium | | UIP | | PPP | | Currency premium | | RIP | |
|---|---|---|---|---|---|---|---|---|---|---|---|---|
| | 1 | \|1\| | 2 | \|2\| | 3=1+2 | \|3\| | 4 | \|4\| | 5=2+4 | \|5\| | 6=1+5 | \|6\| |
| Belgium | -0.96 (0.23) | 1.11 (0.22) | 1.69 (1.12) | 4.88 (0.80) | 0.73 (1.18) | 4.42 (0.85) | 1.12 (1.16) | 4.15 (0.93) | 2.81 (0.49) | 3.39 (0.37) | 1.85 (0.40) | 2.65 (0.27) |
| Denmark | -0.94 (0.26) | 1.63 (0.22) | 2.21 (1.02) | 5.82 (0.61) | 1.26 (1.07) | 5.82 (0.59) | -0.16 (1.05) | 5.77 (0.61) | 2.05 (0.62) | 3.54 (0.44) | 1.11 (0.60) | 3.55 (0.34) |
| France | -2.68 (0.47) | 2.76 (0.47) | 2.24 (1.05) | 6.60 (0.72) | -0.44 (1.09) | 5.10 (0.68) | -0.29 (1.20) | 5.63 (0.74) | 1.96 (0.74) | 3.55 (0.51) | -0.72 (0.54) | 2.57 (0.29) |
| Greece[a] | – | – | – | – | -7.64 (3.24) | 14.55 (2.60) | 2.75 (3.14) | 14.94 (2.26) | – | – | -4.89 (1.12) | 8.00 (0.74) |
| Ireland | -0.75 (0.12) | 0.98 (0.13) | 3.49 (1.26) | 6.63 (0.83) | 2.74 (1.25) | 6.14 (0.85) | -2.76 (1.48) | 6.68 (0.99) | 0.73 (0.82) | 3.82 (0.43) | -0.02 (0.86) | 3.86 (0.47) |
| Italy | -2.34 (0.58) | 2.66 (0.50) | 4.73 (1.05) | 7.84 (0.66) | 2.39 (1.01) | 6.39 (0.52) | -2.56 (1.16) | 6.65 (0.71) | 2.17 (0.73) | 4.15 (0.43) | -0.17 (0.84) | 3.55 (0.50) |
| The Netherlands | -0.32 (0.06) | 0.54 (0.09) | 0.40 (0.55) | 2.78 (0.36) | 0.08 (0.54) | 2.69 (0.36) | 0.32 (0.64) | 3.54 (0.35) | 0.73 (0.36) | 2.56 (0.22) | 0.41 (0.37) | 2.43 (0.22) |
| Portugal | -7.62 (1.13) | 7.72 (1.12) | 3.73 (2.07) | 12.03 (1.41) | -3.89 (2.21) | 10.51 (1.44) | 0.62 (2.42) | 11.99 (1.46) | 4.35 (1.43) | 7.42 (0.93) | -3.27 (1.12) | 6.49 (0.61) |
| Spain | -3.27 (0.50) | 3.78 (0.49) | 3.89 (2.19) | 11.43 (1.32) | 0.62 (2.36) | 11.24 (1.42) | -0.26 (2.22) | 10.51 (1.36) | 3.63 (0.83) | 4.87 (0.65) | 0.36 (0.80) | 3.81 (0.44) |
| United Kingdom | -0.57 (0.10) | 0.72 (0.09) | 2.58 (3.53) | 18.13 (1.83) | 2.02 (3.48) | 17.85 (1.80) | -1.63 (3.77) | 18.83 (2.03) | 0.95 (0.67) | 3.49 (0.37) | 0.38 (0.70) | 3.42 (0.41) |

| October 1987–August 1992 | CIP | | Exchange risk premium | | UIP | | PPP | | Currency premium | | RIP | |
|---|---|---|---|---|---|---|---|---|---|---|---|---|
| | 1 | \|1\| | 2 | \|2\| | 3=1+2 | \|3\| | 4 | \|4\| | 5=2+4 | \|5\| | 6=1+5 | \|6\| |
| Belgium | 0.06 (0.03) | 0.12 (0.01) | 1.31 (0.43) | 1.56 (0.38) | 1.37 (0.42) | 1.59 (0.38) | 0.04 (0.51) | 2.00 (0.24) | 1.34 (0.45) | 2.11 (0.29) | 1.40 (0.44) | 2.12 (0.27) |
| Denmark | -0.12 (0.07) | 0.24 (0.05) | 2.16 (0.77) | 3.14 (0.55) | 2.04 (0.73) | 3.05 (0.51) | -0.34 (0.70) | 2.96 (0.26) | 1.83 (0.43) | 2.38 (0.35) | 1.71 (0.44) | 2.32 (0.35) |
| France | -0.10 (0.06) | 0.17 (0.05) | 1.68 (0.58) | 2.84 (0.30) | 1.58 (0.56) | 2.78 (0.29) | 0.02 (0.56) | 2.49 (0.27) | 1.70 (0.58) | 1.97 (0.32) | 1.60 (0.36) | 1.89 (0.29) |
| Greece | -3.41 (0.66) | 3.96 (0.53) | 4.04 (1.28) | 6.20 (0.69) | 0.63 (1.36) | 5.36 (0.61) | -1.39 (1.49) | 6.34 (0.87) | 2.65 (1.06) | 6.46 (0.51) | -0.76 (1.09) | 5.87 (0.50) |
| Ireland | 0.32 (0.08) | 0.44 (0.05) | 1.93 (0.52) | 2.36 (0.42) | 2.25 (0.52) | 2.49 (0.47) | -0.24 (0.43) | 1.93 (0.19) | 1.69 (0.37) | 2.08 (0.26) | 2.01 (0.38) | 2.29 (0.29) |
| Italy | 0.02 (0.08) | 0.30 (0.05) | 3.47 (1.00) | 4.79 (0.66) | 3.50 (0.97) | 4.72 (0.66) | -1.93 (0.92) | 3.93 (0.56) | 1.54 (0.46) | 2.01 (0.35) | 1.57 (0.42) | 1.92 (0.34) |
| The Netherlands | 0.07 (0.02) | 0.11 (0.02) | 0.19 (0.17) | 0.67 (0.11) | 0.26 (0.17) | 0.65 (0.11) | 0.45 (0.51) | 2.35 (0.31) | 0.64 (0.56) | 2.37 (0.34) | 0.71 (0.55) | 2.34 (0.34) |
| Portugal | 0.55 (0.45) | 1.60 (0.24) | 5.33 (1.10) | 7.02 (0.74) | 5.88 (1.31) | 7.72 (0.88) | -5.95 (1.44) | 8.39 (0.89) | -0.62 (0.67) | 3.08 (0.28) | -0.07 (0.74) | 2.92 (0.41) |
| Spain | 0.13 (0.10) | 0.34 (0.09) | 6.84 (1.69) | 8.20 (1.43) | 6.97 (1.74) | 8.38 (1.48) | -4.22 (1.58) | 7.49 (1.02) | 2.62 (0.58) | 3.58 (0.35) | 2.75 (0.61) | 3.70 (0.38) |
| United Kingdom | 0.18 (0.16) | 0.45 (0.13) | 3.36 (2.52) | 9.40 (1.48) | 3.55 (2.52) | 9.46 (1.47) | -2.55 (2.77) | 9.85 (1.56) | 0.81 (0.58) | 2.98 (0.36) | 1.00 (0.60) | 3.06 (0.37) |

| March 1979–August 1992 | CIP | | Exchange risk premium | | UIP | | PPP | | Currency premium | | RIP | |
|---|---|---|---|---|---|---|---|---|---|---|---|---|
| | 1 | \|1\| | 2 | \|2\| | 3=1+2 | \|3\| | 4 | \|4\| | 5=2+4 | \|5\| | 6=1+5 | \|6\| |
| Belgium | -0.59 (0.17) | 0.75 (0.16) | 1.55 (0.73) | 3.67 (0.58) | 0.96 (0.77) | 3.39 (0.59) | 0.73 (0.76) | 3.37 (0.62) | 2.28 (0.37) | 2.93 (0.28) | 1.69 (0.30) | 2.46 (0.20) |
| Denmark | -0.64 (0.18) | 1.13 (0.17) | 2.19 (0.70) | 4.85 (0.48) | 1.55 (0.73) | 4.81 (0.47) | -0.22 (0.71) | 4.75 (0.45) | 1.97 (0.42) | 3.12 (0.31) | 1.33 (0.42) | 3.10 (0.27) |
| France | -1.74 (0.36) | 1.82 (0.36) | 2.04 (0.70) | 5.23 (0.55) | 0.30 (0.74) | 4.25 (0.48) | -0.17 (0.79) | 4.48 (0.54) | 1.86 (0.49) | 2.98 (0.36) | 0.12 (0.41) | 2.32 (0.22) |
| Greece[b] | -2.35 (1.05) | 5.13 (0.55) | -1.07 (3.16) | 10.27 (2.46) | -3.42 (2.58) | 8.62 (2.12) | 1.55 (2.31) | 9.39 (1.74) | 0.48 (1.53) | 7.57 (0.81) | -1.87 (0.93) | 6.20 (0.52) |
| Ireland | -0.36 (0.12) | 0.78 (0.09) | 2.92 (0.83) | 5.08 (0.63) | 2.56 (0.81) | 4.81 (0.63) | -1.84 (0.97) | 4.95 (0.73) | 1.08 (0.54) | 3.18 (0.32) | 0.72 (0.58) | 3.29 (0.34) |
| Italy | -1.48 (0.41) | 1.80 (0.38) | 4.27 (0.77) | 6.72 (0.53) | 2.80 (0.74) | 5.78 (0.43) | -2.33 (0.81) | 5.66 (0.53) | 1.94 (0.49) | 3.37 (0.34) | 0.46 (0.57) | 2.95 (0.36) |
| The Netherlands | -0.18 (0.05) | 0.38 (0.07) | 0.32 (0.36) | 2.01 (0.28) | 0.15 (0.35) | 1.95 (0.28) | 0.37 (0.45) | 3.10 (0.26) | 0.69 (0.30) | 2.49 (0.19) | 0.52 (0.31) | 2.40 (0.19) |
| Portugal | -4.64 (0.96) | 5.49 (0.85) | 4.31 (1.38) | 10.21 (1.01) | -0.33 (1.66) | 9.49 (0.99) | -1.77 (1.70) | 10.68 (1.03) | 2.54 (1.00) | 5.84 (0.68) | -2.11 (0.80) | 5.19 (0.49) |
| Spain | -2.03 (0.41) | 2.53 (0.41) | 4.97 (1.56) | 10.26 (1.02) | 2.94 (1.72) | 10.20 (1.08) | -1.70 (1.57) | 9.41 (0.97) | 3.26 (0.57) | 4.40 (0.44) | 1.23 (0.58) | 3.77 (0.31) |
| United Kingdom | 0.29 (0.10) | 0.62 (0.08) | 2.87 (2.42) | 14.95 (1.44) | 2.57 (2.39) | 14.80 (1.42) | -1.97 (2.59) | 15.56 (1.57) | 0.90 (0.47) | 3.31 (0.27) | 0.61 (0.50) | 3.29 (0.30) |

*Notes:*

[a] Calculated over the period May 1980–September 1987.
[b] Calculated over the period September 1984–August 1992.

Newey–West (1987) standard errors of mean (absolute) deviations are indicated in parentheses.

*Source:* See Appendix 2A1.

ber 1984–August 1992), Belgium, France, Denmark, the United Kingdom, Ireland, Italy, Portugal and Spain. With respect to the size of *mean absolute ex post* exchange risk premia [|2|] over the period March 1979–August 1992, we may list the countries in ascending order as follows: The Netherlands, Belgium, Denmark, Ireland, France, Italy, Portugal, Spain, Greece (calculated over the period September 1984–August 1992) and the United Kingdom. Notice the difference between the ascending orders of [2] and [|2|]. Large outliers bias mean *ex post* exchange risk premia. Forecast errors in predicting future spot exchange rates are quite sizeable; so differences in expected and realized returns can also be quite sizeable in any period. But with respect to The Netherlands an insignificant mean exchange risk premium seems plausible due to a relative stable Dutch guilder/DM exchange rate.

Although the *ex post* exchange risk premium declined in the core-EMS countries after September 1987, it remained rather persistent despite relatively large intra-European exchange rate stability (compare the subperiods March 1979–September 1987 and October 1987–August 1992). The Netherlands is the only country with a relative small exchange risk premium *vis-à-vis* Germany in all (sub)periods. Furthermore, note that mean (absolute) country premia are smaller and less variable than mean (absolute) exchange risk premia. Moreover, non-core-EMS countries show higher exchange risk premia than core-EMS countries. Although some exchange rates of EMS countries are within a small band, the possibility of an exchange rate realignment in the EMS always influences nominal exchange rate expectations which cause short-term (and long-term) nominal interest rate divergences. Exchange rate volatility makes domestic money market instruments and German money market instruments less than perfect substitutes. German investors are only *willing* to hold the foreign assets if they obtain compensation in the form of an exchange risk premium. This argument assumes that CIP holds continuously and the *ex post* exchange risk premium is a good measure of the willingness to hold foreign assets. If exchange risk is just priced risk, investors will be perfectly willing to invest abroad since the exchange risk premium is just a fair reward for the exchange risk they bear. Of course, capital was far from immobile during the EMS exchange crisis of September 1992. Consequently, large exchange risk premia do not always mean that capital is immobile. Exchange risk which not priced hampers capital mobility.

### (3) Deviations from *ex post* UIP
A stronger criterion for money market integration is the UIP condition. UIP measures the ability and willingness to move money market assets across national borders. A positive deviation from *ex post* UIP means that the market requires a higher return from domestic investments than from German investments. With respect to the size of mean deviations from *ex post* UIP [3]

over the period March 1979–August 1992 – measured as the positive or negative difference from zero in absolute value – we may list the countries in ascending order of estimated degree of UIP integration as follows: Greece (calculated over the period September 1984–August 1992), Spain, Italy, the United Kingdom, Ireland, Denmark, Belgium, Portugal, France and The Netherlands. With respect to the size of mean absolute deviations from *ex post* UIP [|3|] over the period March 1979–August 1992, we may list the countries in ascending order of estimated degree of UIP integration as follows: the United Kingdom, Spain, Portugal, Greece (calculated (over the period September 1984–August 1992), Italy, Ireland, Denmark, France, Belgium and The Netherlands. According to Table 2.4, the smallest mean (absolute) deviation from *ex post* UIP relative to Germany over all (sub)periods is that of The Netherlands.

Next, we briefly discuss some critical measurement issues. Clearly, large outliers bias the results with respect to mean deviations from *ex post* UIP. Outliers are caused by large nominal exchange rate variability. The money market of the United Kingdom is not very well integrated with the money market of Germany according to the UIP condition in contrast with the integration according to the CIP condition. German investors who invest in the United Kingdom apparently demand an exchange risk premium before they are willing to invest in the United Kingdom. German investors are risk averse and demand compensation in the form of an (possibly time-varying) exchange risk premium to hold the more risky assets of other EC countries. In general, the relative strengths of risk aversion in the two countries will play a key role in determining the exchange risk premium. Another factor will be the relative size of asset positions. More risk averse German investors will only hold those assets of EC countries with less frequent and sizeable realignments (that is, devaluations) or will demand a higher exchange risk premium. The additional assumption required for UIP (that is, zero exchange risk premium) dilutes the inference from the UIP condition with respect to the degree of money market integration. The interpretation of *ex post* UIP deviations remains unclear because it entails a joint test of two underlying hypotheses. Deviations from *ex post* UIP may reflect a lack of short-term capital mobility of type II and/or expectational errors. Consequently, inference of the degree of money market integration based upon *ex post* UIP differentials must be done with caution.

Note also that inference of the degree of money market integration based upon one segment of the domestic and foreign money markets corresponding with two comparable money market assets is not always wise. Segmentation within the *domestic* financial market may affect the representative money market interest rate (Obstfeld, 1994a, p. 19). Assets may differ considerably in terms of quality of debtor, size, depth and segmentation of markets.

Moreover, in the EMS, short-term nominal interest rates are used as policy instruments to keep exchange rates within the allowed fluctuation margin. Fukao and Hanazaki (1987, p. 75) argue: 'Under an actual adjustable peg system such as the EMS, the nominal interest rates are not equalized in the short-run. This divergence of interest rates is due to the allowed margin of movements in the exchange rates and possible future changes in the parity rates'. When financial markets expect an exchange rate devaluation, high short-term nominal interest rate differentials with respect to Germany are needed to maintain the exchange rate in the allowed fluctuation margins of the EMS. Short-term nominal interest rates not only fluctuate in response to *market* forces but to *policy* forces as well. Therefore, it is hard to isolate the market induced effect of money market integration from the policy induced effect of money market integration.[28] Consequently, declining *ex post* UIP (and CIP and *ex post* RIP) differentials may also be attributed to convergence in the implementation and performance of monetary policies of EMS countries as measured by the development of four key variables: inflation rates, real exchange rates, real short-term interest rates (money market rates) and real long-term interest rates (capital market rates) (Eijffinger, 1993, p. 182). Eijffinger (1994, pp. 10-3) argues that the integration of financial markets also makes high demands on institutional convergence, that is, the convergence of *financial market structure* and *monetary responsibilities*. Financial market structure is related to, among others, the maturities, techniques and volumes of the national money and capital markets and the organization of financial transactions and operations. Monetary responsibilities apply to the final authority in monetary policy making, the presence of statutory requirements concerning monetary stability and the relationship between the central bank and the government in the formulation of monetary policy.

Furthermore, European money market interest rates are not only influenced by *intra-EMS* capital mobility, but also by *extra-EMS* capital mobility in accordance with international interest arbitrage relationships. Capital mobility between Europe and the rest of the world may confuse the issue of measurement of capital mobility within Europe. Changing demand for short-term capital in Europe may change the supply of capital from abroad.

In addition, note that even under the rational expectation assumption, exchange rate forecast errors can have a sample average different from zero for a long time as a consequence of the existence of a *peso problem* in foreign exchange markets where jumps in exchange rates are expected but not realized in a particular sample period (Krasker, 1980). Peso problems can be found in fixed exchange rate periods when parity changes are expected.[29] Market participants may systematically over- or underestimate changes in exchange rates until the exchange rate change occurs.[30] Peso problems are particularly relevant for exchange rates of currencies belonging to the ERM in which realignments do not occur very frequently. Consider the evidence on uncovered interest differentials in Table 2.4. The third column measures the excess uncovered return on ten currencies relative to the DM. Table 2.4 shows high positive deviations from UIP for the Irish pound, the Italian lira, the Portuguese escudo, the Spanish peseta and the British pound sterling over the period September 1987 (the period after the Basle–Nyborg agreement) and August 1992 (the period prior to the first EMS exchange crisis). Interestingly, those are the currencies that suffered from important depreciations since September 1992 as a consequence of ERM realignments (or abandonments of the ERM). Interest rate differentials could have been discounting these unusual events, that is, a peso problem, rather than an exchange risk premium arises. For example, the excess return on the Italian lira conforms closely to the peso model. Prior to dropping out of the ERM, an Italian lira deposit earns 3.5 per cent more than a mark deposit both measured in Italian lira. The higher return on Italian lira deposits compensated the DM based investor for the expected capital loss due to the devaluation of the Italian lira. With the exchange crisis of September 1992 these excess returns are eliminated.

An important issue is the question what will happen with *ex post* UIP deviations if the system of fixed but adjustable exchange rates changes into a system with irrevocably fixed exchange rates? That is, European countries adopt a single currency and form a monetary union. The Delors Report (1989, p. 10) outlines three necessary conditions for a monetary union: (1) the assurance of total and irreversible convertibility of currencies (2) the complete liberalization of capital transactions and full integration of banking and other financial markets and (3) the elimination of margins of fluctuations and the irrevocable locking of exchange rate parities. In the terminology of Table 2.1, perfect monetary integration implies short-term nominal interest parity. Short-term interest rate differentials carry important information about the extent of monetary integration and integration of foreign exchange markets.[31] Perfect monetary integration may be seen as a special case of UIP.[32] If exchange rate parities are irrevocably fixed and fluctuation margins are eliminated perfect monetary integration implies short-term nominal interest rate parity:

$$i_{t,t+k} = i^{*}_{t,t+k} \tag{2.8}$$

Consequently, the expected exchange rate change equals the realized exchange rate change and is zero by definition $[E_t(s_{t+k}-s_t)=(s_{t+k}-s_t)=0]$.[33] That is, investors have *perfect foresight*. Subsequently, we may decompose short-term nominal interest parity as follows:

$$i_{t,t+k} - i^{*}_{t,t+k} = [i_{t,t+k} - i^{*}_{t,t+k} - (f_t^{t+k} - s_t)] + [(f_t^{t+k} - s_t) - E_t(s_{t+k}-s_t)] +$$
$$E_t(s_{t+k}-s_t) \tag{2.9}$$

However, as Table 2.4 indicates, exchange risk premia are far from zero. Fixed nominal exchange rates are not feasible (yet).

## (4) Deviations from *ex post* relative PPP

The *ex post* relative PPP condition holds if the *ex post* real exchange rate between two countries remains constant. This means that the domestic currency depreciates at a rate equal to the *ex post* inflation differential. It also means that in the absence of relative price changes the nominal exchange rate change equals the real exchange rate change. Branson (1988, p. 1119) links the failure of PPP to the failure of goods market integration. Observe that movements in real exchange rates in the short-run tend to be dominated by nominal exchange rate changes rather than by relative price level changes. Mean deviations from UIP and mean deviations from *ex post* relative PPP often have opposite signs and partly cancel out. Exchange rates adjust much faster than interest rates and prices.

The failure of *ex post* relative PPP in the short-run is evident from Table 2.4 for most of the European countries. *Short-term ex post* PPP may be an unrealistic assumption with respect to money market integration, because as was argued by Boughton (1988, p. 18) it has '(...) little or no bearing on short- or medium-term developments'. That is, relative prices of domestic and foreign goods may be sticky in the short-run. In the short-run the real exchange rate may fluctuate around its equilibrium value while in the long-run we have mean reversion of the real exchange rate. However, the size and variability of mean (absolute) deviations from *ex post* PPP declined after the Basle–Nyborg agreement.

With respect to the size of mean deviations from *ex post* PPP [4] over the period March 1979–August 1992 – measured as the positive or negative difference from zero in absolute value – we may list the countries in ascending order as follows: France, Denmark, The Netherlands, Belgium, Greece (calculated over the period September 1984–August 1992), Spain, Portugal, Ireland, the United Kingdom and Italy. With respect to the size of mean absolute deviations from *ex post* PPP [|4|] over the period March 1979–August 1992, we may list the countries in ascending order as follows: The Netherlands, Belgium, France, Denmark, Ireland, Italy, Greece (calculated over the period September 1984–August 1992), Spain, Portugal and the United Kingdom. Again, outliers may bias the results with respect to mean *ex post* PPP deviations. Moreover, outliers may not only be caused by large nominal exchange rate variability but by large inflation rate variability as well. The calculations of *ex post* PPP require approximation of expected exchange rate changes and also approximation of expected relative price changes (Commission of the European Communities, 1990, p. 160). In addition, deviations from *ex post* PPP may be due to relative price changes of tradables and non-tradables in the consumption basket. Countries such as Ireland, Italy, Portugal, Spain and the United Kingdom show highly negative *ex post* deviations from PPP. As it is well known, during the EMS period these countries were depreciating their currency at a rate lower than their inflation differential with Germany. However, this is more a feature of the EMS of fixed but adjustable exchange rates than a measure of financial integration. Table 2.3 illustrated that the size and frequency of realignments had decreased until the exchange crisis of September 1992. Given divergent inflation rates, these realignments were necessary to preserve real exchange rate equilibrium within the EMS (Collins, 1988, p. 112). Theoretical work on the credibility of monetary policy suggests that if countries with higher inflation rates are to gain anti-inflation credibility through EMS membership in order to reduce their inflation rates to German levels, they need a real appreciating exchange rate with Germany. This is because full adjustment of exchange rates would amount to accommodation of domestic inflationary pressures, whereas less than full adjustment of exchange rates would involve an element of punishment for excess domestic inflation by squeezing profits margins of producers of tradable goods (Bleany, 1992, p. 66). Under a fixed but adjustable exchange rate regime such as the EMS, relative high inflation rates are expected to translate into a worsening in competitiveness (real appreciation), which in turn dampens prices and hence promotes inflation convergence (see also Kool and Koedijk, 1992). Giavazzi and Pagano (1988, p. 1055) argue: 'First, between successive realignments, excess inflation (combining with the fixity of the nominal exchange rate) results in one-for-one appreciation of the real exchange rate. Second, at realignment dates, excess inflation countries obtain devaluations which are generally insufficient to make up for the real appreciation experienced since the previous realignment. The first factor introduces real exchange rate fluctuation between realignments while the second factor introduces a trend of real appreciation in the exchange rates of high inflation countries'.

Table 2.4 illustrates that nominal exchange rates did not fully adjust to compensate for inflation differentials. Mean deviations from *ex post* PPP over the period October 1987-August 1992 were negative for almost all European countries. The depreciation of the domestic currency is smaller than needed to maintain competitiveness which was lost due to the higher inflation relative to German inflation.[34] Therefore, the real exchange rate appreciates (where the domestic inflation exceeds the German inflation and the nominal exchange rate depreciation is relatively small). This implies that a country imports deflation. The relative small depreciation may be explained by the stabilization of nominal exchange rates to enhance credibility and achieve monetary convergence.

Unfortunately, the efforts following the EMS exchange crisis of September 1992 to defend the exchange rates within pre-specified bands by manipulation of nominal money market interest rates and exchange market intervention lacked credibility (see also Figure 2A3.1).[35] On 1 August 1993, ERM bands were widened to ± 15 per cent except for the band between The Netherlands and Germany which remained unchanged at ± 2.25 per cent. Now all currencies, except the Dutch guilder, are effectively freely floating against the DM.

## (5) *Ex post* **currency premia**

It is expected that financial markets translate monetary uncertainties into higher currency premia, consisting of exchange risk premia and deviations from PPP. With respect to the size of mean *ex post* currency premia [5] over the period March 1979–August 1992 – measured as the positive or negative difference from zero in absolute value – we may list the countries in ascending order as follows: Greece (calculated over the period September 1984–August 1992), The Netherlands, the United Kingdom, Ireland, France, Italy, Denmark, Belgium, Portugal and Spain. With respect to the size of mean absolute *ex post* currency premia [|5|] over the period March 1979–August 1992, we may list the countries in ascending order as follows: The Netherlands, Belgium, France, Denmark, Ireland, the United Kingdom, Italy, Spain, Portugal and Greece (calculated over the period September 1984–August 1992). Notice the difference in the ascending orders. Notable declines in currency premia occurred for Portugal, Spain and the United Kingdom when they entered the ERM of the EMS (comparing the subperiod March 1979–September 1987 with the subperiod October 1987–August 1992). EMS discipline may have helped to limit previous nominal devaluation tendencies. However, the overall result is that currency premia remain rather persistent. Since country premia are almost zero, currency premia, that is, deviations from *ex post* PPP and *ex post* exchange risk premia are the main sources of real interest differentials.

## (6) **Deviations from** *ex post* **RIP**

The RIP condition is the strongest criterion for money market integration. In fact, the RIP condition not only measures financial integration but non-financial integration as well (see Section 2.2). Deviations from *ex post* RIP are due to country and currency factors. Table 2.4 shows that currency factors dominate country factors in explaining real interest rate differentials with respect to Germany. With respect to the size of mean deviations from *ex post* RIP [6] over the period March 1979–August 1992 – measured as the positive or negative difference from zero in absolute value – we may list the countries in ascending order of estimated degree of RIP integration as follows: Portugal, Greece (calculated over the period September 1984–August 1992), Belgium, Denmark, Spain, Ireland, the United Kingdom, The Netherlands, Italy and France. With respect to the size of mean absolute deviations from *ex post* RIP [|6|] over the period March 1979–August 1992, we may list the countries in ascending order of estimated degree of RIP integration as follows: Greece (calculated over the period September 1984–August 1992), Portugal, Spain, Ireland, the United

Kingdom, Denmark, Italy, Belgium, The Netherlands and France. The worse record of inflation and concomitant devaluation tendencies required countries like Greece, Ireland, Italy, Portugal, Spain and the United Kingdom to keep their money market interest rates above those in Germany, causing large real interest differentials.[36]

Declining real interest rate differentials may point to monetary convergence and to increased cross-border trade in goods and services in Europe. Real interest convergence may be explained by the Single Market project to complete an internal market for persons, goods, services and capital in Europe. In general, Table 2.4 shows that *ex post* RIP has been violated because the components of *ex post* RIP, that is, *ex post* UIP and *ex post* PPP have been violated. Real interest differentials remain rather persistent.[37] There is no clear pattern of lower real interest differentials *vis-à-vis* Germany in one country or another. The interpretation of the RIP condition is even more complicated than the interpretation of the UIP condition. The Economist (1992, p. 23) argues: '(...) the criterion of real interest parity is much more demanding than it seems to be. Exchange rate volatility undermines it in two ways: first by adding a risk premium to the cost of cover in the foreign exchange market [so UIP does not hold], and second by breaking the link between exchange rates and differences in inflation rates [so PPP does not hold]'.

## 2.5   The Speed of Money Market Integration[38]

In Table 2.4 we analyzed the *degree* of money market integration by regressing mean (absolute) deviations from CIP, *ex post* UIP and *ex post* RIP against a constant. It also may be worthwhile to examine the *speed* of money market integration by regressing absolute deviations from CIP, *ex post* UIP and *ex post* RIP over the period March 1979–August 1992 against a constant (coefficient $\beta_0$) and a time trend (coefficient $\beta_1$) (see Frankel, 1990, p. 22 and Frankel, Phillips and Chinn, 1993, pp. 274-5):

$$/y_t/ = \beta_0 + \beta_1 \times t + \varepsilon_t \qquad (2.10)$$

Table 2.5 reports the coefficient estimates and corresponding Newey–West (1987) standard errors of equation (2.10). The speed of money market integration is captured by the magnitude of the negative trend coefficient.[39] [40] The more ne-gative the trend coefficient the larger the downward trend in mean absolute deviations from CIP, ex post UIP or *ex post* RIP. Or in other words, the trend coefficient $\beta_1$ captures the *monthly* change in the degree of money market integration. For example, the monthly decline of absolute CIP differentials with respect to Belgium amounts to 0.013 per cent per year over the period March

*Table 2.5 Time trends in mean absolute deviations from CIP, ex post UIP and ex post RIP over the period March 1979-August 1992 (percentages per year)*

$$|y_t| = \beta_0 + \beta_1 \times t + \varepsilon_t$$

| | | $\beta_0$ | $\beta_1$ | $\bar{R}^2$ |
|---|---|---|---|---|
| Belgium | CIP | 1.793 (0.381)** | −0.013 (0.003)** | 0.224 |
| | UIP | 6.048 (1.421)** | −0.033 (0.011)** | 0.094 |
| | RIP | 3.406 (0.435)** | −0.012 (0.004)** | 0.084 |
| Denmark | CIP | 2.760 (0.220)** | −0.020 (0.002)** | 0.445 |
| | UIP | 8.006 (0.854)** | −0.039 (0.008)** | 0.247 |
| | RIP | 3.959 (0.466)** | −0.010 (0.005)** | 0.032 |
| France | CIP | 4.082 (0.761)** | −0.028 (0.006)** | 0.228 |
| | UIP | 5.721 (1.162)** | −0.018 (0.010)* | 0.033 |
| | RIP | 3.280 (0.509)** | −0.012 (0.005)** | 0.088 |
| Greece[a] | CIP | 7.648 (0.947)** | −0.052 (0.013)** | 0.167 |
| | UIP | 15.522 (5.856)** | −0.142 (0.083)* | 0.087 |
| | RIP | 6.720 (1.240)** | −0.011 (0.018) | −0.055 |
| Ireland | CIP | 1.496 (0.162)** | −0.009 (0.001)** | 0.259 |
| | UIP | 7.403 (1.055)** | −0.032 (0.009)** | 0.077 |
| | RIP | 4.667 (0.791)** | −0.017 (0.007)** | 0.089 |
| Italy | CIP | 4.628 (0.771)** | −0.035 (0.007)** | 0.329 |
| | UIP | 7.747 (0.814)** | −0.024 (0.008)** | 0.067 |
| | RIP | 4.885 (0.946)** | −0.024 (0.009)** | 0.147 |
| The Netherlands | CIP | 0.938 (0.125)** | −0.007 (0.001)** | 0.350 |
| | UIP | 4.175 (0.495)** | −0.027 (0.004)** | 0.331 |
| | RIP | 2.467 (0.314)** | −0.001 (0.004) | −0.006 |
| Portugal | CIP | 9.335 (1.832)** | −0.047 (0.014)** | 0.124 |
| | UIP | 12.599 (2.292)** | −0.038 (0.020)* | 0.031 |
| | RIP | 8.051 (1.092)** | −0.035 (0.010)** | 0.146 |
| Spain | CIP | 6.075 (0.722)** | −0.043 (0.006)** | 0.419 |
| | UIP | 13.961 (2.191)** | −0.046 (0.021)** | 0.049 |
| | RIP | 3.599 (0.483)** | −0.002 (0.005) | −0.005 |
| United Kingdom | CIP | 1.100 (0.122)** | −0.006 (0.001)** | 0.149 |
| | UIP | 22.527 (2.391)** | −0.095 (0.021)** | 0.124 |
| | RIP | 3.708 (0.763)** | −0.005 (0.007) | 0.002 |

*Notes*

[a]  Calculated over the period September 1984–August 1992.
*    Coefficient differs significantly from zero at the 95 per cent level of confidence (one-tailed test)
**   Coefficient differs significantly from zero at the 99 per cent level of confidence (one-tailed test)

Newey–West (1987) standard errors are indicated in parentheses. $\bar{R}^2$ is the coefficient of determination adjusted for degrees of freedom.

*Source:* See Appendix 2A1.

1979 –August 1992. We call this the *catching up* with respect to CIP integration.

The picture of estimated speed of integration is as follows. All ten European countries show significant negative trend coefficients with respect to absolute deviations from CIP at either 95 or 99 per cent level of confidence. The same holds for the negative trend coefficient of absolute deviations from *ex post* UIP. Notice that the speed of UIP integration generally exceeds the speed of CIP and RIP integration. With respect to absolute deviations from CIP, we may list the countries in ascending order of estimated speed of CIP integration over the period March 1979–August 1992: the United Kingdom, The Netherlands, Ireland, Belgium, Denmark, France, Italy, Spain, Portugal and Greece (calculated over the period September 1984–August 1992). The relatively low speed of CIP integration of The Netherlands and the United Kingdom may be explained by the already high degree of CIP integration in the beginning of the sample period. Greece, Portugal and Spain had a lot to catch up with respect to the reference country Germany in terms of CIP integration. With respect to absolute deviations from UIP over the period March 1979–August 1992, we may list the countries in ascending order of estimated speed of UIP integration as follows: France, Italy, The Netherlands, Ireland, Belgium, Portugal, Denmark, Spain, the United Kingdom and Greece (calculated over the period September 1984–August 1992). With respect to absolute deviations from RIP over the period March 1979–August 1992 we may list the countries in ascending order of estimated speed of RIP integration as follows: The Netherlands, Spain, the United Kingdom, Denmark, Greece (calculated over the period September 1984–August 1992), Belgium, France, Ireland, Italy and Portugal.

## 2.6    The Trade-off Between the Degree and Speed of Money Market Integration

This section combines the two previous sections on the degree and speed of money market integration in Europe. A *negative* trade-off between the degree and speed of CIP integration exists. Countries with a relatively low degree of CIP integration show a relatively high speed of CIP integration, and vice versa. That is, the higher the speed of integration, the lower the degree of integration and vice versa. The trade-off may be motivated by the political will to form an economic and monetary union in Europe. We infer the degree of money market integration from Table 2.4 and the speed of money market integration from Table 2.5.

Figure 2.1 illustrates the trade-off between the degree and speed of CIP, UIP and RIP integration in Europe over the period March 1979–August 1992. Greece is excluded from Figure 2.1 because of the lack of comparability of the sample period. The speed of integration is graphed on the vertical axis and the degree of integration is graphed on the horizontal axis. The degree of integration is measured as coefficient $\beta_0$ in the regression of mean absolute deviations against a constant term (see Section 2.4). The speed of integration is measured as coefficient $\beta_1$ in the regression of mean absolute deviations

*The Measurement of Financial Integration*

*Figure 2.1  The trade-off between the degree and speed of CIP, UIP and RIP
          integration over the period March 1979–August 1992 (excluding
          Greece)*

*Degree of integration measured as coefficient* $\beta_0$ *of* $|y_t| = \beta_0 + e_t$
*Speed of integration measured as coefficient* $\beta_1$ *of* $|y_t| = \beta_0 + \beta_1 \times t + \varepsilon_t$

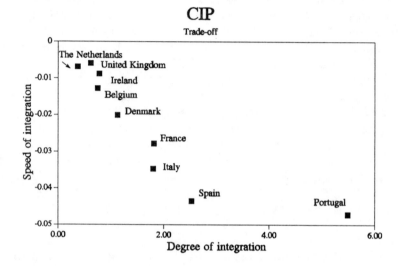

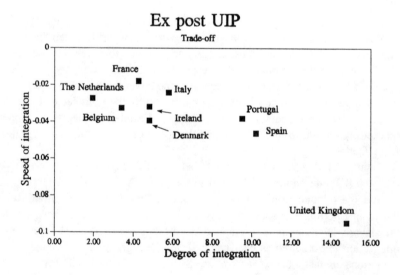

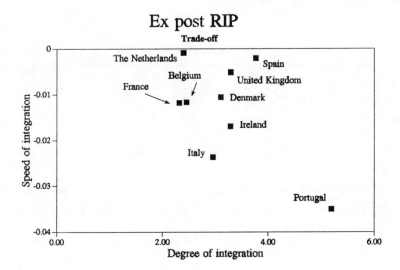

against a constant and a time trend (see Section 2.5). The degree of integration declines if the coefficient values on the horizontal axis increase. The speed of integration increases if the coefficient values on the vertical axis become more negative.

Figure 2.1 for the CIP trade-off shows that countries like France, Italy, Spain, Portugal and Greece starting from a lower degree of CIP integration in the beginning of the sample period rapidly eliminated capital controls during the remainder of the sample period. The United Kingdom and The Netherlands already showed small absolute deviations from CIP in the beginning of the sample period. Consequently, the speed of CIP integration – or in other words the catching up with respect to CIP integration – for those countries is low. Equivalently, the catching up with respect to UIP integration is large for Portugal, Spain and the United Kingdom. The catching up with respect to RIP is particularly large for Portugal.

Table 2.6 assesses the strength of the CIP, UIP and RIP trade-off by regressing the speed of integration against a constant term and the degree of integration. The larger the $\overline{R}^2$ and the more negative coefficient $\lambda_I$ the stronger the trade-off. Since both the dependent and the independent variable are truncated (absolute deviations are always non-negative), we apply a one-tailed t-test to determine the strength of the trade-off. The results indicate a significant negative CIP and UIP trade-off. The CIP and UIP trade-off are strongest. However, the significance of $\lambda_I$ in Table 2.6 may depend on the outliers which show up in Figure 2.1, that is, Portugal for CIP and RIP and the United Kingdom for UIP. The regressions in Table 2.6 are meant as a simple illustra-

*Table 2.6 The strength of the trade-off between the degree and speed of integration over the period March 1979–August 1992 (excluding Greece)*

$$Speed = \lambda_0 + \lambda_1 \times Degree + v_t$$

| Speed of integration | Constant | Degree of integration | $DW$ | $\bar{R}^2$ |
|---|---|---|---|---|
| CIP | −0.008 (0.004)[*] | −0.009 (0.002)[**] | 2.45 | 0.71 |
| UIP | −0.008 (0.008) | −0.005 (0.001)[**] | 2.80 | 0.69 |
| RIP | 0.010 (0.012) | −0.007 (0.004) | 2.18 | 0.25 |

*Notes:*

[*]   Coefficient differs significantly from zero at the 95 per cent level of confidence (one-tailed test)

[**]   Coefficient differs significantly from zero at the 99 per cent level of confidence (one-tailed test)

OLS standard errors are indicated in parentheses. *DW* is the Durbin-Watson statistic for first-order serial correlation and $\bar{R}^2$ is the coefficient of determination adjusted for degrees of freedom.

tion of the negative trade-off. The capital liberalization directive of 24 June, 1988 has certainly enhanced the CIP trade-off. The ERM has stabilized nominal exchange rates within Europe. The RIP trade-off is only marginally significant at the 95 per cent level of confidence. The stringent assumptions required for RIP undoubtedly have contributed to this result. The weak RIP trade-off may be explained by the Single Market project to complete an internal market for persons, goods, services and capital in Europe. Goods market integration lags financial market integration. First liberalizing capital movements (by 1990), then goods and labour movements (by 1992) may create large *real exchange rate movements*, if financial integration is far ahead of goods and labour market integration.

## 2.7   Conclusions

This chapter analyzed money market integration between ten European countries and Germany. We defined three interest parity conditions, that is CIP, *ex ante* UIP and *ex ante* RIP, to assess the degree of money market integration in Europe. Subsequently, we introduced the decomposition method of Frankel and MacArthur (1988). The evidence in this chapter allows us to draw a few conclusions about money market integration in Europe.

1.   Average *ex post* real interest differentials can be decomposed into *ex post* uncovered nominal interest differentials and deviations from *ex post* relative PPP. *Ex post* uncovered nominal interest differentials can be decomposed

into covered interest differentials and *ex post* exchange risk premia.

2.   We find strong support for an increasing degree of geographical money market integration in Europe as measured by the CIP condition. Empirical results indicate that the size and variability of mean (absolute) country premia declined significantly after the Basle–Nyborg agreement of September 1987. Perfect capital mobility of type I can be said to exist between eight European countries and Germany. Portugal and Greece are the exceptions to the rule and are not (yet) completely integrated with Germany. The initial low degree of CIP integration urged countries like France, Greece, Italy, Portugal and Spain to catch up with the rest of the European countries during the 1980s. Finally, CIP deviations are much smaller than *ex post* UIP and *ex post* RIP deviations.

3.   Deviations from *ex post* UIP when compared to those deviations from CIP are highly variable when devaluations (are expected to) take place. Countries like Greece, Italy, Portugal, Spain and the United Kingdom, with initial low degrees of UIP integration, definitely showed larger speed of UIP integration. *Ex post* UIP deviations have declined due to the exchange rate stabilization influence of the ERM.

4.   CIP, *ex post* UIP and *ex post* RIP deviations of core-EMS countries generally are more stable than those deviations of non-core-EMS countries. Throughout the sample period, deviations from *ex post* RIP and *ex post* UIP are more volatile than deviations from CIP.

5.   Although the Basle–Nyborg agreement limited the scope for realignments, *ex post* exchange risk premia remain rather persistent, and so remain *ex post* UIP deviations.

6.   Short-term *ex post* PPP may be an unrealistic assumption with respect to money market integration. That is, relative prices of domestic and foreign goods may be sticky in the short-run. Especially, in the short-run the real exchange rate may fluctuate around its equilibrium value while in the long-run we have mean reversion of the real exchange rate. In addition, movements in real exchange rates tend to be dominated by nominal exchange rate changes rather than by relative price level changes.

7.   Deviations from *ex post* UIP and *ex post* PPP are negatively correlated. This evidence is consistent with there being a common factor, exchange rate changes, driving both differentials. Exchange rates adjust much faster than interest rates and prices.

8.   Despite the fact that the size and variability of mean (absolute) deviations from *ex post* RIP have declined after the Basle–Nyborg agreement, real interest differentials remain rather persistent. In addition, there is no clear pattern of lower real interest differentials *vis-à-vis* Germany. Real interest differentials are not comparable across countries because they are denominated in their own national currency. Consequently, they do not

offer profit opportunities for an individual investor or borrower since no single agent compares real interest rates across countries. Furthermore, lack of goods markets integration imply the violation of PPP (and therefore RIP), even when financial markets are perfectly integrated.

9. Contrary to the CIP condition, the UIP and the RIP conditions can only give an *indirect* indication of money market integration in Europe. In fact, perfect capital mobility of type I is compatible with both, zero and nonzero exchange risk premia and/or zero and nonzero deviations from PPP.

10. Since the present chapter tends to reject UIP and RIP it offers fairly strong conclusions about the inappropriateness of various exchange rate models.

## Notes

1. Up to the time of writing, the EC consisted of 12 member states. Nowadays, the EC is known as the European Union (EU). The EU consists of 15 member states. See Lemmen and Eijffinger (1995d) for the analysis of money market integration with respect to the three new member states (Austria, Finland and Sweden).

2. Discussion of policy implications of financial integration is beyond the scope of this chapter. See, for example, Lamfalussy (1990), The Economist (1992), De Groof and Van Tuijl (1993), Eijffinger and Gerards (1993), Gruijters (1995) and Chapter 5 of this book.

3. See Commission of the European Communities (1990, pp. 160–1) for a first assessment of money market integration in Europe based upon Frankel (1989). See Lemmen and Eijffinger (1993) and Frankel, Phillips and Chinn (1993, pp. 270–9) for a more recent assessment of money market integration in Europe.

4. Van Gemert and Gruijters (1994) study interest rate differentials after the breakdown of the Bretton Woods system of fixed exchange rates using historical data of OECD countries. Holmes and Pentecost (1996) examine financial integration in the EU based on covered and nominal interest rate differentials between March 1979 and August 1992 using cointegration and time-varying parameter econometric techniques.

5. Interest parity conditions are not the only valid tests for the degree of financial integration. For example, Feldstein and Horioka (1980) apply *savings-investment correlations* to assess the degree of financial integration. We shall apply savings-investment correlations to assess the degree of financial integration in Chapter 3. Alternatively, Obstfeld (1986) proposes another test based upon the *Euler equation* for intertemporal consumption behaviour. We shall apply Euler equation-based tests of financial integration in Chapter 4. Goldstein and Mussa (1993) and Obstfeld (1994a) provide excellent surveys of the existing literature.

6. Or in other words, the forward exchange rate is an unbiased predictor of the expected future spot exchange rate (MacDonald and Taylor, 1992, p. 38). Goodhart, McMahon and Lawan Ngama (1992), however, reject the forward exchange rate unbiasedness hypothesis. *Ex ante* UIP also assumes that foreign exchange markets operate efficiently.

7. The term 'arbitrage' should be confined to riskless operations rather than to the risky positions required to ensure that *ex ante* UIP holds.

8. The argument assumes that CIP holds continuously. Moreover, note that deviations from *ex post* UIP do not necessarily imply an exchange risk premium. Deviations from *ex post* UIP might also reflect expectational errors.

9. If *ex ante* UIP holds, *ex ante* RIP between two countries reflects differences in inflationary expectations.

10. Most German restrictions on capital export were lifted in 1973 and 1974. Since the beginning of the 1980s, there have been no restrictions on capital import either. So capital flows to and from German financial markets were unrestricted for most of the sample period. The German controls are described in Dooley and Isard (1980) and Deutsche Bundesbank (1985).

11. Luxemburg is excluded from the analysis because Luxemburg and Belgium form a monetary union, that is, they share the same short-term interest rate and exchange rate. The exchange rate of the British pound sterling has been inverted to conform with the continental definition of the exchange rate.

12. Note that the spot and forward exchange rates are defined as the EC member state's external value *vis-à-vis* the DM to conform with the continental definition of the exchange rate.

13. Concerning the data, the use of *average monthly* data may raise problems. However, since we are interested in the longer-term trends, average monthly data are in order.

14. Euro markets are almost free of capital controls (Fukao and Hanazaki, 1987, p. 48).

15. Lemmen and Eijffinger (1993) note that money market interest rates are more policy determined than capital market interest rates.

16. The use of survey data suffers from the methodological problem that brokers in foreign exchange markets do not reveal their real interests. Survey data may not be an accurate measure of market participants true expectations or people do not act on the expectations they express (Boughton, 1988, p. 13).

17. We agree with Tease, Dean, Elsmekov and Hoeller (1991, p. 119) who argue that 'The precise choice of the method to measure inflationary expectations is unlikely to alter the longer–term trends in the data although it may affect the timing and turning points'.

18. Thus, exchange rate forecast errors must be added to deviations from *ex post* UIP (see Obstfeld, 1994a, pp. 4–5): $i_{t,t+k} - i^*_{t,t+k} - (s_{t+k} - s_t) = [i_{t,t+k} - i^*_{t,t+k} - (f^{t+k}_t - s_t)] + [(f^{t+k}_t - s_t) - E_t(s_{t+k} - s_t)] + [E_t(s_{t+k} - s_t) - (s_{t+k} - s_t)]$.

19. Throughout this book, all interest parity conditions will be expressed in percentages per year.

20. The equation $[ln(1 + i_{t,t+3}) - ln(1 + i^*_{t,t+3}) - (12/3)(f^{t+3}_t - s_t)] \times 100$ may be interpreted alternatively as measuring returns in DM. In that case the realized return on domestic bonds measured in DM, defined as $[ln(1 + i_{t,t+3}) - (12/3)(f^{t+3}_t - s_t)] \times 100$ is equal to the certain return on German bonds $ln(1 + i^*_{t,t+3})$, where spot and forward exchange rates are defined in accordance with the continental definition of the exchange rate. But as pointed out by Siegel (1972), if covered interest differentials are equal when expressed in domestic currency, then because of Jensen's inequality covered interest differentials cannot be equal when re-expressed in DM. McCulloch (1975) argues that the discrepancy between returns due to Jensens's inequality is empirically insignificant.

21. Again, the equation $[ln(1 + i_{t,t+3}) - ln(1 + i^*_{t,t+3}) - (12/3)(s^{t+3}_t - s_t)] \times 100$ may be interpreted alternatively as measuring returns in DM. In that case the expected return on domestic bonds measured in DM, defined as $[ln(1 + i_{t,t+3}) - (12/3)(s^{t+3}_t - s_t)] \times 100$ is equal to the certain return on German bonds $ln(1 + i^*_{t,t+3})$, where spot and forward exchange rates are defined conform the continental definition of the exchange rate.

22. Of course, the forward premium (discount) and the expected devaluation (revaluation) incorporate market participants' expectations about the differences between domestic and German inflation rates.

23. Note that it is possible that (some of) these components may add up to zero while in fact they differ from zero.

24. We have not explicitly performed t-tests in Table 2.4. Though, it is relatively easy to perform t-tests for both mean and mean absolute deviations applying Newey–West (1987) standard errors (see Appendix 2A2).

25. Interested readers can find an excellent overview of recent regulatory and institutional developments which have produced financial integration in Grilli (1989), Shepherd (1994), Gruijters (1995), Herring and Litan (1995) and Marston (1995).

26. Contrary to De Haan, Pilat and Zelhorst (1991), we find significant mean (absolute) deviations from CIP with respect to the Netherlands. Using direct DM–Dutch guilder spot and forward exchange rates, De Haan et al. find insignificant deviations from CIP over the period October 1979–June 1989. The use of indirect DM calculations of spot and forward exchange rates in Table 2.4 may have caused artificially high mean (absolute) deviations from CIP due to the influence of transaction costs in triangular arbitrage.

27. Lemmen and Eijffinger (1993) reproduce the calculations of the Commission of the European Communities (1990).

28. We agree with Pigott (1993, pp. 31–2) that the interaction of changes in capital controls, the exchange rate regime and the coordination of monetary policies considerably affected money market integration in Europe.

29. Peso problems may also occur in flexible exchange rate periods if major shifts in policy regimes are expected.

30. See also Gärtner (1993, p. 221).

31. Knot and De Haan (1995) analyze interest rate differentials of Austria, Belgium and the Netherlands *vis-à-vis* Germany. Interest differentials consist of three parts: expected exchange rate movements within the band, expected changes of the central rates and a risk premium.

32. Gruijters (1995, pp. 10–1) calls monetary integration perfect if capital controls have been abolished *and* market participants no longer expect the bilateral exchange rate to change at all. Observe – as was noted by Gruijters – the subtle difference between perfect capital mobility of type II and perfect monetary integration. With perfect capital mobility of type II the exchange risk premium drops out because investors are assumed to be risk-neutral. With perfect monetary integration the exchange risk premium drops out because exchange rate expectations are held with certainty.

33. See also Goodhart (1992, p. 121).

34. Of course, competitive real depreciations may have negative spill-over effects to other EC countries.

35. Van Aarle, Eijffinger and Lemmen (1995) found evidence for a decline in credibility just before the exchange crisis of September 1992. For Ireland, Italy, Portugal, Spain and the United Kingdom, expected exchange rate movements within the band were positively correlated with expected changes of the central rate. Or in other words, 'divorcement' effects dominated 'honeymoon' effects.

36. The history of high inflation has made these countries more dependent on short-term financing than Germany, and thus more sensitive to shifts in short-term nominal interest rates.

37. Future research should investigate whether the size and variability of real interest differentials are sensitive to the choice of the price index.

38. This section is based on Lemmen and Eijffinger (1994) and Eijffinger and Lemmen (1995).

39. Non–linear specifcations which overcome the problem that absolute deviations may become negative as time increases ($/ y_t / < 0$ if $t \to \infty$) did not perform better in terms of $R^2$ and level of significance than the linear specification. We estimated the following non-linear specifications (where $/ y_t / \geq 0$ if $t \to \infty$):

$$/y_t/ = \beta_0 + \beta_1 \times \frac{1}{\sqrt{t}} + \varepsilon_t$$

$$/y_t/ = \beta_0 + \beta_1 \times \frac{1}{t} + \varepsilon_t$$

40. The following specifications also did not perform better than the linear specification (where $|y_t| < 0$ if $t \to \infty$):

$$|y_t| = \beta_0 + \beta_1 \times \sqrt{t} + \varepsilon_t$$

$$|y_t| = \beta_0 + \beta_1 \times t + \beta_2 \times t^2 + \varepsilon_t$$

$$|y_t| = \beta_0 + \beta_1 \times t^2 + \varepsilon_t$$

## Appendix 2A1: Data Sources

*Money market interest rates*

| Countries | Period | Description | Source |
|---|---|---|---|
| Germany, France, Belgium, The Netherlands, United Kingdom, Denmark, Spain, Portugal, Italy and Ireland | March 1979–June 1993 | Three-month money market interest rates in percentages per year, monthly average, monthly series | Eurostat |
| Greece | May 1980–June 1993 | Three-month money market interest rates in percentages per year, monthly average, monthly series | Eurostat |

*Consumer price indices*

| Countries | Period | Description | Source |
|---|---|---|---|
| Germany, France, Belgium, The Netherlands, United Kingdom, Denmark, Spain, Portugal and Italy | March 1979–June 1993 | Consumer price indices, general index (1985=100), monthly series | Eurostat |
| Ireland | March 1979–June 1993 | Consumer price indices, general index (1985=100), quarterly series. Monthly Irish consumer price indices were arrived at by three-month centred moving-average of the quarterly series | Datastream, IMF |
| Greece | May 1980–June 1993 | Consumer price indices, general index, monthly series (1985=100) | Eurostat |

*Forward exchange rates*

| Countries | Period | Description | Source |
|---|---|---|---|
| Germany, France, Belgium, The Netherlands, United Kingdom, Denmark, Italy and Ireland | March 1979–June 1983 | Own cross-rate calculations of forward exchange rates *vis-à-vis* the DM based upon three-month forward exchange rates to the British pound sterling, middle rate, monthly series | Datastream, Bank of England |
| Spain and Portugal | March 1979–February 1986 | Own cross-rate calculations of forward exchange rates *vis-à-vis* the DM based upon three-month forward exchange rates to the British pound sterling, middle rate, monthly series | Datastream, Bank of England |

| Germany, France, Belgium, The Netherlands, United Kingdom, Denmark, Italy and Ireland | July 1983–June 1993 | Own cross-rate calculations of forward exchange rates *vis-à-vis* the DM based upon three-month forward exchange rates *vis-à-vis* the United States dollar, monthly average, monthly series | Eurostat, BIS |
|---|---|---|---|
| Greece | September 1984–June 1993 | Own cross-rate calculations of forward exchange rates *vis-à-vis* the DM based upon three-month forward exchange rates *vis-à-vis* the United States dollar, monthly average, monthly series | Eurostat, BIS |
| Spain and Portugal | March 1986–June 1993 | Own cross-rate calculations of forward exchange rates *vis-à-vis* the DM based upon three-month forward exchange rates *vis-à-vis* the United States dollar, monthly average, monthly series | Eurostat, BIS |

## Spot exchange rates

| Countries | Period | Description | Source |
|---|---|---|---|
| France, Belgium, The Netherlands, United Kingdom, Denmark, Italy and Ireland | March 1979–June 1983 | Own cross-rate calculations of spot exchange rates *vis-à-vis* the DM based upon spot exchange rates to the British pound sterling, middle rate, monthly series | Datastream, Bank of England |
| Greece | May 1980–August 1984 | Own cross-rate calculations of spot exchange rates *vis-à-vis* the DM based upon spot exchange rates to the British pound sterling, middle rate, monthly series | Datastream, Bank of England |
| Spain and Portugal | March 1979–February 1986 | Own cross-rate calculations of spot exchange rates *vis-à-vis* the DM based upon spot exchange rates to the British pound sterling, middle rate, monthly series | Datastream, Bank of England |
| France, Belgium, The Netherlands, United Kingdom, Denmark, Italy and Ireland | July 1983–June 1993 | Own cross-rate calculations of spot exchange rates *vis-à-vis* the DM based upon spot exchange rate *vis-à-vis* the United States dollar, monthly average, monthly series | Eurostat |

| | | | |
|---|---|---|---|
| Greece | September 1984– June 1993 | Own cross-rate calculations of spot exchange rates *vis-à-vis* the DM based upon spot exchange rate *vis-à-vis* the United States dollar, monthly average, monthly series | Eurostat |
| Spain and Portugal | March 1986– June 1993 | Own cross-rate calculations of spot exchange rates *vis-à-vis* the DM based upon spot exchange rate *vis-à-vis* the United States dollar, monthly average, monthly series | Eurostat |

# Appendix 2A2: Newey–West (1987) Standard Errors

The use of overlapping monthly observations of three-month holding period returns introduces a moving-average term of order two to the residuals (Hansen and Hodrick, 1980). The standard errors reported in Tables 2.4 and 2.5 have been adjusted for serial correlation as well as heteroscedasticity. For example, in order to be able to apply t-tests in case of heteroscedasticity and autocorrelation in the error term $e_t$ in equation (2.6), the variance-covariance matrix of the OLS estimator has to be defined as

$$S_{Newey-West} = (T-K)^{-1} (\Sigma_{t=1}^{T} x_t x_t')^{-1} \Sigma_{l=-k}^{k} w_l \Sigma_{t=1}^{T} \hat{e}_t \hat{e}_{t-l}' x_t x_{t-l}'$$

$$(\Sigma_{t=1}^{T} x_t x_t')^{-1} \qquad (2A2.1)$$

with Bartlett weights $w_l$ defined as

$$w_l = 1 - \frac{|l|}{k+1} \qquad (2A2.2)$$

The Bartlett weights $w_l$ ensure that the middle part of equation (1) is positive definite in finite samples. The middle part allows for autocorrelation up to lag length $|l|$. The errors $e_t$ and $e_{t-l}$ are correlated $[E(e_t e_{t-l}) \neq 0]$ if $|l| < 3$ and uncorrelated $[E(e_t e_{t-l}) = 0]$ if $|l| \geq 3$. Because the autocorrelations are zero for lag lengths larger than three $|l| \geq 3$, we choose $|l| = 3$ as the maximum lag length. The choice of $|l|$ is a reflection of how far back in time one must go to consider the autocorrelation negligible. The use of such a set of weights is clearly compatible with the idea that the impact of the autocorrelations diminishes with $|l|$. With only a constant term $\beta_0$, $x_t$ is simply the unit vector and we have $T-1$ degrees of freedom ($K=1$). Standard errors that are computed in this way are known as Newey–West standard errors. Table 2.4 reports Newey–West standard errors for $\beta_0$. Similarly, Table 2.5 reports Newey–West standard errors for $\beta_0$ and $\beta_1$.

We have not explicitly performed t-tests in Table 2.4. It is relatively easy to perform t-tests for both mean and mean absolute deviations applying Newey–West standard errors. It can be shown that if the OLS standard errors are corrected for autocorrelation and heteroscedasticity as proposed by Newey and West, all the usual results (t-, F-tests, and so on) would hold true in large samples. For example, let (2A2.3) be the mean deviation

$$\bar{y} = \frac{1}{T} \Sigma_{t=1}^{t=T} y_t \qquad (2A2.3)$$

with variance-covariance matrix as indicated in (2A2.1). Then, the t-statistic for the *mean deviations* is defined as (see Krasker, 1980, pp. 270-1):

$$t = \frac{\bar{y} - 0}{s_{Newey-West} \, / \, \sqrt{T}} = \frac{\bar{y}\sqrt{T}}{s_{Newey-West}} \qquad t \sim t_{T-1} \text{ -distribution} \qquad (2A2.4)$$

As indicated in footnote 22 of Popper (1993), the statistical significance of the *mean absolute deviations* should be tested with a t-statistic that is modified slightly to reflect the use of absolute values. For a standard random variable $x$, with a symmetric distribution and a mean of zero (as under the null hypothesis here) the density of $x = /y /$ is twice that of $x$. The t-statistics are given by dividing the mean absolute deviations by the sample standard deviations. The standard probability values must be doubled.

# Appendix 2A3

*Figure 2A3.1:*    *Deviations from CIP, ex post UIP and ex post RIP of ten EC member states relative to Germany (percentages per year)*

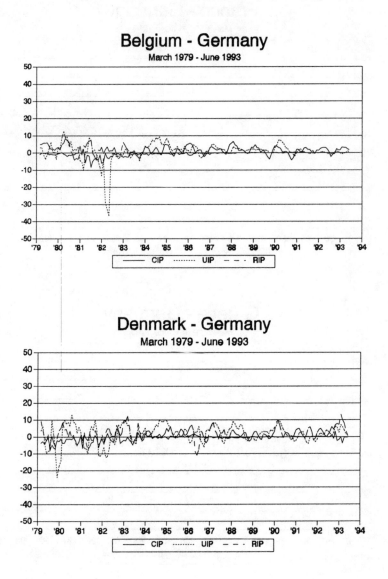

# France - Germany

### March 1979 - June 1993

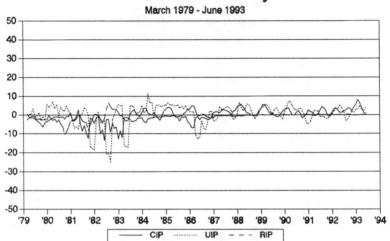

CIP      UIP      RIP

# Greece - Germany

### March 1979 - June 1993

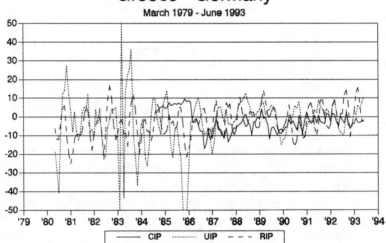

CIP      UIP      RIP

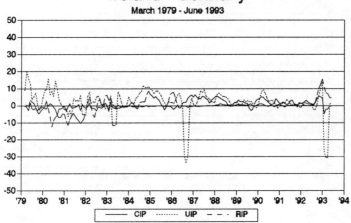

## Ireland - Germany
### March 1979 - June 1993

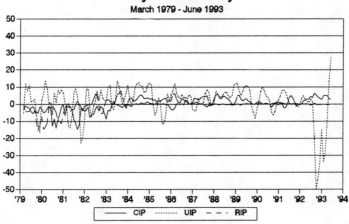

## Italy - Germany
### March 1979 - June 1993

## The Netherlands - Germany

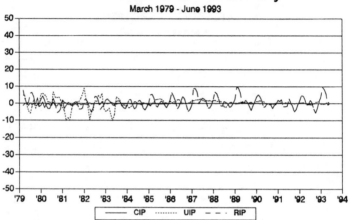

## Portugal - Germany

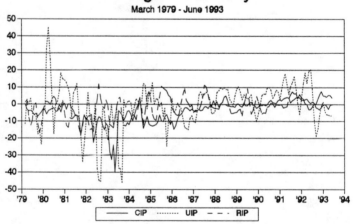

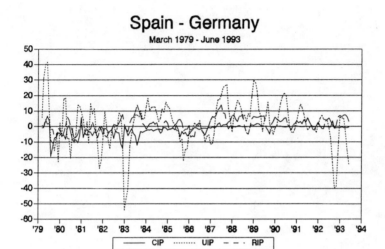

## Spain - Germany
### March 1979 - June 1993

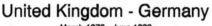

## United Kingdom - Germany
### March 1979 - June 1993

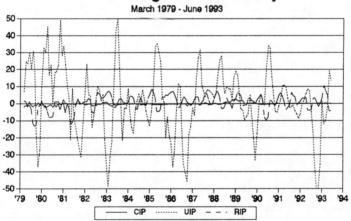

# 3. The Quantity Approach to Financial Integration: The Feldstein–Horioka Criterion Revisited

## 3.1 Introduction

This chapter deals with the theoretical and empirical analysis of the extent of financial integration in the EU. The measurement of financial integration relies on the Feldstein–Horioka (hereafter F–H) criterion which originated in 1980 when Feldstein and Horioka asserted that one could deduce from the national accounting framework the degree of financial integration. By examining the correlation between national savings and domestic investment, F–H were able to quantify the degree of financial integration. F–H hypothesize that changes in gross national savings and/or gross domestic investment generate changes in the current account balance, thus exploiting the definition that the current account is equal to national savings minus domestic investment (see Appendix 3A1 at the end of this chapter).[1] In a perfectly integrated financial market, a current account deficit (surplus) will be balanced by a corresponding capital inflow (outflow) and a country's savings decisions will be separated from its investment decisions. It is this criterion for financial integration that we shall address in this chapter. This chapter develops additional evidence on the integration of European financial markets. Contrary to what is usually found for world financial markets, savings-investment correlations in the EU are relatively small. Although, the F–H criterion is controversial it may provide evidence of an increasing degree of financial integration in the EU.

Chapter 3 is organized as follows. In Section 3.2 we repeat the three alternative criteria for financial integration which were discussed in Chapter 2, that is, covered, uncovered and real interest parity. Subsequently, we establish a link between these interest parity conditions and the F–H criterion. Section 3.3 further elaborates on the interpretation of the F–H criterion for financial integration. We evaluate the F–H criterion for financial integration on the basis of its underlying assumptions. Section 3.4 applies the F–H criterion for financial integration to three cross-sectional samples of EU countries. In Section 3.5 we employ the concept of cointegration to ascertain the existence of a long-run equilibrium relationship between savings and investment ratios of individual EU countries. We formulate an error-correction model of savings-investment correlations to distinguish between short- and long-run savings-investment correlations. Finally, Section 3.6 concludes.

## 3.2    The Link Between Interest Parity Conditions and the Feldstein–Horioka Criterion

Following Dooley, Frankel and Mathieson (1987, pp. 505–6), we set out the link between interest parity conditions and the F–H criterion. The F–H criterion is closely related to three interest parity conditions that correspond to three different criteria for financial integration that have been put forward in the literature. Table 3.1 summarizes algebraically the three different interest parity conditions and the F–H criterion. In addition, Table 3.1 sets out the cumulative assumptions to be fulfilled for each condition to hold. Note that the first three criteria in Table 3.1 rely on the co-movement of domestic and foreign *prices* and fit into the price approach. Criterion IV, however, relies on the co-movement of domestic *quantities* and fits into the quantity approach (see Feldman, 1986).

The first criterion – CIP – examines perfect capital mobility of type I. If CIP holds the forward premium/discount $f_t^{t+k} - s_t$ equals the difference between the domestic and foreign nominal interest rate at the appropriate maturity $i_{t,t+k} - i_{t,t+k}^*$. Investors cover themselves against exchange risk in the forward exchange market. The first criterion can be framed in terms of the decomposition method of Frankel and MacArthur (1988). Perfect capital mobility of type I requires a zero covered nominal interest differential or in other words a zero country premium $i_{t,t+k} - i_{t,t+k}^* - (f_t^{t+k} - s_t) = 0$.

The second criterion – *ex ante* UIP – examines perfect capital mobility of type II. We replace the forward exchange rate by the expected spot exchange rate $E_t s_{t+k} = f_t^{t+k}$. The expected nominal exchange rate change $E_t(s_{t+k} - s_t)$ equals the nominal interest differential at the appropriate maturity $i_{t,t+k} - i_{t,t+k}^*$. The second criterion can also be framed in terms of the decomposition method of Frankel and MacArthur. Frankel and MacArthur decompose the UIP differential in the following way: $i_{t,t+k} - i_{t,t+k}^* - E_t(s_{t+k} - s_t) = [i_{t,t+k} - i_{t,t+k}^* - (f_t^{t+k} - s_t)] + [(f_t^{t+k} - s_t) - E_t(s_{t+k} - s_t)]$. Perfect capital mobility of type II requires a zero country premium and a zero exchange risk premium $[(f_t^{t+k} - s_t) - E_t(s_{t+k} - s_t)] = 0$.

The third criterion – *ex ante* RIP – examines perfect capital mobility of type III or in other words perfect financial and non-financial capital mobility. Non-financial capital mobility refers to the mobility of goods and services and the mobility of the production factors labour and physical capital. *Ex ante* RIP holds if the domestic and foreign real interest rate are equal $E_t r_{t,t+k} = E_t r_{t,t+k}^*$. *Ex*

*Table 3.1 Four criteria for perfect capital mobility and their cumulative assumptions*[a]

---

**I    Covered nominal interest rate parity (CIP)**

Assumption:

$$i_{i,t+k} - i^*_{i,t+k} = f^{t+k}_t - s_t$$

Yields:

$$i_{i,t+k} - i^*_{i,t+k} = f^{t+k}_t - s_t$$

---

**II    *Ex ante* uncovered nominal interest rate parity (UIP)**

Assumptions:

$$i_{i,t+k} - i^*_{i,t+k} = f^{t+k}_t - s_t$$

$$E_t s_{t+k} = f^{t+k}_t$$

Yield:

$$i_{i,t+k} - i^*_{i,t+k} = E_t(s_{t+k} - s_t)$$

---

**III    *Ex ante* real interest rate parity (RIP)**

Assumptions:

$$i_{i,t+k} - i^*_{i,t+k} = f^{t+k}_t - s_t$$

$$E_t s_{t+k} = f^{t+k}_t$$

$$E_t(s_{t+k} - s_t) = E_t(p_{t+k} - p_t) - E_t(p^*_{t+k} - p^*_t)$$

Yield:

$$E_t r_{i,t+k} = E_t r^*_{i,t+k}$$

---

**IV    The Feldstein–Horioka (F–H) Criterion**[b]

Assumptions:

$$i_{i,t+k} - i^*_{i,t+k} = f^{t+k}_t - s_t$$

$$E_t s_{t+k} = f^{t+k}_t$$

$$E_t(s_{t+k} - s_t) = E_t(p_{t+k} - p_t) - E_t(p^*_{t+k} - p^*_t)$$

$$Cov(E_t(r_{i,t+k} - r^*_{i,t+k}), S_{i,t+k}/Y_{i,t+k}) = 0$$

$$Cov(\mu_i, S_{i,t+k}/Y_{i,t+k}) = 0$$

$$Cov(E_t r^*_{i,t+k}, S_{i,t+k}/Y_{i,t+k}) = 0$$

Yield:

$$I_{i,t+k}/Y_{i,t+k} = \alpha + \beta S_{i,t+k}/Y_{i,t+k} + \varepsilon_{i,t+k}$$

**Symbols:**

| | | |
|---|---|---|
| $i_{i,t+k}$ | = | domestic nominal rate of interest at time $t$ on a $k$ period bond held between time $t$ and $t+k$ |
| $f_t^{t+k}$ | = | forward exchange rate at time $t$ for the delivery of foreign currency at time $t+k$ |
| $s_t$ | = | spot exchange rate at time $t$ (that is, domestic currency units per unit of foreign currency) |
| $p_t$ | = | domestic price level at time $t$ |
| $r_{i,t+k}$ | = | expected domestic real rate of interest at time $t$ on a $k$ period bond held between time $t$ and $t+k$ |
| $E_t$ | = | conditional expectations operator based upon the information available at time $t$, that is, $E(./I_t)$ |
| $k$ | = | holding period of the underlying financial instrument |
| * | = | denotes a foreign variable |
| $t$ | = | denotes time $t$ |
| $i$ | = | denotes country $i$ |
| $I$ | = | gross domestic investment |
| $S$ | = | gross national savings |
| $Y$ | = | gross domestic product |
| $\varepsilon$ | = | an error term |
| $\mu$ | = | a stochastic error term that captures all other determinants of the investment ratio uncorrelated with $E_t r_{i,t+k}$ and $S_{i,t+k}/Y_{i,t+k}$ |

*Notes:*

[a]    Table 2.1 is framed according to the terminology introduced by Frankel and MacArthur (1988). All variables except the interest rates are expressed in natural logarithms. Lower-case variables represent natural logarithms. For example, the exact expression of CIP is: $(1+i_{i,t+k})/(1+i_{i,t+k}^*) = F_t^{t+k}/S_t$. We obtain the logarithmic approximation, that is, $i_{i,t+k} - i_{i,t+k}^* = f_t^{t+k} - s_t$, by taking natural logarithms of both sides and applying the approximation that $ln(1+x) \approx x$ for small $x$ where $ln(S_t) = s_t$, $ln(F_t^{t+k}) = f_t^{t+k}$, $ln(1+i_{i,t+k}) \approx i_{i,t+k}$ and $ln(1+i_{i,t+k}^*) \approx i_{i,t+k}^*$.

[b]    For convenience, we apply the cross-section specification of the F–H criterion.

*Sources:* Frankel and MacArthur (1988), Frankel (1989) and Lemmen and Eijffinger (1993).

*ante* RIP not only requires a zero country premium and a zero exchange risk premium but a zero expected real exchange rate change $[(s_{t+k} - s_t) - E_t(p_{t-k} - p_t) + E_t(p_{t-k}^* - p_t^*) = 0]$ as well. This follows from the decomposition of the *ex ante* real interest differential: $E_t(r_{i,t+k} - r_{i,t+k}^*) = [i_{i,t+k} - i_{i,t+k}^* - (f_t^{t+k} - s_t)] + [(f_t^{t+k} - s_t) - E_t(s_{t+k} - s_t)] + [E_t(s_{t+k} - s_t) - E_t(p_{t+k} - p_t) + E_t(p_{t+k}^* - p_t^*)]$.

The fourth criterion – the F–H condition – examines perfect capital mobility of type IV. The F–H condition infers from a regression of the investment ratio $I_{i,t+k}/Y_{i,t+k}$ on the savings ratio $S_{i,t+k}/Y_{i,t+k}$ the degree of capital mobility of type IV. The F–H criterion requires two additional assumptions to the *ex ante* RIP condition and is therefore the strongest criterion for financial integration. If it is true (1) that in each country $i$ the investment rate depends linearly on the expected domestic real interest rate, that is,

$$I_{i,t+k} = -\phi\, E_t(r_{i,t+k}) + \mu_i \tag{3.1}$$

and if it is true (2) that the stochastic error term $\mu_i$ that captures all other determinants of the investment rate is uncorrelated with the savings ratio in that country

$$Cov(\mu_i, S_{i,t+k}/Y_{i,t+k}) = 0 \tag{3.2}$$

and if (3) the savings ratio is not affected by the expected real foreign interest rate

$$Cov(E_t r^{*}_{i,t+k}, S_{i,t+k}/Y_{i,t+k}) = 0 \tag{3.3}$$

and if (4) deviations from *ex ante* RIP are uncorrelated with the savings ratio

$$Cov(E_t(r_{i,t+k} - r^{*}_{i,t+k}), S_{i,t+k}/Y_{i,t+k}) = 0 \tag{3.4}$$

then a regression of the investment ratio $I_{i,t+k}/Y_{i,t+k}$ on the savings ratio $S_{i,t+k}/Y_{i,t+k}$ must yield a zero coefficient $\beta$. Thus, the F–H criterion for perfect capital mobility of type IV requires a zero coefficient $\beta$ in the following equation:

$$I_{i,t+k}/Y_{i,t+k} = \alpha + \beta\, S_{i,t+k}/Y_{i,t+k} + \varepsilon_{i,t+k} \tag{3.5}$$

Equation (3.5) specifies the F–H criterion for testing the degree of capital mobility of type IV. Dooley et al. (1987) summarize these three covariances in the following equation (see also Table 3.1):[2]

$$Cov(I_{i,t+k}/Y_{i,t+k}, S_{i,t+k}/Y_{i,t+k}) =$$
$$Cov(\mu_i, S_{i,t+k}/Y_{i,t+k}) -$$
$$\Phi\, Cov(E_t r^{*}_{i,t+k}, S_{i,t+k}/Y_{i,t+k}) -$$
$$\Phi\, Cov(E_t(r_{i,t+k} - r^{*}_{i,t+k}), S_{i,t+k}/Y_{i,t+k}) = 0 \tag{3.6}$$

Note that real interest parity is not required. If it is assumed as in our chapter, (3.4) is automatically satisfied because the first variable in the covariance, that is, the real interest differential, is nonstochastic. This means that contrary to what is argued in the literature (for example, Blundell-Wignall and Browne, 1991) real interest parity is not a necessary condition for perfect capital mobility of type IV, it is merely a *sufficient* condition for perfect capital mobility of type IV. Furthermore, note that although the regression must yield a zero coefficient $\beta$ if (3.1)–(3.4) hold, a zero coefficient $\beta$ can also be obtained if some terms cancel out.

Using annual data of savings and investment ratios for 16 OECD countries averaged over the period 1960–1974 and the subperiods 1960–1964, 1965–1969 and 1970–1974, F–H estimated with OLS equation (3.5). F–H convert gross national savings $S_{i,t+k}$ and gross domestic investment $I_{i,t+k}$ into relative form by dividing by gross domestic product $Y_{i,t+k}$. F–H argued that, under the null hypothesis of perfect financial integration, $\beta$ should be zero for small countries, whereas for large countries $\beta$ should approximate the country's share of the world capital stock. F–H obtained an estimated value of $\beta$ of 0.887 (with a standard error of 0.074) over the period 1960–1974 which is significantly different from zero and insignificantly different from one at the 95 per cent level of confidence. Resulting, F–H concluded this $\beta$ value to be consistent with a low degree of financial integration among OECD countries during that period.[3] Also their $\beta$ estimates for the subperiods were closely centred around this value. Furthermore, the $\beta$ estimate is above the industrial-country benchmark value of 0.6. This finding was robust to the inclusion of a quadratic term for the savings ratio, to the inclusion of the population growth rate as an additional explanatory variable, to a linear specification for $\beta$ that permitted it to be a function of 'openness' variables such as the share of trade in gross domestic product or the size of the economy, as well as to the use of instrumental variables for the savings ratio.

The findings of F–H have been confirmed by many other researchers, using different samples and different empirical estimation techniques. Bayoumi (1990), for example, examined savings-investment correlations of ten OECD countries over the period 1965–1986, estimating $\beta$ using cross-sectional data for the full period as well as several subperiods. He also found high values of $\beta$, with no clear pattern over time, whether the estimates were conducted in levels or first differences. The view that $\beta$ has not fallen over time among industrial countries, however, has proved to be somewhat less robust than the finding that the value of $\beta$ has been relatively high on average (Montiel, 1993, p. 14). Obstfeld (1986) found that $\beta$ fell after 1973, contrary to the results cited above. Obstfeld used time-series regressions based on quarterly observations of changes in the savings and investment ratios for several OECD countries. These results are consistent with those of Feldstein and Bacchetta (1989) who found $\beta$ declining from 0.914 (with a standard error of 0.063) in the 1960s to 0.607 (with a standard error of 0.126) over the period 1980–1986 for a cross-section sample of 23 OECD countries. The most extreme evidence of a decline in $\beta$ was provided by Frankel (1989), though only for the United States. Using cyclically-adjusted annual data and instrumental variable estimation, he found that the coefficient $\beta$ was 0.67 (with a standard error of 0.19) during 1930–1979 and 0.15 (with a standard error of 0.27) during 1980–1986 which is statistically insignificantly different from zero.

## 3.3   The Interpretation of Savings-Investment Correlations

The empirical and theoretical criticism that has been put forward against the F–H criterion is strongly related to above covariances which represent the underlying assumptions of the F–H criterion. We briefly analyze these covariances (see Dooley et al., 1987 and Tesar, 1991 for a further discussion of these issues). They capture possible explanations for capital immobility, that is, high $\beta$ estimates.

   With reference to the last covariance: Imperfect financial and/or non-financial capital mobility, which means $Cov(E_t(r_{i,t+k}-r_{i,t+k}^*), S_{i,t+k}/Y_{i,t+k})\neq 0$. It is difficult to infer from the F–H results something about the degree of capital mobility of type I, that is, financial integration. The identification problem of the F–H criterion with respect to financial integration either in cross-section or in time-series analysis is problematic. Recall that *ex ante* RIP is a sufficient condition for perfect capital mobility of type IV which means that the *ex ante* real interest differential is zero: $E_t(r_{t,t+k}-r_{t,t+k}^*)=[i_{t,t+k}-i_{t,t+k}^*-(f_t^{t+k}-s_t)] + [(f_t^{t+k}-s_t)-E_t(s_{t+k}-s_t)] + [E_t(s_{t+k}-s_t)-E_t(p_{t+k}-p_t)+E_t(p_{t+k}^*-p_t^*)]=0$. *Ex ante* RIP simply may not hold because *ex ante* PPP is not valid and/or because an exchange risk premium exists. Frankel (1986, 1989) has adopted the view that F–H evidence reflects imperfect integration in goods and factor markets, rather than financial markets. Frankel argues that domestic crowding out occurs via the domestic real interest rate. Even in a world with perfect financial integration and rational exchange rate expectations there can be sizeable short-run deviations among real interest rates across countries because of imperfect substitutability in goods markets. If goods prices and wages are sticky, a fiscal expansion can cause an increase in the domestic interest rate and a simultaneous overshoot in the exchange value of the domestic currency. The expected depreciation back to the long-run equilibrium value of the currency then equates expected returns on domestic and foreign financial assets. But the rise in the domestic interest rate causes crowding out of domestic spending. Frankel therefore attributes the correlation of savings and investment rates to imperfections in goods and factor markets, not to imperfections in financial markets.[4] An increase in institutional restrictions on labour mobility, physical capital mobility or on trade in goods and services may cause positive correlation between savings and investment ratios which may well go together with increasing financial integration.

   Sinn (1992) criticizes the cross-sectional estimation procedure of the F–H criterion. Sinn (1992, p. 1165) argues: 'Since savings and investment shares are approximately equal if averaged over the adjustment period, a correlation coefficient calculated from average savings and investment shares is likely to be higher than one that is not. It would erroneously signal a low degree of international capital mobility because it ignores net capital flows that have occurred in reverse directions during the period over which averages are taken'. Even with perfect capital mobility, high positive cross-sectional correlation may arise when savings and investment ratios are averaged over long periods of time, while low cross-sectional correlation may arise when savings and investment ratios are averaged over short periods of time. That is, cross-sectional analysis of savings and investment ratios averaged over long periods of time causes an upward bias in the estimate for the coefficient $\beta$. In addition, *gross* (two-way) financial and non-financial capital mobility may well be higher than *net* financial and non-financial capital mobility (see also Golub, 1990, p. 428). However, the F–H criterion only examines *net* financial and non-financial capital mobility. Consequently, cross-sectional analysis of savings-investment correlations using averages over long periods of time may underestimate the degree of financial integration.

Furthermore, savings and investment will be perfectly correlated in the *long-run* due to intertemporal budget constraints (Sachs, 1981). A country may run a current account deficit for a short period of time but current account imbalances must accumulate to zero over a long period of time unless the country defaults on its foreign debt (see Coakley, Kulasi and Smith, 1996, p. 621).

Wong (1990, pp. 61–2) comments on another deficiency of the cross-sectional estimation of the F–H criterion. The cross-sectional correlation between savings and investment may be rather sensitive to the inclusion or exclusion of particular countries in the sample. Wong points out that outliers may significantly bias the result when cross-sectional country averages are calculated. Moreover, Wong shows that the existence of non-traded goods can lead to a short-run correlation between savings and investment even under perfect capital mobility of type III.

Finally, Feldstein and Bacchetta (1989, pp. 10–1) give an important interpretation of the cross-sectional savings and investment correlations. The coefficient $\beta$ not only refers to the degree of capital mobility among (a group of) EU countries but also to the degree of capital mobility among (a group of) EU countries and the rest of the world which of course also include(s) countries like the United States and Japan. The same holds for the time-series interpretation of correlations between savings and investment ratios of individual EU countries.

With reference to the second covariance: The foreign expected real interest rate is endogenous, which means $Cov(E_t r^*_{i,t+k}, S_{i,t+k}/Y_{i,t+k}) \neq 0$. The second covariance says that savings and investment ratios may be correlated even in the presence of perfect capital mobility of type III because of the effect of country size. The first interpretation of the country-size argument is as follows. Small countries take the world interest rate as given, while changes in savings and investment behaviour of large countries will have an impact on the world interest rate (Murphy, 1984).[5] Shocks to national savings in large countries could thus affect world interest rates and through them domestic investment. Murphy, in particular, shows that the high value of $\beta$ can be attributed to the inclusion of three large countries in the sample (the United States, Japan and the United Kingdom). When these are removed from the sample, the value of $\beta$ falls to approximately 0.6. The second interpretation of the country-size argument follows from Harberger (1980). Harberger argues that in small less-diversified countries savings and investment shocks do not compensate each other. When a country becomes larger it also becomes more diversified and the need to borrow from abroad in the event of a shock declines.[6] Differences between savings and investment are therefore greater in small than in large countries. These greater differences, however, do not mean that the degree of capital mobility of type IV is higher, or savings-investment correlations are higher – even though type III capital mobility is perfect.

With reference to the first covariance: Savings are endogenous, which means $Cov(\mu_i, S_{i,t-k}/Y_{i,t-k}) \neq 0$. Even with perfect capital mobility of type III savings ratios may be positively correlated for reasons unrelated to capital mobility. This endogeneity of savings arises especially in time-series analysis but may also arise in cross-section analysis. Dooley et al. (1987, p. 508) argue: '*Any* economic variable, in addition to the cost of capital that influences the investment rate, will probably be correlated with the national savings rate'. Essentially, the savings ratio may be correlated with the stochastic error term $\mu_i$ that captures all other determinants of the investment rate – other than the *ex ante* real interest rate of that country. Furthermore, investment may also be endogenous. Although it takes time to adjust investment in equipment (fixed capital formation), investment in inventory can be changed quickly. In time-series, the correlation could arise because both investment and savings are functions of the state of the business cycle – that is, of a third variable. In particular, both investment and savings are known to be procyclical. Investment and savings may be correlated even if RIP holds, because they are both endogenous variables which respond to movements in common factors. Tesar (1991) argues that capital is in fact mobile, but that shocks to the productivity of domestic capital and labour in a country affect both desired savings and desired investment in the same way, leading to a positive correlation between savings and investment. Moreover, other real shocks such as shocks to the prices of imported means of production, or to world real interest rates (see the previous argument) may move savings and investment in the same direction. Similarly, Obstfeld (1986) argues that income and population growth may simultaneously affect savings and investment.

Not only private sector behaviour but also public sector behaviour may cause savings and investment to be positively correlated. Artis and Bayoumi (1991, p. 301) note that common cause variations in savings and investment of the private and public sector (positively correlated shocks) will suffice to induce a high correlation between total savings and investment. For example, the government may use its policy instruments to balance savings and investment of the private sector in the light of its current account target. The government – which aims at long-term current account balance – may react to an incipient current account deficit arising from growing investment relative to savings by raising taxes or lowering their spending (Fieleke, 1982, Westphal, 1983 and Summers, 1988). Taking national savings as the sum of private and public savings, this makes national savings endogenous through its public component.

Gordon and Bovenberg (1996) argue that asymmetric information between investors in different countries provides the most plausible explanation for savings-investment to be correlated. Foreign investors are at a handicap relative to domestic investors due to their poorer knowledge of domestic markets. As a result, they are likely to be less successful when setting up new firms, and they are vulnerable to being overcharged if they acquire existing domestic firms.

An econometric solution to the endogeneity problem of savings is offered by the use of instrumental variables. Instrumental variable estimation requires an instrumental variable that is highly correlated with the savings ratio $S_{i,t-k}/Y_{i,t-k}$ and uncorrelated with the error term $\varepsilon_{i,t-k}$. However, these Two Stage Least Squares (2SLS) estimates of the coefficient $\beta$ do not particularly differ from OLS estimates (Feldstein and Horioka, 1980, p. 312 and Dooley et al., 1987, p. 518). In Section 3.4, however, we shall introduce the concept of cointegration to cope with the endogeneity problem.

To summarize, the use of savings-investment correlations to draw inference about the degree of financial integration is problematic, because there are at least three ways that savings and investment could be correlated even if financial markets are well integrated in the sense that CIP or UIP hold exactly. The interpretation of the F–H criterion depends heavily on three covariances which must be zero before no correlation between savings and investment ratios would be expected. Therefore, the interpretation of the F–H criterion must be made with caution.

## 3.4    The Feldstein–Horioka Criterion and Cross-section Analysis

In spite of the interpretation problems posed by savings-investment correlations as an indicator of the degree of financial integration, it is useful to examine what information such correlations can provide about financial integration in the EU. The coefficient $\beta$ at least represents a direct and simple measure of the degree of capital mobility. The annual data employed in this section are taken from OECD (1995b). A nonzero statistical discrepancy is split equally between savings and investment (see Appendix 3A1). The sample period 1960–1993 is divided into two subperiods: 1960–1978 and 1979–1993.[7] The division reflects the formation of the EMS and the establishment of the ERM in 1979. Ratios of savings and investment to gross domestic product for individual EU countries are averaged over time in order to avoid bias caused by the correlation of savings and investment over the business cycle.

Figure 3.1 plots average savings and investment ratios over the subperiods 1960–1978 and 1979–1993 for EU countries (excluding Luxemburg) similar to Murphy (1984, p. 334) and Tesar (1991, p. 61). The interpretation of Figure 3.1 runs as follows. An observation on the 45° line indicates that the country's current account is balanced, that is, the country's domestic investment equals its supply of national savings. An observation above the 45° line reflects a current account deficit that is, the country's domestic investment exceeds its supply of national savings and the country is a net borrower in the international capital market (Tesar, 1991, p. 61). An observation below the 45° line reflects a current account surplus. National savings exceed domestic investment. The country must have a corresponding capital account deficit (that is, a capital outflow). The capital account is simply the inverse of the current account.

The F–H criterion for testing the degree of financial integration in the EU with cross-section data can be specified as follows:

$$I_{i,t+k}/Y_{i,t+k} = \alpha + \beta S_{i,t+k}/Y_{i,t+k} + \varepsilon_{i,t+k} \qquad (3.7)$$

where $\varepsilon_{i,t+k}$ stands for the error term and $i$ stands for the country index. F–H convert gross national savings $S_{i,t+k}$ and gross domestic investment $I_{i,t+k}$ into relative form by dividing by gross domestic product $Y_{i,t+k}$.[8] The coefficient $\beta$ is called the 'savings retention coefficient' and indicates the proportion of the incremental savings that is invested domestically (Feldstein and Bacchetta, 1989, p. 10). When financial markets are not integrated the current account is forced to balance and the coefficient $\beta$ should be unity. With perfect capital mobility of type IV a zero value of $\beta$ is predicted. We distinguish between three cross-sectional samples of European countries. The first sample consists of 13 EU member states excluding Greece and Luxemburg (EU-13). The scatter plots in Figure 3.1 show that Greece and Luxemburg may have an 'outlier' effect on the results. Luxemburg even lies out of the range of the graph. Furthermore, Greek savings-investment correlations are less comparable with savings-investment correlations of other EU countries. Greece is the only EU member state which national accounting definitions of savings and investment are based on the earlier System of National Accounts definitions (see Appendix 3A1). Greece almost certainly has less claim to be included among the EU-13 countries than either Portugal and Spain. The second sample includes all EU countries except Austria, Finland, Greece, Luxemburg and Sweden (EC-10).

*Figure 3.1   Average gross national savings versus gross domestic investment
ratios over the periods 1960–1978 and 1979–1993 of EU countries
(percentages of gross domestic product) (excluding Luxemburg)*

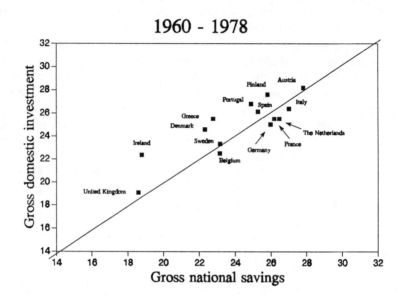

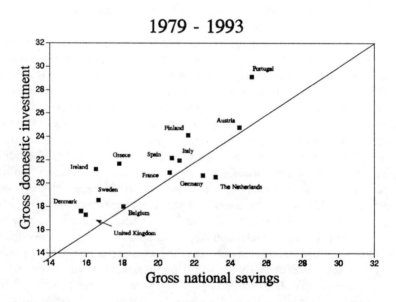

*Source:* OECD (1995b).

The third sample consists of the core ERM countries which entered the EC in 1979 with a small fluctuation margin of ± 2.25 per cent, Belgium, Denmark, France, Germany, Ireland and The Netherlands (ERM-6).

We estimate the standard cross-section specification of the F–H criterion in level form for three cross-sections of EU countries with OLS. The results are summarized in Table 3.2. The results for the EU-13 and EC-10 countries

*Table 3.2 The F–H criterion and cross-section analysis (EU-13, EC-10 and ERM-6)*

$$I_{i,t+k}/Y_{i,t+k} = \alpha + \beta \, S_{i,t+k}/Y_{i,t+k} + \varepsilon_{i,t+k}$$

| EU-13 | $\alpha$ | $\beta$ | $R^2$ |
|---|---|---|---|
| 1960–1993 | 0.06 (0.03) | 0.75 (0.15)** | 0.70 |
| 1960–1978 | 0.07 (0.03) | 0.74 (0.12)** | 0.76 |
| 1979–1993 | 0.05 (0.04) | 0.82 (0.18)** | 0.66 |
| **EC-10** | $\alpha$ | $\beta$ | $R^2$ |
| 1960–1993 | 0.08 (0.04) | 0.68 (0.18)** | 0.63 |
| 1960–1978 | 0.08 (0.03) | 0.67 (0.14)† | 0.74 |
| 1979–1993 | 0.05 (0.05) | 0.79 (0.23)** | 0.59 |
| **ERM-6** | $\alpha$ | $\beta$ | $R^2$ |
| 1960–1993 | 0.16 (0.03) | 0.30 (0.14)* | 0.55 |
| 1960–1978 | 0.15 (0.03) | 0.40 (0.13)† | 0.69 |
| 1979–1993 | 0.15 (0.04) | 0.27 (0.21)* | 0.29 |

*Notes:*

\*    Indicates that the coefficient $\beta$ is insignificantly different from zero and significantly different from one at the 95 per cent level of confidence (two-tailed test).
\*\*   Indicates that the coefficient $\beta$ is significantly different from zero and insignificantly different from one at the 95 per cent level of confidence (two-tailed test).
†    Indicates that the coefficient $\beta$ is imprecisely estimated and differs significantly from zero and significantly from one at the 95 per cent level of confidence (two-tailed test).

Standard errors are shown in parentheses. $R^2$ is the coefficient of determination.

*Source:* OECD (1995b).

in Table 3.2 show a rise in the estimated value of $\beta$ in the period 1979–1993 relative to the period 1960–1978 indicating a declining degree of capital mobility of type IV. The results for the ERM-6 countries show a decline in the estimated value of $\beta$ in the period 1979–1993 relative to the period 1960–1978 indicating an increasing degree of capital mobility of type IV.

Following Feldstein and Horioka (1980) and Feldstein (1983), we simultaneously test the null hypothesis $H_0$: $\beta = 0$ against the alternative hypothesis $H_1$: $\beta \neq 0$ and the null hypothesis $H_0$: $\beta = 1$ against the alternative hypothesis

$H_1$: $\beta \neq 1$ at the 5 per cent level of significance. The results for the EU-13 show that the coefficient $\beta$ is significantly different from zero and insignificantly different from one over the three periods 1960–1993, 1960–1978 and 1979–1993. The results for the EC-10 are comparable to the results for the EU-13. However, the coefficient $\beta$ is imprecisely estimated over the period 1960–1978. The results for the ERM-6 show that the coefficient $\beta$ is insignificantly different from zero and significantly different from one over the period 1960–1993 and the subperiod 1979–1993. Accordingly, for the ERM-6 countries the assumption of perfect capital mobility of type IV cannot be rejected over the period 1960–1993 and subperiod 1979–1993. This result is also illustrated in Figure 3.1 by the greater dispersion of the ERM-6 points around the 45° line in the subperiod 1979–1993 relative to the subperiod 1960–1978. The ERM-6 estimates for $\beta$ are smaller than the EC-10 and EU-13 estimates. We may conclude that capital mobility of type IV between ERM-6 countries is higher than between EC-10 and EU-13 countries. It seems that the ERM-6 countries are already substantially integrated. This may be accounted for by the lack of currency risk and by the strong interdependence of their economies.

As was explained in Section 3.2 the results obtained from F–H regressions are hard to interpret.[9] The results for the EC-10 and EU-13 show a rise in the estimated value of $\beta$ in the period 1979–1993 relative to the period 1960–1978, indicating a decreasing degree of capital mobility of type IV. This increase of savings-investment correlations for the EC-10 and EU-13 countries over the period 1979–1993 relative to the period 1960–1978 bears no relation with the expected increase of integration between European financial markets after 1979. The apparent higher correlation in the period 1979–1993 relative to 1960–1978 for the EC-10 and EU-13 may be explained by emerging investment opportunities in Europe after the formation of the EMS in 1979 (Obstfeld, 1989, p. 151). The formation of the EMS in 1979 and the subsequent preparation for the EMU, may have caused a pattern of investment increases only partly financed by foreign savings. Santillán (1991, p. 33) argues: 'Efforts to stimulate savings and enhance its allocation across countries are at the heart of the process towards Economic and Monetary Union'. The higher values in the latter period simply may be due to the fact that within the EC-10 and EU-13 countries, markets became so integrated that there was little need for capital flows to and from the rest of the world (Leachman, 1991, p. 159).

Although savings-investment correlations are difficult to interpret, the lower cross-sectional savings-investment correlation for the ERM-6 countries do challenge the usual findings for world financial markets. Results obtained by Bhandari and Mayer (1990) have confirmed the higher degree of capital mobility among EMS countries than among other industrial countries. ERM-6 savings-investment correlations are sufficiently far from the value of unity to conclude that financial markets are not closed.

Finally, the cross-sectional β coefficients simply reflect capital mobility between a sample of countries taken as a unit to and from the rest of the world, not capital mobility between individual EC countries (Leachman, 1991, p. 158). A high statistical correlation between savings and investment ratios based upon a sample of EU countries does not necessarily indicate a low degree of capital mobility of type IV for each individual EU country. In fact, cross-section analysis assumes the same degree of capital mobility for each individual country in the sample. Therefore, the next section turns to time-series analysis of savings-investment correlations of individual EU countries.

## 3.5 The Feldstein–Horioka Criterion and Time-series Analysis

In the previous section we performed cross-section analysis for three samples of EU countries to eliminate the procyclical nature of savings and investment even when expressed as a fraction of gross domestic product. Regressions between variables that are averaged over many years measure the long-run correlation between savings and investment. However, we argued that the long-run correlation between savings and investment may be a less relevant indicator for the degree of capital mobility.

First, this section performs time-series analysis with the help of cointegration tests. Cointegration in the context of the F–H criterion deals with the long-run relationship between savings and investment ratios. Two variables are said to be cointegrated if both are non-stationary but there exists a linear combination of the variables that is stationary (see Engle and Granger, 1987, p. 253). Subsequently, if the two variables are cointegrated, we may specify an error-correction model (ECM) to distinguish between the *short-* and *long-run* correlations between savings and investment.

Before turning to the time-series analysis of savings-investment correlations Figure 3A2.1 shows the time-series behaviour of savings and investment as percentage of gross domestic product over the period 1960–1993. Since we know that the difference between savings and investment need to be equal to the current account balance, Figure 3A2.1 also presents the behaviour of the current account as percentage of gross domestic product. The current account may also shed light on the correlation between savings and investment.[10] It is apparent that for some countries the current account has fluctuated considerably in the 1970s and 1980s. The savings and investment ratios of EU countries typically display a sharp downfall after 1973, and a rise at the end of the eighties.[11]

The application of cointegration requires savings and investment ratios to be non-stationary (Engle and Granger, 1987). The original test for unit roots in economic times series was developed by Fuller (1976) and Dickey and Fuller (1979). We have performed Augmented Dickey–Fuller (ADF) tests. A regression model is used to test for a unit root in $Z_{t+k,i} = (I_{t+k,i}/Y_{t+k,i}, S_{t+k,i}/Y_{t+k,i})$:

$$\Delta Z_{t+k,i} = \alpha + \beta t + \pi Z_{t+k-1,i} + \sum_{j=1}^{8} \gamma_j \Delta Z_{t+k-j,i} + \mu_{t+k,i} \qquad (3.8)$$

where $\alpha$ is a constant term, t is a trend term and $\mu_{t+k,i}$ is a white noise error term. The null hypothesis of a unit root $H_0$: $\pi = 0$ is tested using the ADF test. For non-stationarity of $I_{t+k,i}/Y_{t+k,i}$ and $S_{t+k,i}/Y_{t+k,i}$ to be rejected, coefficient $\pi$ has to be significantly negative. A constant has been included since both $I_{t+k,i}/Y_{t+k,i}$ and $S_{t+k,i}/Y_{t+k,i}$ have a nonzero mean. Following De Haan and Siermann (1994, p. 7), we first apply the ADF test with a trend term included. If the coefficient of the trend term does not differ significantly from zero, we apply the ADF test without a trend variable. Furthermore, we include the minimum number of lags necessary to ensure that the residuals $\mu_{t+k,i}$ are white noise, since the power of the test reduces when more lagged differences of the dependent variable are included (see Kremers, Ericsson and Dolado, 1992 and McCallum, 1993). Possible serial correlation of $\mu_{t+k,i}$ in the regression models is corrected for up to eighth-order lags. Recently, MacKinnon (1991) has tabulated Dickey–Fuller critical values for any sample size, with a constant and/or a time trend included. We apply MacKinnon critical values in our unit root tests.

We are aware of the fact that drawing reliable inference from the outcome of the ADF test may be problematic due to the limited number of observations when annual data are used. OECD (1995c) quarterly data of savings and investment ratios are only available for France, West Germany and the United Kingdom from 1970 onwards. The problem is partly overcome due to the relatively long 34 (1960–1993), 19 (1960–1978) and 15 (1979–1993) year spans of annual data and 25 (1970Q1–1994Q4), 9 (1970Q1–1978Q4) of 16 (1979Q1–1994Q4) year spans of quarterly data we examine. Hakkio and Rush (1990) argue that what is relevant for determining long-run relationships is the length of the time-series spanning.

Table 3.3 reports the outcomes of the ADF tests for fifteen EU countries when annual data are used and for three EU countries when quarterly data are used. With respect to the annual data, only for Belgium (1960–1978), Germany (1960–1993), Ireland (1960–1978), Portugal (1960–1993) and the United Kingdom (1960–1993) the null hypothesis of non-stationarity of one or both series was rejected at the 95 per cent and/or 99 per cent level of confidence. Similarly, with respect to the quarterly data, only for Germany (1970Q1–1994 Q4) non-stationarity of the investment series was rejected at the 95 per cent and 99 per cent level of confidence. Interpreting the rejection of non-stationarity as a small sample problem, we may safely conclude from Table 3.3 that in gene-

*Table 3.3 The F–H criterion and time-series analysis: testing for a unit root in $I_{t+k,i}/Y_{t+k,i}$ and $S_{t+k,i}/Y_{t+k,i}$*

| Country | Variable | 1960–1993 | 1960–1978 | 1979–1993 |
|---|---|---|---|---|
| Austria | I/Y | ADF($c$,0)=−1.94 (−2.95) | ADF($c$,0)=−2.27 (−3.05) | ADF($c$,1)=−2.09 (−3.08) |
|  | S/Y | ADF($c$,0)=−1.31 (−2.95) | ADF($c$,0)=−1.22 (−3.05) | ADF($c$,0)=−1.49 (−3.08) |
| Belgium | I/Y | ADF($t$,0)=−2.58 (−3.55) | ADF($c$,0)=−3.17 (−3.05) * | ADF($c$,0)=−1.78 (−3.08) |
|  | S/Y | ADF($c$,0)=−1.24 (−2.95) | ADF($c$,0)=−1.76 (−3.05) | ADF($t$,0)=−2.85 (−3.76) |
| Denmark | I/Y | ADF($t$,0)=−2.72 (−3.55) | ADF($c$,0)=−2.74 (−3.05) | ADF($c$,0)=−1.24 (−3.08) |
|  | S/Y | ADF($c$,1)=−1.40 (−2.96) | ADF($t$,1)=−3.22 (−3.71) | ADF($t$,0)=−3.54 (−3.76) |
| Finland | I/Y | ADF($t$,1)=−3.55 (−3.56) | ADF($c$,1)=−2.77 (−3.05) | ADF($c$,0)=−0.43 (−3.08) |
|  | S/Y | ADF($t$,1)=−2.53 (−3.56) | ADF($c$,0)=−2.08 (−3.05) | ADF($t$,1)=−3.37 (−3.76) |
| France | I/Y | ADF($t$,0)=−2.27 (−3.55) | ADF($c$,0)=−2.41 (−3.05) | ADF($c$,0)=−0.76 (−3.08) |
|  | S/Y | ADF($t$,1)=−2.65 (−3.56) | ADF($c$,0)=−1.44 (−3.05) | ADF($c$,1)=−2.56 (−3.08) |
| Germany | I/Y | ADF($t$,1)=−3.88 (−3.56)* | ADF($c$,0)=−1.02 (−3.05) | ADF($c$,1)=−2.76 (−3.08) |
|  | S/Y | ADF($c$,0)=−1.48 (−2.95) | ADF($c$,0)=−1.08 (−3.05) | ADF($c$,0)=−1.03 (−3.08) |
| Greece | I/Y | ADF($c$,0)=−1.83 (−2.95) | ADF($c$,0)=−2.04 (−3.05) | ADF($c$,0)=−1.54 (−3.08) |
|  | S/Y | ADF($c$,0)=−1.47 (−2.95) | ADF($c$,0)=−1.55 (−3.05) | ADF($c$,0)=−1.56 (−3.08) |
| Ireland | I/Y | ADF($c$,0)=−1.63 (−2.95) | ADF($t$,0)=−3.40 (−3.71) | ADF($c$,0)=−0.74 (−3.08) |
|  | S/Y | ADF($c$,0)=−2.55 (−2.95) | ADF($t$,0)=−4.75 (−3.71)** | ADF($t$,0)=−3.25 (−3.76) |
| Italy | I/Y | ADF($t$,0)=−3.10 (−3.55) | ADF($c$,0)=−2.87 (−3.05) | ADF($t$,1)=−3.16 (−3.76) |
|  | S/Y | ADF($t$,0)=−2.47 (−3.55) | ADF($c$,0)=−2.94 (−3.05) | ADF($t$,0)=−2.14 (−3.76) |
| Luxem-burg | I/Y | ADF($c$,0)=−2.10 (−2.95) | ADF($t$,0)=−1.88 (−3.71) | ADF($c$,0)=−0.84 (−3.08) |
|  | S/Y | ADF($c$,0)=−1.12 (−2.95) | ADF($c$,0)=−1.44 (−3.05) | ADF($c$,0)=−1.77 (−3.08) |
| The Nether-lands | I/Y | ADF($c$,0)=−1.29 (−2.95) | ADF($c$,0)=−1.14 (−3.05) | ADF($c$,0)=−1.69 (−3.08) |
|  | S/Y | ADF($c$,0)=−2.19 (−2.95) | ADF($c$,0)=−0.70 (−3.05) | ADF($c$,0)=−1.32 (−3.08) |
| Portugal | I/Y | ADF($c$,1)=−3.48 (−2.96)* | ADF($c$,0)=−2.34 (−3.05) | ADF($c$,1)=−2.98 (−3.08) |
|  | S/Y | ADF($c$,1)=−4.37 (−2.96)** | ADF($c$,1)=−3.04 (−3.05) | ADF($c$,1)=−3.05 (−3.08) |
| Spain | I/Y | ADF($t$,1)=−2.91 (−3.56) | ADF($c$,0)=−2.01 (−3.05) | ADF($c$,1)=−2.38 (−3.08) |
|  | S/Y | ADF($t$,0)=−2.46 (−3.55) | ADF($t$,0)=−1.28 (−3.71) | ADF($c$,1)=−2.83 (−3.08) |
| Sweden | I/Y | ADF($t$,1)=−3.53 (−3.56) | ADF($t$,1)=−2.80 (−3.71) | ADF($c$,0)=−0.98 (−3.08) |
|  | S/Y | ADF($t$,1)=−2.65 (−3.56) | ADF($c$,0)= 0.38 (−3.05) | ADF($c$,1)=−2.02 (−3.08) |
| United Kingdom | I/Y | ADF($c$,1)=−3.19 (−2.96)* | ADF($c$,0)=−2.91 (−3.05) | ADF($c$,1)=−2.86 (−3.08) |
|  | S/Y | ADF($t$,0)=−2.11 (−3.55) | ADF($c$,0)=−1.99 (−3.05) | ADF($c$,0)=−0.33 (−3.08) |
| Country | Variable | 1970Q1–1994Q4 | 1970Q1–1978Q4 | 1979Q1–1994Q4 |
| France | I/Y | ADF($t$,1)=−2.73 (−3.46) | ADF($t$,1)=−3.51 (−3.55) | ADF($c$,0)=−1.50 (−2.91) |
|  | S/Y | ADF($t$,0)=−1.84 (−3.46) | ADF($t$,0)=−2.04 (−3.55) | ADF($c$,0)=−2.44 (−2.91) |
| Germany | I/Y | ADF($c$,4)=−2.92 (−2.89)* | ADF($c$,4)=−1.59 (−2.96) | ADF($c$,4)=−2.72 (−2.91) |
|  | S/Y | ADF($c$,4)=−2.53 (−2.89) | ADF($t$,4)=−2.91 (−3.56) | ADF($c$,4)=−1.92 (−2.91) |
| United Kingdom | I/Y | ADF($t$,1)=−2.72 (−3.46) | ADF($c$,1)=−1.94 (−2.95) | ADF($c$,0)=−1.82 (−2.91) |
|  | S/Y | ADF($c$,4)=−1.90 (−2.89) | ADF($c$,0)=−2.66 (−2.95) | ADF($t$,0)=−3.38 (−3.48) |

*Notes:*

*  The null hypothesis of a unit root is rejected at the 95 per cent level of confidence (one-tailed test).
** The null hypothesis of a unit root is rejected at the 99 per cent level of confidence (one-tailed test).

ADF stands for the Augmented Dickey–Fuller test with the specification of the test equation between brackets (*c* estimated with constant term or *t* estimated with constant and trend term). In addition, the number of lagged differences of the dependent variable is also indicated between brackets.

MacKinnon critical values at the 95 per cent level of confidence are shown in brackets.

*Sources:* OECD (1995b) and OECD (1995c).

ral savings and investment ratios are non-stationary. If they are, and they are not cointegrated, then a regression in levels may lead to spurious correlation (Granger and Newbold, 1974). This may provide an alternative interpretation for the high correlations between savings and investment. If both savings and investment ratios possess a unit root, first differencing would make them stationary and regressions based on first differences would not exhibit the spurious correlation problem. Therefore cointegration tests are needed.

Cointegration between savings and investment ratios implies the existence of an ECM or, in other words, a long-run equilibrium relationship (see Engle and Granger, 1987). This ECM corresponds with the theoretical prediction that in the long-run, savings and investment need to move together to balance the current account. Theoretical considerations suggest that in the long-run, savings and investment should cointegrate with a unit coefficient, irrespective of the degree of capital mobility. The reason is that the current account provides the resources with which a country repays its external creditors (Sachs, 1981). Solvency thus imposes a constraint which prevents deviations between national savings and domestic investment from becoming permanent. Since gaps between savings and investment must eventually be reversed for the country to remain solvent, we expect these series to be cointegrated. The current account or the capital account are expected to balance over long periods of time. Consequently, in the long-run, savings and investment ratios necessarily have to move together, that is, we have cointegration of savings and investment. The cointegrating regression equation is specified as follows:

$$I_{t+k,i}/Y_{t+k,i} = \alpha + \beta\, S_{t+k,i}/Y_{t+k,i} + \varepsilon_{t+k,i} \qquad (3.9)$$

This equation (3.9) is simply the specification of the F–H criterion with time-series analysis.

Table 3.4 summarizes the estimation results for the cointegrating regression. The coefficient $\beta$ basically represents the long-run savings-investment correlation and therefore it indicates long-run capital mobility. Table 3.4 shows that the *long-run* savings-investment correlation differs substantially among EU countries and over time. It is particularly interesting to compare OLS estimates of $\beta$ in the subperiods before and after the formation of the EMS in 1979. Clearly, the magnitude of the coefficient $\beta$ declined over the period 1979–1993 as opposed to the period 1960–1978 in all EU countries with the exception of Austria, France, Luxemburg and Sweden (annual data) and France (quarterly

*Table 3.4 The F–H criterion and time-series analysis: the cointegrating regression*

$$I_{t+k,i}/Y_{t+k,i} = \alpha + \beta\, S_{t+k,i}/Y_{t+k,i} + \varepsilon_{t+k,i}$$

| Country | Period | $\alpha$ | $\beta$ | DW | $R^2$ |
|---|---|---|---|---|---|
| Austria | 1960–1993 | 0.03 (0.02) | 0.91 (0.08)** | 1.09 | 0.79 |
| | 1960–1978 | 0.09 (0.04) | 0.68 (0.13)‡ | 1.49 | 0.63 |
| | 1979–1993 | −0.05 (0.06) | 1.23 (0.25)** | 1.24 | 0.66 |
| Belgium | 1960–1993 | 0.07 (0.02) | 0.67 (0.08)‡ | 0.41 | 0.69 |
| | 1960–1978[a] | 0.10 (0.02) | 0.53 (0.09)‡ | 1.24 | 0.66 |
| | 1979–1993 | 0.11 (0.03) | 0.38 (0.18)‡ | 0.45 | 0.26 |
| Denmark | 1960–1993 | 0.04 (0.02) | 0.90 (0.09)** | 0.56 | 0.74 |
| | 1960–1978 | 0.10 (0.03) | 0.63 (0.12)‡ | 2.72 | 0.59 |
| | 1979–1993 | 0.16 (0.05) | 0.08 (0.33)* | 0.57 | 0.004 |
| Finland | 1960–1993 | 0.04 (0.02) | 0.92 (0.09)** | 0.92 | 0.76 |
| | 1960–1978 | −0.05 (0.06) | 1.26 (0.25)** | 0.96 | 0.61 |
| | 1979–1993 | 0.05 (0.02) | 0.86 (0.11)** | 0.95 | 0.83 |
| France | 1960–1993 | 0.03 (0.01) | 0.86 (0.05)** | 1.21 | 0.91 |
| | 1960–1978 | 0.003 (0.05) | 0.96 (0.18)** | 1.40 | 0.63 |
| | 1979–1993 | 0.01 (0.03) | 0.98 (0.13)** | 1.01 | 0.82 |
| Germany | 1960–1993[a] | −0.01 (0.02) | 1.00 (0.10)** | 0.50 | 0.75 |
| | 1960–1978 | −0.03 (0.02) | 1.09 (0.09)** | 1.13 | 0.89 |
| | 1979–1993 | 0.18 (0.05) | 0.13 (0.22)* | 0.58 | 0.02 |
| Greece | 1960–1993 | 0.08 (0.01) | 0.78 (0.05)‡ | 1.45 | 0.89 |
| | 1960–1978 | 0.04 (0.02) | 0.96 (0.07)** | 1.56 | 0.91 |
| | 1979–1993 | 0.10 (0.01) | 0.65 (0.07)‡ | 1.69 | 0.87 |
| Ireland | 1960–1993 | 0.23 (0.06) | −0.08 (0.34)* | 0.33 | 0.002 |
| | 1960–1978[b] | 0.01 (0.09) | 1.16 (0.46)‡ | 1.56 | 0.27 |
| | 1979–1993 | 0.38 (0.09) | −0.99 (0.55)* | 0.54 | 0.20 |
| Italy | 1960–1993 | 0.05 (0.02) | 0.80 (0.07)‡ | 1.24 | 0.80 |
| | 1960–1978 | 0.02 (0.06) | 0.91 (0.22)** | 1.09 | 0.51 |
| | 1979–1993 | 0.03 (0.03) | 0.88 (0.14)** | 1.60 | 0.76 |
| Luxemburg | 1960–1993 | 0.22 (0.03) | −0.02 (0.08)* | 0.53 | 0.002 |
| | 1960–1978 | 0.25 (0.09) | −0.09 (0.27)* | 0.58 | 0.01 |
| | 1979–1993 | 0.18 (0.07) | 0.08 (0.15)* | 0.48 | 0.02 |
| The Netherlands | 1960–1993 | −0.02 (0.03) | 1.01 (0.13)** | 0.46 | 0.66 |
| | 1960–1978 | 0.03 (0.05) | 0.84 (0.18)** | 0.62 | 0.57 |
| | 1979–1993 | 0.13 (0.04) | 0.34 (0.19)* | 0.71 | 0.19 |
| Portugal | 1960–1993[ab] | 0.20 (0.03) | 0.33 (0.12)‡ | 0.65 | 0.19 |
| | 1960–1978 | 0.18 (0.02) | 0.35 (0.10)‡ | 1.11 | 0.44 |
| | 1979–1993 | 0.26 (0.10) | 0.12 (0.40)‡ | 0.49 | 0.01 |
| Spain | 1960–1993 | 0.06 (0.03) | 0.79 (0.13)** | 0.62 | 0.54 |
| | 1960–1978 | 0.11 (0.08) | 0.59 (0.30)† | 0.65 | 0.18 |
| | 1979–1993 | 0.11 (0.08) | 0.53 (0.40)† | 0.57 | 0.12 |
| Sweden | 1960–1993 | 0.06 (0.01) | 0.77 (0.05)‡ | 1.39 | 0.87 |
| | 1960–1978 | 0.04 (0.03) | 0.82 (0.11)** | 1.34 | 0.75 |
| | 1979–1993 | 0.04 (0.03) | 0.86 (0.17)** | 1.32 | 0.67 |
| United Kingdom | 1960–1993[a] | 0.11 (0.02) | 0.42 (0.13)‡ | 0.67 | 0.24 |
| | 1960–1978 | 0.12 (0.03) | 0.39 (0.19)* | 1.27 | 0.21 |
| | 1979–1993 | 0.15 (0.04) | 0.15 (0.27)* | 0.59 | 0.02 |

| Country | Period | α | β | DW | R² |
|---------|--------|-----|-----|-----|-----|
| France | 1970Q1–1994Q4 | 0.02 (0.007) | 0.92 (0.03)[‡] | 0.44 | 0.90 |
|        | 1970Q1–1978Q4 | 0.02 (0.03) | 0.92 (0.11)[**] | 0.53 | 0.67 |
|        | 1979Q1–1994Q4 | –0.02 (0.02) | 1.02 (0.07)[**] | 0.42 | 0.80 |
| Germany | 1970Q1–1994Q4[a] | 0.13 (0.006) | 0.80 (0.05)[‡] | 1.22 | 0.69 |
|         | 1970Q1–1978Q4 | 0.10 (0.008) | 1.01 (0.06)[**] | 1.53 | 0.90 |
|         | 1979Q1–1994Q4 | 0.15 (0.01) | 0.61 (0.11)[‡] | 1.32 | 0.34 |
| United Kingdom | 1970Q1–1994Q4 | 0.02 (0.01) | 0.96 (0.07)[**] | 0.29 | 0.63 |
|               | 1970Q1–1978Q4 | 0.07 (0.05) | 0.78 (0.24)[**] | 0.28 | 0.23 |
|               | 1979Q1–1994Q4 | 0.05 (0.02) | 0.77 (0.09)[‡] | 0.23 | 0.52 |

*Notes:*

[*]    Indicates that the coefficient $\beta$ is insignificantly different from zero and significantly different from one at the 95 per cent level of confidence (two-tailed test).

[**]   Indicates that the coefficient $\beta$ is significantly different from zero and insignificantly different from one at the 95 per cent level of confidence (two-tailed test).

[†]    Indicates that the coefficient $\beta$ is imprecisely estimated and differs insignificantly from zero and insignificantly from one at the 95 per cent level of confidence (two-tailed test).

[‡]    Indicates that the coefficient $\beta$ is imprecisely estimated and differs significantly from zero and significantly from one at the 95 per cent level of confidence (two-tailed test).

[a]    Note that in Table 3.3 the null hypothesis of a unit root in $I_{t+k,i}/Y_{t+k,i}$ was rejected at the 95 per cent level of confidence.

[b]    Note that in Table 3.3 the null hypothesis of a unit root in $S_{t+k,i}/Y_{t+k,i}$ was rejected at the 99 per cent level of confidence.

Standard errors are shown in parentheses. $DW$ is the Durbin-Watson statistic for first-order serial correlation and $R^2$ is the coefficient of determination.

data). The empirical results seem consistent with an increasing degree of *long-run* capital mobility of type IV in the 1980s.

Next, we consider two common tests for cointegration. The first test is the Engle-Granger cointegration test. Engle and Granger (1987) proposed the following two-step procedure to test for cointegration between savings and investment. First, one has to test for unit roots in the savings and investment ratios and estimate coefficient $\beta$ in the cointegrating regression as specified in equation (3.9). Subsequently, one has to test for of a unit root in the OLS residuals $\varepsilon_{t+k,i}$ of the cointegrating regression. The test regression is fitted without an intercept since the residuals have zero mean. Again, the null hypothesis of a unit root in the residuals (that is, no cointegration) is rejected if the value of the ADF test exceeds its 5 per cent critical value. Second, if the null hypothesis of a unit root in $\varepsilon_{t+k,i}$ is rejected, then we may specify an ECM where the error-correction term is replaced by $\varepsilon_{t+k,i}$. The second test is the Johansen (1988) cointegration test. Although the Johansen cointegration test is a multivariate test, it is also possible to apply it to the two-dimensional case to discover a unique cointegrating vector $r$ which may exist between savings and investment ratios. If the null hypothesis of $H_0: r=0$ is rejected and the alternative hypothesis $H_1: r=1$ is accepted, we have cointegration.[12] Further details are available in Johansen (1988, 1991) and Johansen and Juselius (1990).

Table 3.5 reports the results for the Engle-Granger and the Johansen cointegration tests. If both the Engle-Granger and the Johansen cointegration tests reject no cointegration, we find the strongest evidence for cointegration of savings and investment ratios. However, it appears rather difficult to reject no cointegration of savings and investment. For the annual data at least two out of three tests (Engle-Granger cointegration test, Johansen cointegration test I, Johansen cointegration test II) reject no cointegration between savings and investment ratios for Denmark (1960–1978), Finland (1960–1993), France (1960–1993), Greece (1960–1993), Ireland (1960–1978), Italy (1960–1993, 1979–1993), Portugal (1979–1993), Spain (1960–1993, 1979–1993) and Sweden (1960–1993). For the quarterly data at least two tests reject no cointegration between savings and investment ratios for France (1970Q1–1994Q4, 1970Q1–1978Q4) and Germany (1970Q1–1978Q4, 1979Q1–1994Q4) and the United Kingdom (1970Q1–1978Q4).

The weak evidence in favour of cointegration of savings and investment could be explained by the low power of the tests. Furthermore, the length of the time-series spanning may still be too short. The outcomes of the Engle-Granger and the Johansen cointegration tests for the subperiods probably have less weight due to the limited number of (annual) data. The Johansen test is biased in small samples because it is based upon asymptotic theory. Therefore, Engle and Granger recommend the ADF test of the residuals. Alternatively, equation (3.9) may be subject to several econometric problems. First, as is often the case with OLS results and time-series data, there is autocorrelation in the error term which introduces bias in the sampling variances and makes estimates inefficient. Second, the savings variable may well be endogenous, implying inconsistent estimates. Third, the small sample size introduces a sample bias. Fourth, results are meaningless if savings and investment are integrated of order one, or have different degree of integration (see Table 3.3) and their linear combination $\varepsilon_{t-k,i}$ is not stationary.

Kremers et al. (1992) argue that a more powerful test of cointegration follows from the direct specification of an error-correction model. To examine the short- and long-run relationship between savings and investment, we derive the following error-correction model. For simplicity, we may start with an Autoregressive Distributed Lag (abbreviated ADL(1,1)) model (see Hendry, Pagan and Sargan, 1984):

$$(I/Y)_{t+k,i} = \phi (I/Y)_{t+k-1,i} + \beta_0 (S/Y)_{t+k,i} + \beta_1 (S/Y)_{t+k-1,i} + \eta_{t+k,i} \qquad (3.10)$$

where disturbance term $\eta$ is white noise. After transformation, we get

*Table 3.5 The F–H criterion and time-series analysis: testing for cointegration between $I_{t+k,i}/Y_{t+k,i}$ and $S_{t+k,i}/Y_{t+k,i}$*

| Country | Period | Engle-Granger cointegration test | Johansen cointegration test I: $H_0: r=0$  $H_1: r=1$ | Johansen cointegration test II: $H_0: r=0$  $H_1: r=1$ |
|---|---|---|---|---|
| Austria | 1960–1993 | ADF(n,0)=–3.54 (–3.53) | 11.98 (15.67) | 14.05 (19.96) |
| | 1960–1978 | ADF(n,0)=–3.20 (–3.70) | 9.24 (15.67) | 11.24 (19.96) |
| | 1979–1993 | ADF(n,0)=–2.45 (–3.81) | 6.33 (15.67) | 9.45 (19.96) |
| Belgium | 1960–1993 | ADF(n,0)=–1.17 (–3.53) | 9.25 (15.67) | 12.57 (19.96) |
| | 1960–1978[a] | ADF(n,0)=–3.22 (–3.70) | 12.40 (15.67) | 14.61 (19.96) |
| | 1979–1993 | ADF(n,0)=–1.82 (–3.81) | 14.48 (15.67) | 17.72 (19.96) |
| Denmark | 1960–1993 | ADF(n,0)=–1.33 (–3.53) | 3.78 (15.67) | 6.26 (19.96) |
| | 1960–1978 | ADF(n,1)=–5.45 (–3.72) | 21.89 (15.67) | 24.60 (19.96) |
| | 1979–1993 | ADF(n,0)=–1.51 (–3.81) | 7.45 (15.67) | 8.47 (19.96) |
| Finland | 1960–1993 | ADF(n,1)=–4.39 (–3.53) | 20.55 (15.67) | 25.14 (19.96) |
| | 1960–1978 | ADF(n,1)=–3.57 (–3.72) | 12.35 (15.67) | 20.18 (19.96) |
| | 1979–1993 | ADF(n,0)=–1.97 (–3.81) | 10.32 (15.67) | 15.31 (19.96) |
| France | 1960–1993 | ADF(n,0)=–4.09 (–3.53) | 17.84 (15.67) | 19.86 (19.96) |
| | 1960–1978 | ADF(n,0)=–3.62 (–3.70) | 11.35 (15.67) | 14.01 (19.96) |
| | 1979–1993 | ADF(n,0)=–2.23 (–3.81) | 15.28 (15.67) | 22.01 (19.96) |
| Germany | 1960–1993[a] | ADF(n,0)=–2.15 (–3.53) | 6.73 (15.67) | 10.67 (19.96) |
| | 1960–1978 | ADF(n,1)=–3.63 (–3.72) | 7.41 (15.67) | 9.50 (19.96) |
| | 1979–1993 | ADF(n,1)=–3.85 (–3.85) | 11.33 (15.67) | 19.94 (19.96) |
| Greece | 1960–1993 | ADF(n,0)=–4.39 (–3.53) | 15.74 (15.67) | 17.98 (19.96) |
| | 1960–1978 | ADF(n,0)=–3.25 (–3.70) | 10.79 (15.67) | 14.70 (19.96) |
| | 1979–1993 | ADF(n,0)=–3.50 (–3.81) | 11.35 (15.67) | 18.76 (19.96) |
| Ireland | 1960–1993 | ADF(n,0)=–1.70 (–3.53) | 10.27 (15.67) | 16.29 (19.96) |
| | 1960–1978[b] | ADF(n,0)=–3.42 (–3.70) | 23.19 (15.67) | 31.16 (19.96) |
| | 1979–1993 | ADF(n,0)=–3.12 (–3.81) | 13.55 (15.67) | 17.65 (19.96) |
| Italy | 1960–1993 | ADF(n,0)=–3.67 (–3.53) | 17.17 (15.67) | 20.29 (19.96) |
| | 1960–1978 | ADF(n,0)=–2.45 (–3.70) | 7.85 (15.67) | 10.65 (19.96) |
| | 1979–1993 | ADF(n,0)=–3.43 (–3.81) | 28.88 (15.67) | 39.20 (19.96) |
| Luxem-burg | 1960–1993 | ADF(n,0)=–2.15 (–3.53) | 7.24 (15.67) | 9.17 (19.96) |
| | 1960–1978 | ADF(n,0)=–1.77 (–3.70) | 5.90 (15.67) | 8.14 (19.96) |
| | 1979–1993 | ADF(n,0)=–1.07 (–3.81) | 7.02 (15.67) | 8.71 (19.96) |
| Nether-lands | 1960–1993 | ADF(n,0)=–1.98 (–3.53) | 7.16 (15.67) | 10.22 (19.96) |
| | 1960–1978 | ADF(n,0)=–1.83 (–3.70) | 6.59 (15.67) | 9.08 (19.96) |
| | 1979–1993 | ADF(n,0)=–2.27 (–3.81) | 8.47 (15.67) | 12.41 (19.96) |
| Portugal | 1960–1993[ab] | ADF(n,0)=–2.56 (–3.53) | 10.61 (15.67) | 16.91 (19.96) |
| | 1960–1978 | ADF(n,0)=–3.32 (–3.70) | 7.10 (15.67) | 9.57 (19.96) |
| | 1979–1993 | ADF(n,1)=–4.28 (–3.85) | 17.71 (15.67) | 30.21 (19.96) |
| Spain | 1960–1993 | ADF(n,1)=–4.04 (–3.53) | 16.72 (15.67) | 18.82 (19.96) |
| | 1960–1978 | ADF(n,0)=–2.81 (–3.72) | 15.50 (15.67) | 21.05 (19.96) |
| | 1979–1993 | ADF(n,1)=–2.75 (–3.85) | 18.19 (15.67) | 24.48 (19.96) |
| Sweden | 1960–1993 | ADF(n,0)=–4.08 (–3.53) | 23.13 (15.67) | 24.90 (19.96) |
| | 1960–1978 | ADF(n,0)=–2.91 (–3.70) | 13.59 (15.67) | 14.67 (19.96) |
| | 1979–1993 | ADF(n,0)=–2.46 (–3.81) | 14.96 (15.67) | 17.98 (19.96) |
| United Kingdom | 1960–1993[a] | ADF(n,1)=–3.55 (–3.53) | 6.11 (15.67) | 7.27 (19.96) |
| | 1960–1978 | ADF(n,1)=–3.76 (–3.72) | 8.77 (15.67) | 12.75 (19.96) |
| | 1979–1993 | ADF(n,1)=–3.16 (–3.85) | 10.18 (15.67) | 11.73 (19.96) |

| Country | Period | Engle–Granger cointegration test | Johansen cointegration test I: $H_0: r=0\ H_1: r=1$ | Johansen cointegration test II: $H_0: r=0\ H_1: r=1$ |
|---|---|---|---|---|
| France | 1970Q1–1994Q4 | ADF($n$,1)=−3.31 (−3.40) | 20.10 (15.67) | 24.41 (19.96) |
| | 1970Q1–1978Q4 | ADF($n$,0)=−2.24 (−3.52) | 23.69 (15.67) | 25.99 (19.96) |
| | 1979Q1–1994Q4 | ADF($n$,0)=−2.97 (−3.43) | 13.23 (15.67) | 20.83 (19.96) |
| Germany | 1970Q1–1994Q4[a] | ADF($n$,0)=−6.58 (−3.40) | 13.27 (15.67) | 16.68 (19.96) |
| | 1970Q1–1978Q4 | ADF($n$,1)=−3.50 (−3.52) | 33.79 (15.67) | 36.56 (19.96) |
| | 1979Q1–1994Q4 | ADF($n$,1)=−3.05 (−3.44) | 17.56 (15.67) | 26.73 (19.96) |
| United Kingdom | 1970Q1–1994Q4 | ADF($n$,0)=−3.02 (−3.40) | 7.23 (15.67) | 13.18 (19.96) |
| | 1970Q1–1978Q4 | ADF($n$,1)=−1.71 (−3.52) | 19.74 (15.67) | 24.34 (19.96) |
| | 1979Q1–1994Q4 | ADF($n$,0)=−2.01 (−3.43) | 8.42 (15.67) | 10.41 (19.96) |

*Notes:*

[a]  Note that in Table 3.3 the null hypothesis of a unit root in $I_{t+k,i}/Y_{t+k,i}$ was rejected at the 95 per cent level of confidence.

[b]  Note that in Table 3.3 the null hypothesis of a unit root in $S_{t+k,i}/Y_{t+k,i}$ was rejected at the 99 per cent level of confidence.

ADF stands for the Augmented Dickey–Fuller test with the specification of the test equation between brackets ($n$ estimated without constant or trend term). In addition, the number of lagged differences of the dependent variable are also shown between brackets. MacKinnon critical values for the ADF test at 95 per cent level of confidence are shown in brackets.

Johansen cointegration test I: cointegration likelihood ratio test based on maximal eigenvalue of the stochastic matrix (non-trended case, maximum lag in VAR is 1 (annual data) and 4 (quarterly data). Johansen cointegration test II: cointegration likelihood ratio test based on the trace of the stochastic matrix (non-trended case, maximum lag in VAR is 1 (annual data) and 4 (quarterly data). Critical values for the Johansen tests at 95 per cent level of confidence are shown in brackets.

$$\Delta (I/Y)_{t+k,i} = (\phi - 1)(I/Y)_{t+k-1,i} + \beta_0 \Delta (S/Y)_{t+k,i} +$$

$$(\beta_0 + \beta_1)(S/Y)_{t+k-1,i} + \eta_{t+k,i} \qquad (3.11)$$

and

$$\Delta (I/Y)_{t+k,i} = \beta_0 \Delta (S/Y)_{t+k,i} + \lambda \left[ (I/Y)_{t+k-1,i} - \theta (S/Y)_{t+k-1,i} \right] + \eta_{t+k,i} \qquad (3.12)$$

with $\lambda = (\phi - 1)$, $\theta = -(\beta_0 + \beta_1)/(\phi - 1)$ and $\eta \sim N(0, \sigma_\eta^2)$. $\beta_0$ is the impact multiplier, $\theta$ is the long-run multiplier and $\left[ (I/Y)_{t+k-1,i} - \theta (S/Y)_{t+k-1,i} \right]$ is the error-correction term. If equation (3.12) is well specified – that is, the error term $\eta$ is white noise – it may be estimated with OLS. Equation (3.12) is a valid error-correction model. The long-run multiplier $\theta$ may be interpreted as a measure for long run savings-investment correlations: if from time $t + k$ it holds that $(S/Y)_{t+k+s,i} = \overline{S/Y}$ and $\eta_{t+k+s,i} = 0$ for $s = 0, 1, 2, \ldots$, then $I_{t+k+s,i}/Y_{t+k+s,i}$ converges to $\overline{I/Y} = \theta \overline{S/Y}$, the long-term solution of the model. The impact multiplier $\beta_0$ may be interpreted as a measure for *short-run* savings-investment correlations while the long-run multiplier $\theta = -(\beta_0 + \beta_1)/(\phi - 1)$ may be interpreted as a measure for *long-run* savings-investment correlations.

Finally, the parameter $\lambda$ is called the error-correction coefficient or adjustment coefficient. If $\lambda = 0$ ($\phi = 1$) error-correction does not take place, and we arrive at a model in first differences, while when $-2 < \lambda < 0$ ($|\phi| < 1$) the model is stable. Notwithstanding the above, many tests of savings-investment correlations are based on regression models in first differences (with $\lambda = 0$):[13]

$$\Delta (I/Y)_{t+k,i} = \beta_0 + \beta_1 \Delta (S/Y)_{t+k,i} + \eta_{t+k,i} \qquad (3.13)$$

However, Engle and Granger (1987) argue, that when the long-run correlations between savings and investment are not included in the model, the estimates of short-run correlations (coefficient $\beta$) in equation (3.13) may be biased due to omitted long-run variables. Equation (3.12) is the appropriate specification since it distinguishes between short- and long-run savings-investment correlations. From the estimation of equation (3.11) one may calculate the short- and long-run savings-investment correlations. Only *short-run* savings-investment correlations may be used as an indication of the degree of capital mobility of type IV.

The existence of cointegration (that is, *long-run* savings-investment correlation close to unity) can be ascertained by testing whether the coefficient on $(I/Y)_{t+k-1,i}$ ($\lambda = (\phi - 1)$) has a significantly negative t-value (Banerjee, Dolado, Hendry and Smith, 1986). Banerjee et al. show in Monte Carlo simulations that in finite samples this test is more efficient and less biased than the Engle-Granger cointegration test. Kremers et al. (1992, p. 7) advise to use the critical values from the standard normal distribution in large samples and the critical values from the Dickey–Fuller distribution in small samples. To ensure that the error term is white noise, up to fourth-order lagged variables of changes in the savings $\Delta(S/Y)_{t+k-j,i}$   $j = 1, \ldots, 4$ and investment ratio $\Delta(I/Y)_{t+k-j,i}$   $j = 1, \ldots, 4$ have been added. Only significant lagged variables have been reported in Table 3.6a. In addition, if significant, a trend term $t$ has been added. Note that we do not set coefficient $\theta$ equal to 1, contrary to Jansen (1995). To increase efficiency we estimate coefficient $\theta$. Table 3.6a presents the results. Furthermore, Table 3.6b also reports various diagnostic tests. The regressions generally pass all diagnostic tests.

If we take critical values from the standard normal distribution at the 95 per cent level of confidence, the results in Table 3.6a indicate that savings and investment are cointegrated in Austria (1960–1993, 1960–1978, 1979–1993), Belgium (1960–1978), Denmark (1960–1993, 1960–1978), Finland (1960–1993, 1960–1978), France (1960–1993, 1960–1978), Germany (1960–1993, 1960–1978), Greece (1960–1993, 1960–1978, 1979–1993), Ireland (1960–1978, 1979–1993), Italy (1960–1993, 1979–1993), Luxemburg (1979–1993), Portugal (1960–1993, 1979–1993), Spain (1960–1993, 1960–1978), Sweden (1960–1993, 1960–1978, 1979–1993) and the United Kingdom (1960–1993, 1960–1978).

Similarly, we find cointegration between savings and investment for France (1970Q1–1994Q4, 1970Q1–1978Q4 1979Q1–1994Q4), Germany (1970Q1– 1994Q4, 1970Q1–1978Q4, 1979Q1–1994Q4) and the United Kingdom (1970Q– 1994Q4, 1970Q1–1978Q4, 1979Q1–1994Q4). If we take the very conservative critical values from the Dickey–Fuller distribution (as calculated by MacKinnon, 1991), we find cointegration between savings and investment for Austria (1960–1993), Denmark (1960–1978), Finland (1960–1978), France (1960–1993, 1960–1978), Greece (1960–1993), Ireland (1960–1978), Italy (1960–1993, 1979–1993), Luxemburg (1979–1993), Spain (1960–1993), Sweden (1960–1993, 1979–1993) and the United Kingdom (1960–1993). Similarly, we find cointegration between savings and investment for France (1970Q1–1994Q4, 1970Q1–1978Q4, 1979Q1–1994Q4) and Germany (1970Q1–1994Q4, 1970Q1– 1978Q4, 1979Q1–1994Q4). The finding of no cointegration is probably due to the small sample size and time span. The results confirm that equation (3.11) is the correct specification.

From Table 3.6a we may calculate the long-run savings-investment correlation $\theta = -(\beta_0 + \beta_1)/(\phi - 1)$ for annual data: Austria (0.96, 0.70, 1.41), Belgium (1.06, 0.37, 0.95), Denmark (0.38, 0.62, −3.20), Finland (0.93, 2.30, 1.29), France (0.91, 1.02, 1.06), Germany (1.22, 1.16, 1.23), Greece (0.78, 0.97, 0.65), Ireland (−1.68, 2.03, 1.15), Italy (0.85, 1.04, 0.86), Luxemburg (0.12, 0.64, −0.28), The Netherlands (1.25, 0.41, 0.87), Portugal (0.68, 0.38, 1.57), Spain (0.95, 0.81, 4.17), Sweden (0.79, 1.09, 1.25) and the United Kingdom (0.30, 0.52, 0.50). Similarly, we may calculate the long-run savings-investment correlation for quarterly data: France (1.00, 0.80, 1.28), Germany (0.61, 0.88, 0.33) and the United Kingdom (1.09, 1.76, 0.62). The long-run correlations are close to one, at least over the longer sample periods.

The short-run correlations differ considerably from the long-run correlations. From Table 3.6a we may obtain the short-run savings-investment correlation $\beta_0$ for annual data: Austria (0.88, 0.78, 1.03), Belgium (0.62, 0.55, 0.44), Denmark (0.70, 0.55, 0.64), Finland (0.74, 1.14, 0.83), France (0.80, 0.90, 1.04), Germany (0.77, 1.03, 0.16), Greece (0.73, 0.94, 0.55), Ireland (−0.11, 0.07, 0.85), Italy (0.71, 1.30, −0.45), Luxemburg (0.03, 0.25, −0.07), The Netherlands (0.63, 0.72, 0.44), Portugal (0.40, 0.43, −0.14), Spain (0.29, 0.27, 0.64), Sweden (0.45, 0.49, 0.49) and the United Kingdom (0.63, 0.49, 1.28). Similarly, we may obtain the short-run savings-investment correlation for quarterly data: France (0.71, 0.21, 0.76), Germany (0.41, 1.18, 0.37) and the United Kingdom (0.55, 0.51, 0.52).

Overall, the short-run correlations are smaller than long-run correlations. Furthermore, the short-run correlation declined over the period 1979–1993 relative to the period 1960–1978 in Belgium, Finland, Germany, Greece, Italy, Luxemburg, The Netherlands and Portugal, while the long-run correlation were relatively stable. Similarly, comparing the subperiods 1970Q1–1978Q4 and 1979-

*Table 3.6a*  The F–H criterion and time-series analysis: an error-correction model

$$\Delta(I/Y)_{t+k,i} = Constant + (\phi-1)(I/Y)_{t+k-1,i} + \beta_0\Delta(S/Y)_{t+k,i} + (\beta_0+\beta_1)(S/Y)_{t+k-1,i} + \sum_{j=1}^{4}A_j\Delta(I/Y)_{t+k-j,i} + \sum_{j=1}^{4}B_j\Delta(S/Y)_{t+k-j,i} + Ct + \eta_{t+k,i}$$

| Country | Period | Constant | $(I/Y)_{t+k-1,i}$ | $\Delta(S/Y)_{t+k,i}$ | $(S/Y)_{t+k-1,i}$ | $\Delta(I/Y)_{t+k-1,i}$ | $\Delta(S/Y)_{t+k-1,i}$ | $\Delta(S/Y)_{t+k-2,i}$ | $\Delta(I/Y)_{t+k-3,i}$ | $\Delta(I/Y)_{t+k-4,i}$ | $t$ |
|---|---|---|---|---|---|---|---|---|---|---|---|
| Austria | 1960–1993 | 0.008 (0.02) | −0.56 (0.17)^ab | 0.88 (0.16)** | 0.54 (0.17) | | | | | | |
| | 1960–1978 | 0.06 (0.05) | −0.71 (0.27)^a | 0.78 (0.21)** | 0.50 (0.22) | | | | | | |
| | 1979–1993 | −0.06 (0.06) | −0.64 (0.27)^a | 1.03 (0.35)** | 0.90 (0.42) | | | | | | |
| Belgium | 1960–1993 | −0.003 (0.01) | −0.16 (0.14) | 0.62 (0.13)‡ | 0.17 (0.10) | | | | | | |
| | 1960–1978 | 0.09 (0.03) | −0.67 (0.23)^a | 0.55 (0.13)‡ | 0.25 (0.15) | | | | | | |
| | 1979–1993 | 0.0002 (0.04) | −0.22 (0.30) | 0.44 (0.38)† | 0.21 (0.17) | | | | | | |
| Denmark | 1960–1993 | 0.08 (0.04) | −0.42 (0.18)^a | 0.70 (0.22)** | 0.16 (0.15) | | | | | | −0.001 (0.0005) |
| | 1960–1978 | 0.15 (0.04) | −1.42 (0.26)^ab | 0.55 (0.22)** | 0.88 (0.20) | | | | | | |
| | 1979–1993 | 0.03 (0.05) | −0.05 (0.20) | 0.64 (0.36)† | −0.16 (0.22) | | | | | | |
| Finland | 1960–1993 | 0.02 (0.03) | −0.58 (0.17)^ab | 0.74 (0.16)** | 0.54 (0.16) | 0.31 (0.12) | | | | | |
| | 1960–1978 | −0.15 (0.06) | −0.47 (0.22)^a | 1.14 (0.27)** | 1.09 (0.30) | | | | | | |
| | 1979–1993 | −0.02 (0.03) | −0.45 (0.27) | 0.83 (0.21)** | 0.58 (0.22) | | | | | | |
| France | 1960–1993 | 0.01 (0.01) | −0.69 (0.18)^ab | 0.80 (0.16)** | 0.63 (0.16) | | | | | | |
| | 1960–1978 | −0.01 (0.05) | −0.81 (0.25)^ab | 0.90 (0.25)** | 0.83 (0.28) | | | | | | |
| | 1979–1993 | −0.04 (0.03) | −0.30 (0.28) | 1.04 (0.24)** | 0.50 (0.23) | | | | | | |
| Germany | 1960–1993 | −0.02 (0.02) | −0.27 (0.12)^a | 0.77 (0.15)** | 0.33 (0.13) | | | | | | −0.002 (0.0008) |
| | 1960–1978 | −0.03 (0.03) | −0.58 (0.24)^a | 1.03 (0.17)** | 0.67 (0.28) | | | | | | |
| | 1979–1993 | 0.01 (0.08) | −0.47 (0.33) | 0.16 (0.33)* | 0.58 (0.18) | | | | | | |
| Greece | 1960–1993 | 0.06 (0.02) | −0.74 (0.18)^ab | 0.73 (0.10)‡ | 0.58 (0.15) | | | | | | |
| | 1960–1978 | 0.03 (0.02) | −0.81 (0.29)^a | 0.94 (0.17)** | 0.79 (0.28) | | | | | | |
| | 1979–1993 | 0.08 (0.03) | −0.83 (0.32)^a | 0.55 (0.15)‡ | 0.54 (0.23) | | | | | | |
| Ireland | 1960–1993 | −0.01 (0.05) | −0.19 (0.11) | −0.11 (0.27)* | −0.32 (0.21) | | | | | | −0.01 (0.004) |
| | 1960–1978 | −0.09 (0.07) | −0.61 (0.15)^ab | 0.07 (0.33)* | 1.24 (0.43) | | | | | | |
| | 1979–1993 | 0.31 (0.12) | −0.71 (0.24)^a | 0.85 (0.41)† | 0.82 (0.36) | | | | | | |

Integrating Financial Markets in the European Union

| Country | Period | | | | | | |
|---|---|---|---|---|---|---|---|
| Italy | 1960–1993 | 0.02 (0.02) | −0.65 (0.19)[ab] | 0.71 (0.27)** | 0.55 (0.16) | | |
| | 1960–1978 | −0.008 (0.06) | −0.45 (0.26) | 1.30 (0.40)** | 0.47 (0.30) | | |
| | 1979–1993 | 0.03 (0.02) | −0.98 (0.19)[ab] | −0.45 (0.28)* | 0.84 (0.14) | | |
| Luxemburg | 1960–1993 | 0.04 (0.04) | −0.25 (0.13) | 0.03 (0.16)* | 0.03 (0.06) | | 0.01 (0.002) |
| | 1960–1978 | 0.002 (0.09) | −0.22 (0.20) | 0.25 (0.30)* | 0.14 (0.23) | | |
| | 1979–1993 | 0.14 (0.04) | −1.18 (0.26)[ab] | −0.07 (0.11)* | −0.33 (0.10) | | |
| Netherlands | 1960–1993 | −0.02 (0.02) | −0.20 (0.11) | 0.63 (0.17)‡ | 0.25 (0.14) | | |
| | 1960–1978 | 0.04 (0.05) | −0.27 (0.21) | 0.72 (0.24)** | 0.11 (0.27) | | |
| | 1979–1993 | −0.0006 (0.05) | −0.31 (0.21) | 0.44 (0.28)† | 0.27 (0.15) | | |
| Portugal | 1960–1993 | 0.03 (0.04) | −0.31 (0.14)* | 0.40 (0.14)‡ | 0.21 (0.10) | | −0.003 (0.001) |
| | 1960–1978 | 0.09 (0.06) | −0.52 (0.29) | 0.43 (0.15)‡ | 0.20 (0.14) | | |
| | 1979–1993 | 0.03 (0.09) | −0.49 (0.17)* | −0.14 (0.30)* | 0.77 (0.18) | | |
| Spain | 1960–1993 | 0.009 (0.02) | −0.42 (0.11)[ab] | 0.29 (0.20)* | 0.40 (0.12) | 0.38 (0.14) | |
| | 1960–1978 | 0.03 (0.08) | −0.54 (0.22)[a] | 0.27 (0.38)† | 0.44 (0.25) | | |
| | 1979–1993 | −0.12 (0.06) | −0.18 (0.19) | 0.64 (0.37)† | 0.75 (0.24) | | |
| Sweden | 1960–1993 | 0.03 (0.02) | −0.66 (0.19)[ab] | 0.45 (0.16)‡ | 0.52 (0.16) | 0.36 (0.17) | |
| | 1960–1978 | −0.02 (0.04) | −0.70 (0.24)[a] | 0.49 (0.20)‡ | 0.76 (0.20) | | |
| | 1979–1993 | −0.02 (0.04) | −0.83 (0.26)[ab] | 0.49 (0.24)† | 1.03 (0.24) | | |
| United Kingdom | 1960–1993 | 0.06 (0.03) | −0.44 (0.14)[ab] | 0.63 (0.19)** | 0.13 (0.11) | 0.38 (0.16) | |
| | 1960–1978 | 0.06 (0.06) | −0.60 (0.27)[a] | 0.49 (0.25)‡ | 0.31 (0.23) | | |
| | 1979–1993 | 0.02 (0.05) | −0.16 (0.20) | 1.28 (0.61)† | 0.08 (0.19) | | |

| Country | Period | Constant | $(I/Y)_{t-k-1,i}$ | $\Delta(S/Y)_{t-k,i}$ | $(S/Y)_{t-k-1,i}$ | $\Delta(I/Y)_{t-k-1,i}$ | $\Delta(S/Y)_{t-k-1,i}$ | $\Delta(S/Y)_{t-k-2,i}$ | $\Delta(I/Y)_{t-k-3,i}$ | $\Delta(I/Y)_{t-k-4,i}$ | $t$ |
|---|---|---|---|---|---|---|---|---|---|---|---|
| France | 1970Q1–1994Q4 | 0.0008 (0.004) | −0.22 (0.06)[ab] | 0.71 (0.10)‡ | 0.22 (0.06) | | | | | | |
| | 1970Q1–1978Q4 | 0.02 (0.02) | −0.44 (0.11)[ab] | 0.21 (0.20)·· | 0.35 (0.12) | 0.80 (0.18) | −0.59 (0.20) | | | | |
| | 1979Q1–1994Q4 | −0.01 (0.008) | −0.21 (0.07)[ab] | 0.76 (0.11)‡ | 0.27 (0.08) | | | | | | |
| Germany | 1970Q1–1994Q4 | 0.03 (0.009) | −0.23 (0.06)[ab] | 0.41 (0.08)‡ | 0.14 (0.05) | −0.11 (0.05) | | −0.16 (0.06) | −0.13 (0.04) | 0.51 (0.06) | |
| | 1970Q1–1978Q4 | 0.08 (0.02) | −0.68 (0.14)[ab] | 1.18 (0.06)‡ | 0.60 (0.14) | | | | | | |
| | 1979Q1–1994Q4 | 0.04 (0.01) | −0.21 (0.07)[ab] | 0.37 (0.10)‡ | 0.07 (0.06) | | | | | 0.69 (0.06) | |
| United Kingdom | 1970Q1–1994Q4 | −0.002 (0.007) | −0.11 (0.05)[a] | 0.55 (0.08)‡ | 0.12 (0.06) | | 0.17 (0.08) | | | | |
| | 1970Q1–1978Q4 | −0.02 (0.03) | −0.17 (0.08)[a] | 0.51 (0.15)‡ | 0.30 (0.14) | | | | | | |
| | 1979Q1–1994Q4 | 0.01 (0.008) | −0.13 (0.06)[a] | 0.52 (0.09)‡ | 0.08 (0.06) | | | | 0.26 (0.10) | | |

*Notes:*

[a] Indicates that the coefficient is significantly negative at the 95% level of confidence (one-tailed test). Critical values are taken from the standard normal distribution (one-tailed test).

[b] Indicates that the coefficient is significantly negative at the 99% level of confidence (one-tailed test). Critical values are taken from the Dickey–Fuller distribution (one-tailed test).

· Indicates that the coefficient is insignificantly different from zero and significantly different from one at the 95 per cent level of confidence (two-tailed test).

·· Indicates that the coefficient is significantly different from zero and insignificantly different from one at the 95 per cent level of confidence (two-tailed test).

† Indicates that the coefficient is imprecisely estimated and differs insignificantly from zero and insignificantly from one at the 95 per cent level of confidence (two-tailed test).

‡ Indicates that the coefficient is imprecisely estimated and differs significantly from zero and significantly from one at the 95 per cent level of confidence (two-tailed test).

Standard errors are indicated in parentheses.

*Table 3.6b  The F–H criterion and time-series analysis: diagnostic tests*

| Country | Period | $\bar{R}^2$ | DW | $LM_{AR}$ (1) | LB | JB | $LM_{ARCH}$ (1) |
|---|---|---|---|---|---|---|---|
| Austria | 1960–1993 | 0.60 | 1.80 | 1.46 (0.23) | 0.35 (0.56) | 1.36 (0.51) | 0.32 (0.57) |
| | 1960–1978 | 0.63 | 1.73 | 3.06 (0.08) | 0.21 (0.65) | 0.20 (0.91) | 0.05 (0.83) |
| | 1979–1993 | 0.50 | 1.61 | 2.85 (0.09) | 0.64 (0.42) | 0.26 (0.88) | 0.37 (0.54) |
| Belgium | 1960–1993 | 0.50 | 1.92 | 0.20 (0.65) | 0.13 (0.72) | 1.19 (0.55) | 0.30 (0.58) |
| | 1960–1978 | 0.73 | 2.01 | 0.01 (0.92) | 0.00 (0.95) | 1.05 (0.25) | 1.33 (0.25) |
| | 1979–1993 | 0.33 | 1.87 | 0.26 (0.61) | 0.18 (0.68) | 1.12 (0.57) | 0.004 (0.95) |
| Denmark | 1960–1993 | 0.35 | 2.22 | 2.10 (0.15) | 0.62 (0.43) | 0.01 (0.99) | 0.19 (0.67) |
| | 1960–1978 | 0.72 | 2.33 | 4.11 (0.04) | 0.76 (0.38) | 0.70 (0.70) | 0.45 (0.50) |
| | 1979–1993 | 0.21 | 2.00 | 0.30 (0.58) | 0.22 (0.64) | 1.55 (0.46) | 0.87 (0.35) |
| Finland | 1960–1993 | 0.72 | 1.89 | 0.21 (0.64) | 0.04 (0.84) | 0.61 (0.74) | 9.03 (0.06) |
| | 1960–1978 | 0.67 | 1.25 | 3.28 (0.07) | 1.94 (0.16) | 1.42 (0.49) | 5.88 (0.21) |
| | 1979–1993 | 0.77 | 1.76 | 0.27 (0.60) | 0.14 (0.70) | 0.12 (0.94) | 1.15 (0.28) |
| France | 1960–1993 | 0.64 | 2.03 | 1.08 (0.29) | 0.26 (0.61) | 0.48 (0.79) | 0.29 (0.59) |
| | 1960–1978 | 0.63 | 2.25 | 3.15 (0.08) | 0.77 (0.36) | 2.01 (0.37) | 0.01 (0.93) |
| | 1979–1993 | 0.68 | 2.04 | 0.99 (0.32) | 0.43 (0.51) | 1.44 (0.49) | 0.10 (0.75) |
| Germany | 1960–1993 | 0.51 | 1.44 | 4.12 (0.04) | 2.76 (0.10) | 0.07 (0.96) | 0.20 (0.65) |
| | 1960–1978 | 0.70 | 1.50 | 1.28 (0.26) | 1.28 (0.26) | 0.32 (0.85) | 0.28 (0.60) |
| | 1979–1993 | 0.47 | 1.47 | 0.74 (0.39) | 0.53 (0.47) | 0.65 (0.72) | 1.26 (0.26) |
| Greece | 1960–1993 | 0.69 | 1.88 | 0.57 (0.45) | 0.07 (0.80) | 2.92 (0.23) | 0.59 (0.44) |
| | 1960–1978 | 0.78 | 1.79 | 2.50 (0.11) | 0.12 (0.73) | 2.09 (0.35) | 0.80 (0.37) |
| | 1979–1993 | 0.53 | 1.89 | 0.53 (0.47) | 0.04 (0.85) | 0.87 (0.65) | 0.55 (0.46) |
| Ireland | 1960–1993 | 0.09 | 1.85 | 0.12 (0.73) | 0.09 (0.77) | 1.22 (0.54) | 0.17 (0.68) |
| | 1960–1978 | 0.54 | 1.72 | 0.17 (0.68) | 0.15 (0.70) | 0.42 (0.81) | 0.01 (0.92) |
| | 1979–1993 | 0.35 | 1.70 | 1.88 (0.17) | 0.33 (0.57) | 1.43 (0.49) | 0.56 (0.46) |
| Italy | 1960–1993 | 0.44 | 1.80 | 0.80 (0.37) | 0.11 (0.74) | 3.06 (0.22) | 2.10 (0.15) |
| | 1960–1978 | 0.53 | 1.62 | 1.98 (0.16) | 0.54 (0.46) | 3.50 (0.17) | 1.42 (0.23) |
| | 1979–1993 | 0.71 | 2.25 | 1.00 (0.32) | 0.94 (0.33) | 1.29 (0.52) | 1.47 (0.23) |
| Luxemburg | 1960–1993 | 0.04 | 1.61 | 0.67 (0.41) | 0.39 (0.53) | 0.30 (0.86) | 1.30 (0.25) |
| | 1960–1978 | 0.02 | 1.35 | 1.79 (0.18) | 1.03 (0.31) | 0.44 (0.80) | 0.001 (0.98) |
| | 1979–1993 | 0.58 | 2.40 | 2.03 (0.15) | 0.85 (0.36) | 2.59 (0.27) | 0.007 (0.93) |
| The Netherlands | 1960–1993 | 0.30 | 1.76 | 0.63 (0.43) | 0.41 (0.52) | 0.78 (0.68) | 0.36 (0.55) |
| | 1960–1978 | 0.34 | 1.70 | 0.90 (0.34) | 0.29 (0.59) | 0.23 (0.89) | 0.53 (0.47) |
| | 1979–1993 | 0.27 | 1.77 | 0.02 (0.90) | 0.01 (0.91) | 1.38 (0.50) | 1.07 (0.30) |
| Portugal | 1960–1993 | 0.34 | 1.66 | 1.57 (0.21) | 0.82 (0.37) | 0.77 (0.68) | 5.78 (0.02) |
| | 1960–1978 | 0.47 | 2.03 | 0.37 (0.54) | 0.05 (0.82) | 0.99 (0.60) | 1.15 (0.28) |
| | 1979–1993 | 0.63 | 1.64 | 0.35 (0.55) | 0.32 (0.57) | 0.20 (0.90) | 1.40 (0.24) |
| Spain | 1960–1993 | 0.45 | 1.99 | 0.02 (0.88) | 0.01 (0.94) | 0.76 (0.68) | 1.28 (0.26) |
| | 1960–1978 | 0.38 | 1.28 | 2.48 (0.12) | 1.56 (0.21) | 0.15 (0.93) | 0.35 (0.55) |
| | 1979–1993 | 0.40 | 1.43 | 0.45 (0.50) | 0.26 (0.61) | 0.99 (0.61) | 0.50 (0.48) |
| Sweden | 1960–1993 | 0.61 | 1.82 | 0.86 (0.35) | 0.14 (0.71) | 1.10 (0.58) | 0.03 (0.87) |
| | 1960–1978 | 0.55 | 1.58 | 2.35 (0.13) | 0.82 (0.37) | 1.00 (0.61) | 5.32 (0.02) |
| | 1979–1993 | 0.69 | 1.86 | 0.04 (0.84) | 0.02 (0.89) | 0.95 (0.62) | 1.35 (0.25) |
| United Kingdom | 1960–1993 | 0.43 | 1.72 | 1.69 (0.19) | 0.52 (0.47) | 1.30 (0.52) | 0.02 (0.90) |
| | 1960–1978 | 0.40 | 1.58 | 4.59 (0.03) | 0.74 (0.39) | 2.63 (0.27) | 1.47 (0.23) |
| | 1979–1993 | 0.21 | 1.47 | 3.12 (0.08) | 1.17 (0.28) | 0.64 (0.73) | 0.43 (0.51) |

| Country | Period | $\bar{R}^2$ | DW | $LM_{AR}$ (4) | LB | JB | $LM_{ARCH}$ (4) |
|---------|--------|-------------|-----|---------------|-----|-----|-----------------|
| France | 1970Q1–1994Q4 | 0.40 | 1.74 | 4.67 (0.32) | 3.56 (0.47) | 3.75 (0.15) | 9.03 (0.06) |
|  | 1970Q1–1978Q4 | 0.55 | 2.15 | 2.25 (0.69) | 1.36 (0.85) | 2.25 (0.32) | 5.88 (0.21) |
|  | 1979Q1–1994Q4 | 0.47 | 2.35 | 3.63 (0.46) | 3.52 (0.48) | 2.33 (0.31) | 2.27 (0.69) |
| Germany | 1970Q1–1994Q4 | 0.94 | 2.27 | 5.71 (0.22) | 5.66 (0.23) | 5.62 (0.06) | 4.60 (0.33) |
|  | 1970Q1–1978Q4 | 0.95 | 2.05 | 5.58 (0.23) | 5.87 (0.21) | 0.62 (0.73) | 2.50 (0.65) |
|  | 1979Q1–1994Q4 | 0.92 | 2.55 | 11.27(0.02) | 8.98 (0.06) | 3.32 (0.19) | 1.02 (0.91) |
| United | 1970Q1–1994Q4 | 0.33 | 1.96 | 1.29 (0.86) | 0.82 (0.94) | 8.32 (0.02) | 12.55 (0.01) |
| Kingdom | 1970Q1–1978Q4 | 0.27 | 1.79 | 3.92 (0.42) | 3.65 (0.46) | 1.05 (0.60) | 5.90 (0.21) |
|  | 1979Q1–1994Q4 | 0.41 | 2.01 | 1.11 (0.89) | 0.74 (0.95) | 0.07 (0.97) | 2.90 (0.58) |

*Symbols:*

| | | |
|---|---|---|
| $\bar{R}^2$ | = | the coefficient of determination adjusted for degrees of freedom. |
| DW | = | he Durbin–Watson test statistic for first-order serial correlation. |
| $LM_{AR}$ (p) | = | the Lagrange Multiplier test for serial correlation of order p. |
| $LM_{ARCH}$ (p) | = | the Lagrange Multiplier test for autoregressive conditional heteroscedasticity of order p. |
| JB | = | the Jarque–Bera test statistic for normality. |

Probability values of the test statistic are indicated between parentheses.

Q1–1994Q4, the short-run correlation declined in France and Germany.

Using the error-correction estimates for coefficien $\beta_0$, perfect short-term capital mobility could not be rejected at the 95 per cent level of confidence with respect to Germany (1979–1993), Ireland (1960–1993, 1960–1978), Italy (1979–1993), Luxemburg (1960–1993, 1960–1978, 1979–1993), Portugal (1979–1993) and Spain (1960–1993). Similarly, perfect short-term capital immobility could not be rejected at the 99 per cent level of confidence with respect to Austria (1960–1993, 1960–1978, 1979–1993), Denmark (1960–1993, 1960–1978), Finland (1960–1993, 1960-1978, 1979–1993), France (1960–1993, 1960–1978, 1979–1993), Germany (1960–1993, 1960–1978), Greece (1960–1978), Italy (1960–1993, 1960–1978), The Netherlands (1960–1978), the United Kingdom (1960–1993) and France (1960Q1–1978Q4). The other $\beta_0$ estimates are too imprecise to be useful.

Furthermore, the F–H methodology indicates that EU countries tend to differ substantially among themselves with respect to the extent of short- and long-run correlations between savings and investment. If we take the EU countries with below industrial-country benchmark value estimates for $\beta_0$ (that is, 0.6) to be financially integrated, we find below 0.6 $\beta_0$ for Belgium (1960–1978, 1979–1993), Denmark (1960–1978), Greece (1979–1993), Italy (1979–1993), Luxemburg (1960–1993, 1960–1978, 1979–1993), The Netherlands (1979–1993), Portugal (1960–1993, 1960–1978, 1979–1993), Spain (1960–1993, 1960–1978), Sweden (1960–1993, 1960–1978, 1979–1993), the United Kingdom (1960–1978), France (1970Q1–1978Q4), Germany (1960Q1–1993Q4, 1979Q1–1993Q4) and the United Kingdom (1960Q1–1993Q4, 1960Q1–1978Q4, 1979Q1–1993Q4).

## 3.6 Conclusions

In this chapter we examined the extent of financial integration on the basis of savings-investment correlations. It is difficult to accept that most evidence from savings-investment correlations with respect to a sample of OECD countries often contradicts the finding of high capital flows in world financial markets. We stressed that many of these high correlations may be due to the underlying assumptions of the F–H criterion. Importantly, we stressed that the F–H criterion measures more than *financial* capital mobility alone. Furthermore, we apply an error-correction specification of savings-investment correlations to distinguish between short- and long-run savings-investment correlations. The evidence in this chapter allows us to draw a few conclusions about financial integration in the EU.

1.  The results for the EU-13 and EC-10 countries in Table 3.2 show a rise in the estimated value of $\beta$ in the period 1979–1993 relative to the period 1960–1978 indicating a declining degree of capital mobility of type IV. The results for the ERM-6 countries show a decline in the estimated value of $\beta$ in the period 1979–1993 relative to the period 1960–1978 indicating an increasing degree of capital mobility of type IV.
2.  It is important to account for non-stationarity of the underlying time-series of savings and investment.
3.  An error-correction specification of savings-investment correlations is to be preferred as it distinguishes between short- and long-run correlations between savings and investment. Theoretically, long-run savings-investment correlations should be close to one, while short-run correlations may differ from one. A country may run a current account deficit for a short period of time but current account imbalances must accumulate to zero over a long period of time unless the country defaults on its foreign debt. That is, the current account should be stationary. Only *short-run* savings-investment correlations may be used as an indication of the degree of capital mobility of type IV.
4.  From the time-series analysis based upon cointegration techniques, we concluded that savings and investment ratios of EU countries are cointegrated. The finding of no cointegration is probably due to the small sample size and time span. The results confirm that our error-correction specification is the correct specification.
5.  From Section 3.2 we know that departures from perfect capital mobility of type IV may be caused by investors who are risk averse with respect to exchange risk. Therefore, an important explanation for an increasing degree of financial integration in the EU may be the smoothing of exchange rate volatility. Bhandari and Mayer (1990, p. 5) conclude '(...)

it appears that the exchange rate stability achieved in the EMS has been an important factor promoting capital mobility'. Feldstein and Bacchetta (1989, p. 12) argue: 'Although capital might in principle flow with equal ease among all countries or at least all industrial countries, the availability of market information, the existence of institutional relationships, and the perception of risk might make capital flows greater among some pairs of countries than among others'. Another important explanation for an increasing degree of financial integration is the gradual elimination of all barriers to short- and long-term capital mobility in the EU.

6.  Furthermore, the F–H methodology indicates that EU countries tend to differ substantially among themselves with respect to the extent of short- and long-run correlations between savings and investment. The short-run correlations are smaller than long-run correlations. The short-run correlation declined over the period 1979–1993 relative to the period 1960–1978 in Belgium, Finland, Germany, Greece, Italy, Luxemburg, The Netherlands and Portugal, while the long-run correlation were relatively stable. Similarly, comparing the subperiods 1970Q1–1978Q4 and 1979Q1–1994Q4, the short-run correlation declined in France and Germany.

In summary, the F–H criterion has some meaning in quantifying the degree of financial integration in the EU. Its value will further increase when it is examined in combination with related criteria for financial integration such as those examined in the previous chapter. Financial markets may be divided into two segments: one segment with highly rated financial instruments traded in liquid wholesale markets and one segment with low rated financial instruments traded in less liquid retail markets. Clearly, the F–H criterion is more concerned with this latter segment whereas interest parity conditions are more concerned with the former segment. Overall, the apparent decline of short-run savings-investment correlations indicates that an increasing share of total savings and investment is held in internationally traded securities.

# Notes

1. Because any international transaction automatically gives rise to two offsetting entries in the balance of payments, the current account balance and the capital account balance automatically add up to zero.

2. The equation is based on the specification of the F–H criterion used with *cross-section* analysis. The equation could equally well be specified in a time-series context.

3. Penati and Dooley (1983), however, show that the F–H findings are not very stable. Results differ from one estimation period to another and from one country to another.

4. Frankel's argument can hold only for the short-to-medium run, since goods prices and wages are flexible in the long run.

5. Large countries are countries with a large share of world output and likely have a large share in the world's savings and investment.

6. Montiel (1993) finds lower $\beta$ coefficients in samples of developing countries.

7. Although the focus of our study is on the decade of the eighties, restricting the sample period to this decade would have left too few degrees of freedom in regressions based on annual data. Moreover, currency convertibility with respect to the current account was restored in December 1958.

8. We examine gross savings and investment ratios, rather than net savings and investment ratios, because the depreciation data used to calculate the net savings and investment ratios are very unreliable.

9. To accept the null hypothesis of perfect capital mobility of type IV ($H_0$: $\beta = 0$), we require all three covariances set out in Section 3.2 to be zero or at least to cancel out.

10. Tests of cointegration between savings and investment effectively look at the time-series properties of the current account.

11. Dean, Durand, Fallon and Hoeller (1990) give a detailed description of these trends.

12. Johansen tests of $H_0$: $r = 1$ against $H_1$: $r = 2$ should also reject the alternative hypothesis.

13. See, for instance, Obstfeld (1986), Feldstein and Bacchetta (1989) and Bayoumi (1990).

## Appendix 3A1: Data Sources

Data of gross national savings, gross domestic investment and gross domestic product are taken from OECD (1995b), *National Accounts of OECD Countries*, Main Aggregates 1960–1993, Vol. I, Paris and OECD (1995c), *Quarterly National Accounts*, No. 1, Paris. Gross national savings, gross domestic investment and gross domestic product are taken at current prices. The OECD definitions of gross national savings, gross domestic investment and gross domestic product of all EU member states except Greece are the one used in the United Nations *Present* System of National Accounts. Definitions of Greece are based on an earlier system. The national accounting framework underlying the F–H criterion can be specified as follows (Krugman and Obstfeld, 1994, pp. 309–13):

$$S = GNP - C + NCT$$
$$GNP = C + I + X - M + NFI$$
$$S = I + X - M + NFI + NCT$$

Now, the current account can be written as the difference between savings and investment which is equal to the difference between exports and imports plus net factor income and net current transfers from abroad.

$$CA = S - I = X - M + NFI + NCT$$
$$I = FCF + ST$$

EU countries reporting a nonzero value for the statistical discrepancy include Italy, The Netherlands, Portugal, Spain and the United Kingdom. The statistical discrepancy is split equally between savings and investment so that the identity containing only the three aggregate variables, S, I and the CA, holds exactly across all countries.

$$CA = (S + 1/2 \times statistical\ discrepancy) - (I - 1/2 \times statistical\ discrepancy) = S - I$$

Following Feldstein and Horioka (1980), gross national savings and gross domestic investment are converted into relative form by dividing by gross domestic product.

$$Y = GNP + NCT$$

*Symbols:*

| | | |
|---|---|---|
| S | = | total national savings |
| I | = | total domestic investment |
| C | = | total final consumption expenditure |
| M | = | import of goods and services |
| X | = | export of goods and services |
| Y | = | gross domestic product |
| CA | = | current account of the balance of payments |
| GNP | = | gross national product |
| NCT | = | net current transfers from the rest of the world |
| NFI | = | net factor income from the rest of the world |
| FCF | = | fixed capital formation |
| ST | = | increase in stocks |
| | = | corrected for a nonzero value of the statistical discrepancy |

## Appendix 3A2

*Figure 3A2.1:   Gross national savings, gross domestic investment and current account balance (percentages of gross domestic product)*

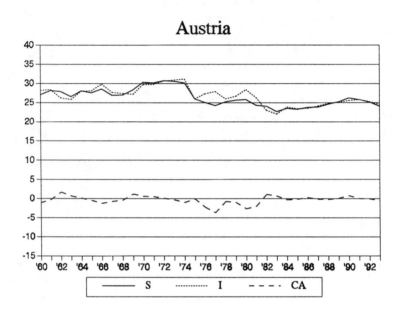

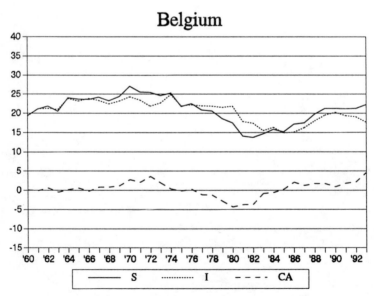

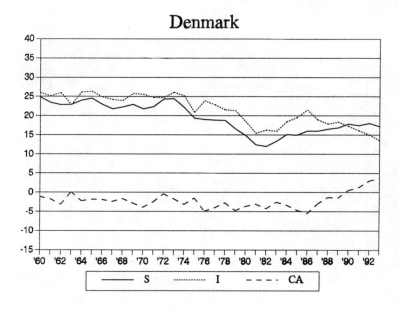

Denmark

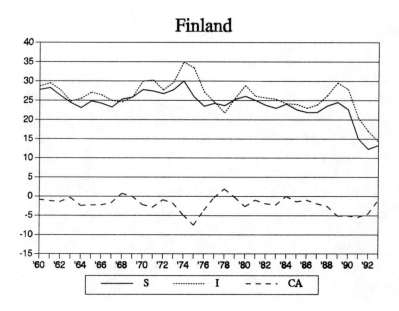

Finland

## France

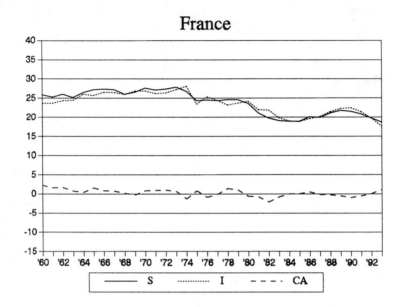

## Germany

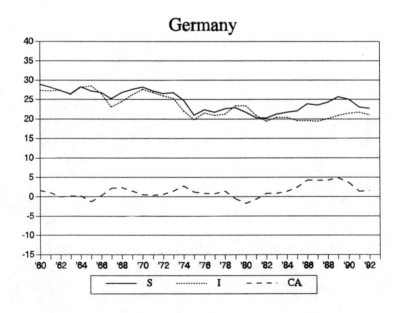

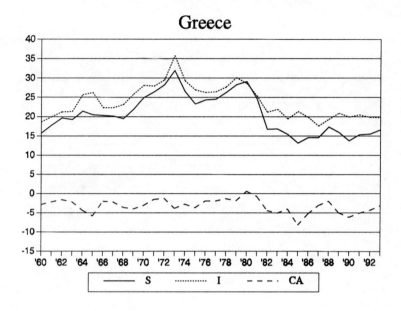

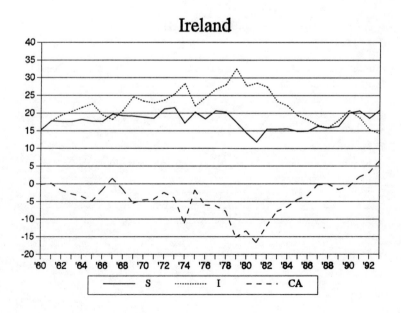

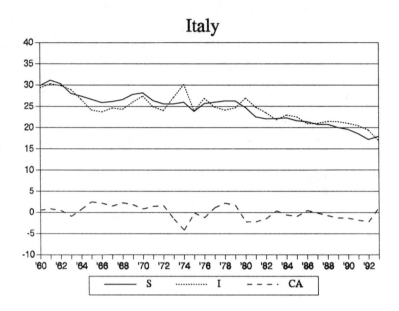

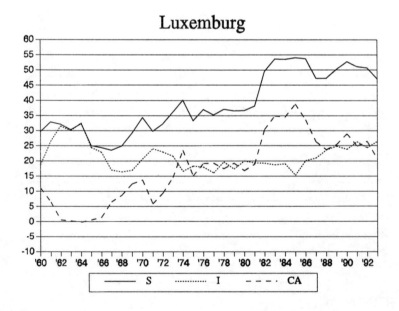

## The Netherlands

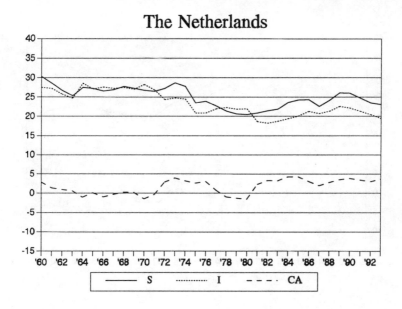

## Portugal

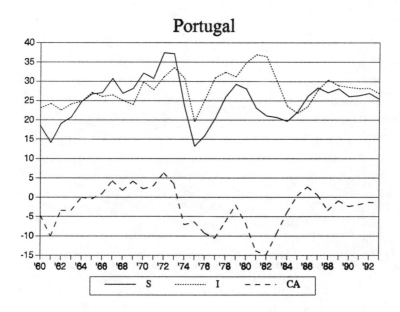

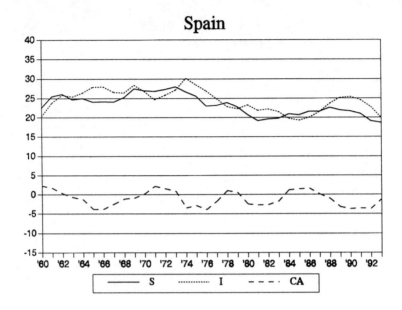

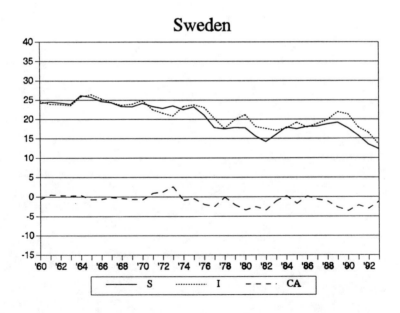

## United Kingdom

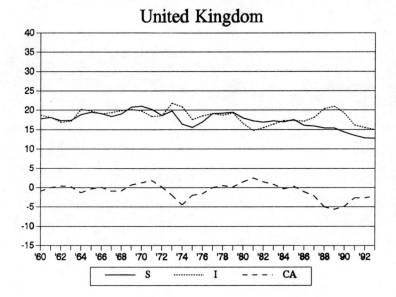

# 4. Financial Integration in Europe: Evidence from Euler Equation Tests

## 4.1 Introduction

This chapter contributes to the ongoing debate on the theory and measurement of financial integration. In combination with other criteria for financial integration such as arbitrage conditions and savings-investment correlations, Euler equation tests may be valuable. This chapter examines the relationship between returns on financial assets and consumption growth rates across countries to test for the extent of financial integration in the European Union. Traditional tests of financial integration have compared interest rates across countries (Frankel and MacArthur, 1988, Eijffinger and Lemmen, 1995) and provided measures of the correlation of savings and investment (Feldstein and Horioka, 1980, Lemmen and Eijffinger, 1995a). Recently, Obstfeld (1986, 1989 and 1994a, 1994b) proposed a third test to assess the degree of financial integration. Obstfeld's test is based upon the *Euler equation* that characterizes optimal intertemporal consumption between period $t$ and $t+1$.

The plan of this chapter is as follows. Section 4.2 derives three Euler equation-based tests of financial integration. Test I – Obstfeld's (1986, 1989) Euler equation test – attempts to detect whether residents of different political jurisdictions have access to the same *risk-free* asset of the home country (the law of one price holds). Specifically, this test evaluates whether markets for nominal risk-free bonds are integrated for a given pair of countries. The test implies that the expected marginal rates of substitution in consumption will be equalized. Test II – Obstfeld's (1994a, 1994b) Euler equation test – assumes trade in a set of Arrow–Debreu securities. Capital movements more realistically take the form of trade in both risk-free and risky assets. The idea here is that if an integrated international market for state-contingent claims existed, then consumption growth rates would be perfectly correlated across countries *ex post*, as well as *ex ante* (provided that all countries have identical iso-elastic preferences and consume the same good). This concept of consumption risk sharing is the cross-country counterpart of the Permanent Income Hypothesis (PIH) in the presence of *complete* markets. Each agent (country) hedges his or her positions against any idiosyncratic shock not suffered by the group of agents (countries) with which the pooling of risks exists (Brennan and Solnik, 1989). Test III focuses on the prediction that, in the presence of integrated financial markets, cross-country differences in expected real returns are linearly related to expected consumption growth rates in these countries under certain auxiliary assumptions. It can be applied to a broad set of financial assets (bonds and equities) without imposing the unrealistic assumption of trade in a complete set of contingent claims. Using data from the latest Penn World Table, *Mark 6*, Section 4.3 tests for financial integration in the EU. Tests I and III are applied to country pairs which include Germany. Test II is applied to any possible country pair. Section 4.4 evaluates the three Euler equation tests of financial integration. Finally, Section 4.5 concludes.

## 4.2   Theory

### 4.2.1   Obstfeld's (1986, 1989) Euler equation test of financial integration: trade in risk-free assets of the home country

This chapter first applies Obstfeld's (1986, 1989) Euler equation test to assess the degree of financial integration in the EU.[1] The idea of this test is essentially as follows. Usual intertemporal utility maximization gives rise to the Lucas (1978) asset-pricing equation or Euler equation,[2]

$$1 = E_t(R_{t+1} m_{t+1}) \tag{4.1}$$

where $R_{t+1}$ is the real return on some traded asset between time $t$ and $t+1$, and $m_{t+1}$ is the marginal rate of intertemporal substitution of any consumer participating in this market, usually given by,

$$m_{t+1} = \beta \frac{U_c(C_{t+1})}{U_c(C_t)} \tag{4.2}$$

for some instantaneous utility function $U(C)$ and some discount factor $\beta < 1$. Now, consider two countries, a home country (no asterisk) and a foreign country (asterisk). Further, consider a nominal bond, denominated in the *home* currency, paying a nominal interest rate of $i_{t+1}$ known at date $t$. Let $P_t$, $P_t^*$ denote price levels and $S_t$ the exchange rate. Then,

$$R_{t+1} = (1 + i_{t+1}) \frac{P_t}{P_{t+1}} \tag{4.3}$$

or

$$R_{t+1} = (1 + i_{t+1}) \frac{P_t^*}{P_{t+1}^*} \frac{S_t}{S_{t+1}} \tag{4.4}$$

by definition of $S_t$. Define,

$$\eta_{t+1} = \frac{P_t}{P_{t+1}} m_{t+1} - \frac{S_t}{S_{t+1}} \frac{P_t^*}{P_{t+1}^*} m_{t+1}^* \qquad (4.5)$$

then the Euler equation implies that,

$$E_t[(1+i_{t+1}) \eta_{t+1}] = 0 \qquad (4.6)$$

where $E_t$ is the conditional expectation, given information available at date $t$.[3] Hence,

$$E_t(\eta_{t+1}) = 0 \qquad (4.7)$$

since the *nominal* interest rate $i_{t+1}$ is known at date $t$. Now assume, a convenient utility function that takes the particular form,[4]

$$U(C) = \frac{C^{1-\alpha}}{1-\alpha} \qquad \alpha > 0 \qquad (4.8)$$

where $\alpha$ is the relative risk-aversion coefficient. Taking $C_t$ and $C_t^*$ to be aggregate consumption in the home and the foreign country (the representative agent assumption), one can write $m_{t+1}$ as

$$m_{t+1} = \beta \left( \frac{C_{t+1}}{C_t} \right)^{-\alpha} \qquad (4.9)$$

and likewise for $m_{t+1}^*$.[5] Thus, the restriction $E_t(\eta_{t+1}^*) = 0$ becomes testable. Assuming the asset to be the risk-free asset, the degree of financial integration ('law of one price') can be tested as follows,

$$\eta_t = \gamma_0 + \sum_{i=1}^{N} \gamma_i \eta_{t-i} + v_t \qquad (4.10)$$

Perfect financial integration with respect to the risk-free asset in the home country implies,

$$H_0: \gamma_0 = 0 \ \wedge \ \gamma_i = 0 \qquad i = 1, \dots, N \qquad (4.11)$$

Condition (4.11) states that $\eta_t$ must be orthogonal to the lagged information available represented by $\eta_{t-i}$. No variable contained in the information set available prior to time $t$ should help to predict the time $t$ value of $\eta_t$

$(E(\eta_t/I_{t-i})=0).$[6] Obstfeld's (1986, 1989) Euler equation test only takes into account trade in risk-free assets of the home country. One can go a step further.

### 4.2.2  Obstfeld's (1994a, 1994b) Euler equation test of financial integration: trade in a set of Arrow–Debreu securities

Obstfeld's (1994a, 1994b) Euler equation test of financial integration allows countries to trade differential consumption risks. That is, international financial markets provide mutual insurance against purely idiosyncratic national consumption fluctuations. The insurance function of financial markets is best analyzed by assuming that countries trade a set of Arrow–Debreu securities.[7] To that end, assume that there are finitely many states of the world. Let the state at date $t$ be denoted by $x_t$, and assume further that $x_t$ follows a Markov process (that is, the probability $\pi(x_t, x_{t+1})$ for a particular state $x_{t+1}$ to occur at date $t+1$ depends solely on $x_t$) with $\pi(x_t, x_{t+1}) > 0$ for all $x_t$ and $x_{t+1}$. Marginal rates of substitution become a function of the states $x_t$ and $x_{t+1}$,

$$m_{t+1} = m(x_t, x_{t+1}) \qquad (4.12)$$

and the same holds true for returns. As a result, the Euler equation can be written as

$$1 = E[R(x_t, x_{t+1}) m(x_t, x_{t+1}) / x_t = x] \qquad (4.13)$$

$$= \sum_{x_{t+1}} \pi(x, x_{t+1}) R(x, x_{t+1}) m(x, x_{t+1}) \qquad (4.14)$$

for all states $x$. Now assume (and this is a 'big' assumption) that at date $t$, all state-contingent securities are actually traded.[8] Thus, for any state $x'$, there is an asset $a$ that pays one unit of the consumption good, should the state $x_{t+1} = x'$ be realized, and nothing in all other states, $x_{t+1} \neq x'$. This asset will be exchanged for a certain amount $q_t(x')$ of the consumption good at date $t$ and its return is given by

$$R(a_{t+1}) = \begin{cases} \dfrac{1}{q_t(x')} & \text{if } x' = x_{t+1} \\ 0 & \text{otherwise} \end{cases} \qquad (4.15)$$

Substituting this into the Euler equation above yields the following,

$$1 = \frac{\pi(x, x')}{q_t(x')} m(x, x') \qquad (4.16)$$

Thus for two different consumers $i$ and $j$, say, one gets,

$$m_i(x, x') = m_j(x, x') \qquad (4.17)$$

for all states of the world $x$ and $x'$. In other words, if insurance against any state of the world is traded on the financial market (perfect financial integration), then one gets the strong result that marginal rates of substitution of different consumers must be perfectly correlated. This result holds if there is free and costless international asset trade, and if the set of securities available is complete, so that all consumption risks are insurable.[9] Accordingly, Obstfeld's (1994a, 1994b) Euler equation test is a joint test of *perfect* financial integration and *complete* financial markets.

### 4.2.3  The New Euler Equation Test of Financial Integration

Our Euler equation test is intimately related to Obstfeld's (1994a, 1994b) Euler equation test. Consider two countries, a home country (no asterisk) and a foreign country (asterisk) each issuing their own country-specific nominal bond. The nominal bond, denominated in the home currency, pays a nominal interest rate of $i_{t-1}$ known at date $t$, and the nominal bond denominated in the foreign currency pays a nominal interest rate of $i_{t-1}^*$. Again, let $P_t$ and $P_t^*$ denote price levels

$$R_{t+1} = (1 + i_{t+1}) \frac{P_t}{P_{t+1}} \qquad (4.18)$$

and

$$R_{t+1}^* = (1 + i_{t+1}^*) \frac{P_t^*}{P_{t+1}^*} \qquad (4.19)$$

Then, for simplicity omitting the variables denoting the different states of the world, one gets

$$E_t(m_{t+1} R_{t+1}) = E_t(m_{t+1}^* R_{t+1}^*) = 1 \qquad (4.20)$$

Again assuming that the home country and the foreign country apply the constant relative risk aversion (CRRA) utility function[10]

$$E_t[\beta(\frac{C_{t+1}}{C_t})^{-\alpha} R_{t+1}] = E_t[\beta^*(\frac{C_{t+1}^*}{C_t^*})^{-\alpha^*} R_{t+1}^*] = 1 \qquad (4.21)$$

we obtain equation (4.22) by assuming that consumption growth rates and rates of return are jointly lognormally distributed[11]

$$E_t[-\alpha(c_{t+1}-c_t)+\log\beta+r_{t+1}]+\frac{1}{2}Var[-\alpha(c_{t+1}-c_t)+\log\beta+r_{t+1}]=$$

$$E_t[-\alpha^*(c_{t+1}^*-c_t^*)+\log\beta^*+r_{t+1}^*]+\frac{1}{2}Var[-\alpha^*(c_{t+1}^*-c_t^*)+$$

$$\log\beta^*+r_{t+1}^*]=1 \qquad (4.22)$$

where lower-case variables represent logarithms. Thus $log(C_{t-1})=c_{t-1}$, $log(C_{t-1}^*)=c_{t-1}^*$, $log(R_{t-1})=r_{t-1}$, $log(R_{t-1}^*)=r_{t-1}^*$, $\Delta$ is the first difference operator and *Var* is the abbreviation of variance. Rearranging leads to

$$E_t(r_{t+1}-r_{t+1}^*)=\frac{1}{2}Var(-\alpha^*\Delta c_{t+1}^*+\log\beta^*+r_{t+1}^*)-$$

$$\frac{1}{2}Var(-\alpha\Delta c_{t+1}+\log\beta+r_{t+1})+$$

$$\log\beta^*-\log\beta+\alpha E_t(\Delta c_{t+1})-\alpha^*(E_t\Delta c_{t+1}^*) \qquad (4.23)$$

where $E_t r_{t+1}$ and $E_t r_{t+1}^*$ are the expectations of the logarithms of the real returns on some traded asset in the home and the foreign country and $E_t(\Delta c_{t+1})$ and $E_t(\Delta c_{t+1}^*)$ are expected consumption growth rates in the home and the foreign country, respectively.

Clearly, the expected real return differential depends negatively on the value of $\beta$, positively on the value of $\beta^*$, positively on expected consumption growth in the home country, negatively on expected consumption growth in the foreign country, negatively on the variance of home-country-specific factors and positively on the variance of foreign-country-specific factors. Equation (4.21) should hold for any asset.[12] To get rid of the conditional expectations one has to assume rational expectations. Assuming rational expectations gives rise to an estimating equation

$$r_{t+1}-r_{t+1}^*=Constant+\alpha\Delta c_{t+1}-\alpha^*\Delta c_{t+1}^*+\varepsilon_{t+1} \qquad (4.24)$$

where $\varepsilon_{t-1}$ is the forecast error which satisfies $E_t(\varepsilon_{t+1})=0$ and where the constant entails the difference between the variance terms and the $\beta$'s. Financial markets are perfectly integrated when no information prior to time $t+1$ may help to explain the real return differential[13]

$$r_{t+1} - r_{t-1}^* = Constant + \alpha [\Delta c_{t+1}] - \alpha^* [\Delta c_{t+1}^*] + \Sigma_{i=1}^{N} \gamma_i [\Delta c_{t+1-i}] -$$

$$\Sigma_{j=1}^{N} \gamma_j^* [\Delta c_{t+1-j}^*] + \upsilon_{t+1} \qquad (4.25)$$

Thus, perfect financial integration implies[14]

$$H_0 : \quad \gamma_i = \gamma_j = 0 \qquad i = 1, \dots, N \qquad j = 1, \dots, N \qquad (4.26)$$

The definition of financial integration incorporated in Test III differs from the one presented in Chapter 1. Test III is a test of real interest parity. The next section applies the three Euler equation tests to quantify the degree of financial integration in the EU.

## 4.3 Empirical Results and Interpretation

This section applies the three Euler equations to test for the degree of financial integration in the EU.[15] Obstfeld's (1986, 1989) Euler equation test requires real (per capita) consumption, national price level and exchange rate data. The Penn World Table, *Mark 6* provides easy-to-use annual real per capita private consumption data in 1985 international prices, the corresponding price level of private consumption and US dollar exchanges rates (see Appendix 4A1 at the end of this chapter).[16] The 14 European countries considered are Austria, Belgium, Denmark, Finland, France, Germany, Greece, Ireland, Italy, The Netherlands, Portugal, Spain, Sweden and the United Kingdom.[17] Test I assumes common risk aversion and time preference in all countries.[18] Test I needs additional assumptions about the numerical values of the degree of risk aversion ($\alpha = \alpha^*$). We calculate the marginal rates of intertemporal substitution and test if they are equalized across countries. That is, we constructed the variable $\eta_t$ as defined in equation (4.5) of Section 4.2 for the EU countries (no asterisk) *vis-à-vis* Germany (asterisk). Three alternatives were chosen for the risk aversion parameter $\alpha$, which equals $\alpha^*$: $\alpha = 0.75$, $\alpha = 1$ and $\alpha = 2$. These values for $\alpha$ may be seen as reasonable benchmark values.[19] Furthermore, test I assumes that domestic and foreign agents apply the same rate of time preference ($\beta = \beta^*$).

Table 4.1 summarizes t- and F-statistics of bilateral tests of perfect financial integration between EU countries (home countries) and Germany (foreign country).[20] The sample period is divided into two subperiods 1963–1978 and 1979–1992, reflecting the start of the EMS. As explained in Section 4.2, the test procedure involves determining whether variables contained in the information set available prior to time $t$ can help to predict $\eta_t$. The sample period begins in 1963, since three degrees of freedom are lost in estimation.

*The Measurement of Financial Integration*

*Table 4.1 Obstfeld's (1986, 1989) Euler equation test of financial integration: 1963–1978 and 1979–1992[a]*

$$\eta_t = \gamma_0 + \sum_{i=1}^{2} \gamma_i \eta_{t-i} + v_t$$

| Country | Year of full liberalization of capital controls[c] | | 1963–1978 $\gamma_0=0$ t | 1963–1978 $\gamma_1=\gamma_2=0$ $F_{(2,15)}$ | 1979–1992 $\gamma_0=0$ t | 1979–1992 $\gamma_1=\gamma_2=0$ $F_{(2,13)}$ |
|---|---|---|---|---|---|---|
| Austria–Germany | 1991 | $\alpha=0.5$ | 0.01 | 0.62 | $-2.79^*$ | $4.39^\dagger$ |
| | | $\alpha=1.0$ | $-0.20$ | 0.80 | $-2.56^*$ | 2.27 |
| | | $\alpha=2.0$ | $-0.69$ | 0.91 | $-1.76$ | 0.08 |
| Belgium–Germany | 1990 | $\alpha=0.5$ | 0.73 | 0.71 | 1.01 | 1.42 |
| | | $\alpha=1.0$ | 0.19 | 1.55 | 0.77 | 1.97 |
| | | $\alpha=2.0$ | $-1.02$ | 1.57 | $-2.06$ | 0.41 |
| Denmark–Germany | 1988 | $\alpha=0.5$ | 0.66 | 0.42 | 0.96 | 0.32 |
| | | $\alpha=1.0$ | 0.25 | 0.30 | 0.40 | 0.33 |
| | | $\alpha=2.0$ | $-0.86$ | 0.01 | $-0.43$ | 1.60 |
| Finland–Germany | 1991 | $\alpha=0.5$ | 1.35 | 0.27 | 0.09 | 2.45 |
| | | $\alpha=1.0$ | 0.81 | 0.11 | $-0.15$ | $3.82^\dagger$ |
| | | $\alpha=2.0$ | $-2.06$ | 0.70 | 0.22 | $13.16^{\dagger\dagger}$ |
| France–Germany | 1993 | $\alpha=0.5$ | 1.59 | 0.97 | 1.77 | $8.94^{\dagger\dagger}$ |
| | | $\alpha=1.0$ | 0.70 | 1.34 | $-0.46$ | $5.39^\dagger$ |
| | | $\alpha=2.0$ | $-2.92^*$ | 2.38 | $-0.58$ | $5.01^\dagger$ |
| Greece–Germany[a] | 1994 | $\alpha=0.5$ | 1.16 | 1.44 | 1.78 | 0.15 |
| | | $\alpha=1.0$ | 0.41 | 0.82 | $-0.01$ | 0.17 |
| | | $\alpha=2.0$ | 0.79 | 2.95 | 1.55 | 0.55 |
| Ireland–Germany | 1992 | $\alpha=0.5$ | 1.49 | 0.32 | $-0.03$ | $3.89^\dagger$ |
| | | $\alpha=1.0$ | 1.59 | 0.25 | $-1.12$ | 2.51 |
| | | $\alpha=2.0$ | $-1.80$ | 2.31 | $-1.34$ | 0.42 |
| Italy–Germany | 1992 | $\alpha=0.5$ | 1.42 | 0.96 | $-0.94$ | 2.44 |
| | | $\alpha=1.0$ | 0.82 | 1.86 | $-2.69^*$ | 2.98 |
| | | $\alpha=2.0$ | $-2.95^{**}$ | 1.96 | $-1.38$ | $4.13^\dagger$ |
| The Netherlands–Germany | 1975 | $\alpha=0.5$ | $-0.97$ | 0.14 | $2.65^*$ | 0.70 |
| | | $\alpha=1.0$ | $-1.67$ | 0.49 | $2.81^*$ | 0.51 |
| | | $\alpha=2.0$ | $-3.19^{**}$ | 1.63 | $2.21^*$ | 0.20 |
| Portugal–Germany[b] | 1993 | $\alpha=0.5$ | 0.76 | $4.77^\dagger$ | $2.23^*$ | $7.91^{\dagger\dagger}$ |
| | | $\alpha=1.0$ | 0.12 | 0.06 | $-1.27$ | $8.14^{\dagger\dagger}$ |
| | | $\alpha=2.0$ | $-2.52^*$ | 0.75 | $-2.77^*$ | $5.37^\dagger$ |
| Spain–Germany | 1994 | $\alpha=0.5$ | 0.75 | 0.69 | $-0.23$ | 0.36 |
| | | $\alpha=1.0$ | $-0.22$ | 0.72 | $-1.54$ | 0.33 |
| | | $\alpha=2.0$ | $-2.12$ | 0.74 | $-2.35^*$ | 0.95 |
| Sweden–Germany | 1993 | $\alpha=0.5$ | 1.85 | $5.00^\dagger$ | 1.15 | $4.65^\dagger$ |
| | | $\alpha=1.0$ | 1.52 | $4.32^\dagger$ | 0.09 | 3.19 |
| | | $\alpha=2.0$ | 0.06 | 2.12 | $-0.53$ | 1.57 |
| United Kingdom–Germany | 1979 | $\alpha=0.5$ | $2.19^*$ | 0.09 | $-0.30$ | 1.76 |
| | | $\alpha=1.0$ | $2.86^*$ | 1.14 | $-0.89$ | 1.94 |
| | | $\alpha=2.0$ | $-0.73$ | 0.91 | $-1.51$ | $4.11^\dagger$ |

*Notes:*

[a]   Calculated over the period 1963–1978 and 1979–1991 due to data availability.
[b]   Calculated over the period 1963–1978 and 1979–1990 due to data availability.
[c]   Year of full liberalization of capital controls with respect to the home country (Restrictions on payments for capital transactions + Separate exchange rate(s) for some or all capital transactions and/or some or all invisibles). Full liberalization of capital controls with respect to Germany in 1973.

\* Significantly different from zero at the 95 per cent level of confidence (two-tailed t-test).
\*\* Significantly different from zero at the 99 per cent level of confidence (two-tailed t-test).
† Significantly different from zero at the 95 per cent level of confidence (F-test).
†† Significantly different from zero at the 99 per cent level of confidence (F-test).

The estimation method for the results in the table was OLS. See Dougherty (1992, pp. 364–71) for the critical values of the t- and F- distribution at the 95 per cent and 99 per cent levels of confidence.

*Source:* Penn World Table, *Mark 6.*

If the null hypothesis $\gamma_0 = 0$ is rejected and/or the null hypothesis $\gamma_1 = \gamma_2 = 0$ is rejected, financial markets are said to be imperfectly integrated. The number of rejections of the null hypotheses over the period 1963–1978 are: Austria (0x), Belgium (0x), Denmark (0x), Finland (0x), Greece (0x), Ireland (0x), Spain (0x), France (1x), Italy (1x), The Netherlands (1x), the United Kingdom (2x), Portugal (2x) and Sweden (2x). The number of rejections of the null hypotheses over the period 1979–1992 are: Denmark (0x), Belgium (0x), Greece (0x), Ireland (1x), Spain (1x), Sweden (1x), the United Kingdom (1x), Finland (2x), Italy (2x), Austria (3x), France (3x), The Netherlands (3x) and Portugal (5x). As is clear, the interpretation of these results is complicated by few degrees of freedom. Somewhat surprisingly, financial integration appears to have been stronger during the 1963–1978 period than during the 1979–1992 period. This is quite surprising, as many European countries (including Germany) had relatively more stringent capital controls during much of the 1963–1978 period (see IMF, *Annual Report on Exchange Arrangements and Exchange Restrictions* and Krugman and Obstfeld, 1994, Chapter 20) than during the 1979–1992 period. Hence, the non-rejection of the null of financial integration in test I is most likely due to the fact that test I has low power.

The second test is Obstfeld's (1994a, 1994b) Euler equation test of financial integration. This test assumes trade in risk-free and risky assets. Table 4.2 summarizes simple cross-correlation coefficients of per capita consumption growth rates on a country-by-country base. Furthermore, we report absolute t-statistics for the null hypothesis that there is *no* association between consumption growth rates, that is, the null hypothesis of perfect capital immobility.[21] In contrast to tests I and III, test II considers all pairs of countries in the sample. The sample period 1961–1992 is split into two subperiods: 1961–1978 and 1979–1992. To ensure comparability, we calculate growth rates from per capita private consumption denominated in US dollars.

The null hypothesis of perfect capital immobility over the period 1961–1992 is rejected for: Austria–Belgium, Austria–The Netherlands, Austria–Portugal, Austria–Spain, Belgium–France, Belgium–Germany, Belgium–Italy, Belgium–The Netherlands, Belgium–Spain, Belgium–Sweden, Denmark–Finland, Denmark–France, Denmark–Germany, Denmark–The Netherlands, Denmark–Sweden, Finland–France, Finland–Germany, Finland–Sweden, Finland–United Kingdom, France–Greece, France–Italy, France–The Netherlands, France–Spain, France–

*The Measurement of Financial Integration*

### Table 4.2  Obstfeld's (1994a, 1994b) Euler equation test of financial integration: I: 1961–1992, II: 1961–1978 and III: 1979–1992, respectively

$$m_i(x, x') = m_j(x, x')$$

|        |     | BEL | DEN | FIN | FRA | GER | GRE |
|--------|-----|-----|-----|-----|-----|-----|-----|
| AUS | I   | 0.40 (2.35)* | 0.09 (0.49) | 0.22 (1.21) | 0.34 (1.95) | 0.34 (1.95) | 0.24 (1.31)ᵃ |
|     | II  | 0.22 (0.87) | –0.08 (0.31) | 0.00 (0.00) | –0.08 (0.31) | –0.04 (0.16) | 0.30 (1.22) |
|     | III | 0.28 (0.97) | 0.00 (0.00) | 0.54 (2.13) | 0.28 (0.97) | 0.44 (1.63) | –0.21 (0.71)ᵇ |
| BEL | I   |     | 0.04 (0.22) | 0.26 (1.45) | 0.50 (3.11)** | 0.48 (2.95)* | 0.15 (0.80)ᵃ |
|     | II  |     | –0.11 (0.43) | 0.23 (0.92) | 0.21 (0.83) | 0.19 (0.75) | –0.03 (0.12) |
|     | III |     | –0.11 (0.37) | 0.21 (0.71) | 0.42 (1.53) | 0.53 (2.07) | –0.12 (0.38)ᵇ |
| DEN | I   |     |     | 0.47 (2.87)* | 0.51 (3.19)** | 0.46 (2.79)* | 0.12 (0.64)ᵃ |
|     | II  |     |     | 0.60 (2.90)* | 0.57 (2.69)* | 0.44 (1.90) | 0.05 (0.19) |
|     | III |     |     | 0.15 (0.50) | 0.19 (0.64) | 0.28 (0.97) | –0.08 (0.25)ᵇ |
| FIN | I   |     |     |     | 0.52 (3.28)** | 0.36 (2.08)* | 0.24 (1.31)ᵃ |
|     | II  |     |     |     | 0.67 (3.50)** | 0.36 (1.49) | 0.32 (1.31) |
|     | III |     |     |     | 0.54 (2.13) | 0.33 (1.16) | 0.13 (0.41)ᵇ |
| FRA | I   |     |     |     |     | 0.56 (3.64) | 0.52 (3.22)ᵃ** |
|     | II  |     |     |     |     | 0.34 (1.40) | 0.35 (1.45) |
|     | III |     |     |     |     | 0.22 (0.75) | 0.30 (0.99)ᵇ |
| GER | I   |     |     |     |     |     | 0.23 (1.25)ᵃ |
|     | II  |     |     |     |     |     | 0.37 (1.54) |
|     | III |     |     |     |     |     | –0.45 (1.59)ᵇ |
| GRE | I   |     |     |     |     |     |     |
|     | II  |     |     |     |     |     |     |
|     | III |     |     |     |     |     |     |
| IRE | I   |     |     |     |     |     |     |
|     | II  |     |     |     |     |     |     |
|     | III |     |     |     |     |     |     |
| ITA | I   |     |     |     |     |     |     |
|     | II  |     |     |     |     |     |     |
|     | III |     |     |     |     |     |     |
| NET | I   |     |     |     |     |     |     |
|     | II  |     |     |     |     |     |     |
|     | III |     |     |     |     |     |     |
| POR | I   |     |     |     |     |     |     |
|     | II  |     |     |     |     |     |     |
|     | III |     |     |     |     |     |     |
| SPA | I   |     |     |     |     |     |     |
|     | II  |     |     |     |     |     |     |
|     | III |     |     |     |     |     |     |
| SWE | I   |     |     |     |     |     |     |
|     | II  |     |     |     |     |     |     |
|     | III |     |     |     |     |     |     |

*Notes:*

ᵃ   Correlations over the period 1961–1991 due to data availability.
ᵇ   Correlations over the period 1979–1991 due to data availability.
ᶜ   Correlations over the period 1961–1990 due to data availability.
ᵈ   Correlations over the period 1979–1990 due to data availability.
*   Significantly different from zero at the 95 per cent level of confidence (two-tailed test).
**  Significantly different from zero at the 99 per cent level of confidence (two-tailed test).

The absolute t-values for the sample correlation coefficient are in parentheses. The t-statistic for the correlation coefficient $r$ is calculated as follows:

$t = r \times \sqrt{(n-2/1-r^2)}$ where $n-2$ are the degrees of freedom (see Dougherty, 1992, p. 112).

*Source:* Penn World Table, *Mark 6.*

| IRE | ITA | NET | POR | SPA | SWE | UK |
|---|---|---|---|---|---|---|
| 0.01 (0.05) | 0.24 (1.33) | 0.40 (2.35)* | 0.41 (2.34)^{c*} | 0.50 (3.11)** | 0.30 (1.69) | 0.17 (0.93) |
| −0.41 (1.74) | −0.04 (0.16) | −0.06 (0.23) | 0.51 (2.30)* | 0.37 (1.54) | 0.26 (1.04) | −0.04 (0.16) |
| 0.18 (0.61) | 0.28 (0.97) | 0.33 (1.16) | 0.35 (1.12)^d | 0.34 (1.20) | 0.03 (0.10) | 0.54 (1.12) |
| 0.27 (1.51) | 0.53 (3.37)** | 0.57 (3.74)** | 0.36 (2.01)^c | 0.52 (3.28)** | 0.38 (2.21)* | 0.21 (1.16) |
| 0.05 (0.19) | 0.29 (1.17) | 0.25 (1.00) | 0.47 (2.06) | 0.31 (1.26) | 0.22 (0.87) | 0.37 (1.54) |
| 0.34 (1.20) | 0.71 (3.34)** | 0.60 (2.49)* | 0.26 (0.81)^d | 0.52 (2.02) | 0.31 (1.08) | 0.18 (0.61) |
| −0.01 (0.05) | 0.14 (0.76) | 0.37 (2.14)* | −0.34 (1.88)^c | 0.31 (1.76) | 0.41 (2.42)* | 0.02 (0.11) |
| −0.12 (0.47) | 0.16 (0.63) | 0.22 (0.87) | −0.41 (1.74) | 0.29 (1.17) | 0.45 (1.95) | −0.13 (0.51) |
| −0.08 (0.27) | −0.30 (1.04) | 0.28 (0.97) | −0.24 (0.74)^d | 0.02 (0.07) | 0.22 (0.75) | 0.27 (0.93) |
| 0.01 (0.05) | 0.24 (1.33) | 0.17 (0.93) | −0.07 (0.36)^c | 0.36 (2.08) | 0.53 (3.37)** | 0.45 (3.46)** |
| −0.12 (0.47) | 0.16 (0.63) | 0.19 (0.75) | −0.16 (0.63) | 0.39 (1.64) | 0.47 (2.06) | 0.27 (1.09) |
| 0.08 (0.27) | 0.30 (1.04) | 0.03 (0.10) | 0.32 (1.01)^d | 0.24 (0.82) | 0.64 (2.76)* | 0.78 (4.13)** |
| 0.28 (1.57) | 0.60 (4.04)** | 0.66 (4.73)** | 0.01 (0.05)^c | 0.65 (4.61)** | 0.55 (3.55)** | 0.21 (1.16) |
| 0.23 (0.92) | 0.54 (2.48)* | 0.40 (1.69) | −0.12 (0.47) | 0.51 (2.30)* | 0.37 (1.54) | 0.33 (1.35) |
| −0.01 (0.03) | 0.26 (0.89) | 0.12 (0.40) | 0.42 (1.39)^d | 0.39 (1.40) | 0.56 (2.24)* | 0.59 (2.42)* |
| 0.43 (2.56)* | 0.36 (2.08) | 0.74 (5.92)** | 0.07 (0.36)^c | 0.42 (2.49)* | 0.39 (2.28)* | 0.17 (0.93) |
| 0.18 (0.71) | 0.03 (0.12) | 0.46 (2.01) | −0.10 (0.39) | −0.02 (0.08) | 0.01 (0.04) | 0.10 (0.39) |
| 0.55 (2.18) | 0.46 (1.72) | 0.80 (4.42)** | 0.46 (1.55)^d | 0.61 (2.55)* | 0.51 (1.97) | 0.44 (1.63) |
| 0.10 (0.53)^a | 0.16 (0.86)^a | 0.41 (2.38)^{a*} | 0.18 (0.95)^c | 0.34 (1.91)^a | 0.23 (1.25)^a | −0.01 (0.05)^a |
| −0.01 (0.04) | 0.16 (0.63) | 0.36 (1.49) | 0.19 (0.75) | 0.18 (0.71) | 0.22 (0.87) | 0.29 (1.17) |
| −0.04 (0.13)^b | −0.32 (1.07)^b | −0.05 (0.18)^b | 0.23 (0.71)^d | 0.13 (0.41)^b | −0.03 (0.09)^b | −0.17 (0.55)^b |
| | 0.26 (1.45) | 0.47 (2.87)* | 0.21 (1.12)^c | 0.27 (1.51) | 0.13 (0.71) | 0.32 (1.82) |
| | −0.01 (0.04) | 0.15 (0.59) | −0.03 (0.12) | −0.26 (1.04) | −0.15 (0.59) | 0.46 (2.01) |
| | 0.43 (1.58) | 0.61 (2.55)* | 0.58 (2.14)^d | 0.68 (3.08)* | 0.17 (0.57) | 0.28 (0.97) |
| | | 0.52 (3.28)** | 0.16 (0.84)^c | 0.56 (3.64)** | 0.42 (2.19)* | 0.12 (0.65) |
| | | 0.42 (1.79) | 0.20 (0.79) | 0.53 (2.42)* | 0.26 (1.04) | 0.05 (0.19) |
| | | 0.28 (0.97) | 0.11 (0.33)^d | 0.28 (0.97) | 0.40 (1.45) | 0.36 (1.28) |
| | | | 0.18 (0.95)^c | 0.64 (4.49)** | 0.48 (2.95)* | −0.05 (0.27) |
| | | | 0.13 (0.51) | 0.31 (1.26) | 0.53 (2.42)* | −0.10 (0.39) |
| | | | 0.47 (1.60)^d | 0.69 (3.16)** | 0.16 (0.54) | 0.10 (0.33) |
| | | | | 0.45 (2.62)^{c*} | 0.26 (1.40)^c | 0.14 (0.73)^c |
| | | | | 0.36 (1.49) | 0.27 (1.09) | −0.02 (0.08) |
| | | | | 0.87 (5.29)^{d**} | 0.31 (0.98)^d | 0.40 (1.16)^d |
| | | | | | 0.63 (4.37)** | 0.11 (0.60) |
| | | | | | 0.73 (4.14)** | 0.05 (0.19) |
| | | | | | 0.36 (1.28) | 0.36 (1.28) |
| | | | | | | 0.28 (1.57) |
| | | | | | | −0.02 (0.08) |
| | | | | | | 0.63 (2.59)* |

120     *The Measurement of Financial Integration*

Sweden, Germany–Ireland, Germany–The Netherlands, Germany–Spain, Germany–Sweden, Greece–The Netherlands, Ireland–The Netherlands, Italy–The Netherlands, Italy–Spain, Italy–Sweden, The Netherlands–Spain, The Netherlands–Sweden, Portugal–Spain and Spain–Sweden. The null hypothesis of perfect capital immobility over the period 1961–1978 is rejected for: Austria–Portugal, Denmark–Finland, Denmark–France, Finland–France, France–Italy, France–Spain, Italy–Spain, The Netherlands–Spain and Spain–Sweden. Finally, the null hypothesis of perfect capital immobility over the period 1979–1992 is rejected for: Belgium–Italy, Belgium–The Netherlands, Finland–Sweden, Finland–United Kingdom, France–Sweden, France–United Kingdom, Germany–The Netherlands, Germany–Spain, Ireland–The Netherlands, Ireland–Spain, The Netherlands–Spain, Portugal–Spain and Sweden–United Kingdom.

The number of rejections of the null hypothesis of perfect capital immobility over the period 1961–1992 of individual countries with respect to any country pair in ascending order are: the United Kingdom (1x), Greece (2x), Portugal (2x), Austria (4x), Denmark (5x), Finland (5x), Italy (5x), Belgium (7x), Germany (7x), France (8x), Sweden (8x), Spain (8x) and The Netherlands (10x). The number of rejections of the null hypothesis of perfect capital immobility over the period 1961–1978 of individual countries with respect to any country pair in ascending order are: Belgium (0x), Germany (0x), Greece (0x), Ireland (0x), the United Kingdom (0x), Austria (1x), The Netherlands (1x), Portugal (1x), Spain (1x), Denmark (2x), Finland (2x), Italy (2x), Sweden (2x) and France (4x). The number of rejections of the null hypothesis of perfect capital immobility over the period 1979–1992 of individual countries with respect to any country pair in ascending order are: Austria (0), Denmark (0x), Italy (1x), Portugal (1x), Belgium (2x), Finland (2x), France (2x), Germany (2x), Ireland (2x), Spain (3x), Sweden (3x), the United Kingdom (3x) and The Netherlands (4x).

The main finding from test II is that cross-country consumption correlations have typically been larger during the 1979–1992 period than during the 1961–1978 period, which might be viewed as an indication of closer financial integration in the second half of the sample period. Clearly, this result may point at increased risk sharing through the European financial markets. However, all correlation coefficients are still substantially below unity. Low correlation coefficients may indicate imperfect financial market integration and/or market incompleteness. Although simple correlation coefficients are never conclusive since a third factor may be important, Table 4.2 may give valuable insights about differences in the degree of capital mobility among EU countries and the scope for risk diversification.[22] International trade in assets may reduce the riskiness of the return by allowing countries' residents to diversify their portfolio. The simple correlations coefficients in Table 4.2 indicate that there is still significant room for risk diversification among EU countries.

Test III focuses on the prediction that, in the presence of integrated financial markets, cross-country differences in expected asset returns are linearly related to expected consumption growth rates in these countries. The use of *annual* data renders the lognormality of consumption growth and rates of return (more) realistic. Moreover, the use of annual data avoids the problem of seasonality in consumption. Representative short-term and long-term interest rates were obtained from the OECD *Main Economic Indicators*. Unfortunately, consistent long series of short-term interest rates (Greece and Portugal), long-term interest rates (Greece, Portugal and Spain) and stock market indices (Portugal) were not available. Representative stock market indices to calculate rate of returns were also obtained from the OECD *Main Economic Indicators* (see Appendix 4A1). Subsequently, annual realized real interest rates and real stock returns were calculated using the Penn World Table, *Mark 6* implicit price deflator of private consumption. We calculate growth rates from per capita private consumption denominated *in national currency units* using the Penn World Table, *Mark 6* exchanges rate with respect to the US dollar – since rates of return are also denominated in national currency units. So, home and foreign country returns are priced according to their *own* national consumption behaviour. To increase degrees of freedom, the sample period of test III (1961–1992) differs from the sample periods of tests I and II.

Table 4.3 reports the results of our Euler equation test of financial integration for the EU countries over the period 1961–1992 with Germany as the reference country. OLS may not be a valid estimation technique of equation (4.25). This is due to the fact that the error term $\varepsilon_{t+1}$ is correlated with the regressors $\Delta c_{t+1}$ and $\Delta c_{t+1}^*$. Hence, OLS estimates of $\alpha$ and $\alpha^*$ are inconsistent. To preserve degrees of freedom, we do not perform 2SLS estimation. Therefore, we present simple OLS estimates of equation (4.25). Furthermore, we use one-year lagged information.[23]

Evidently, the pricing performance of the Euler equation with respect to the short-term bond, the long-term bond and the stock market is reasonably sound, as is clear from the significant coefficients for $\Delta c_{t+1}$ and $\Delta c_{t+1}^*$ – indicating a significant relationship between rates of return and consumption growth. Perfect integration between the short-term bond markets is rejected for the following country pairs: Austria–Germany, Finland–Germany, Ireland–Germany and The Netherlands–Germany. Perfect integration between the long-term bond markets is rejected for the following country pairs: Austria–Germany and Finland–Germany. Perfect integration between the stock markets is rejected for the following country pairs: Finland–Germany, Ireland–Germany and Italy–Germany. For the other country pairs perfect financial integration cannot be rejected.

However, some estimates for $\alpha$ and $\alpha^*$ may be inaccurate and/or have the wrong sign. Furthermore, standard errors are high. Consequently, the power

*Table 4.3 The new Euler equation test of financial integration: 1961–1992*

$$r_{t+1} - r_{t+1}^* = constant + \alpha\,\Delta c_{t+1} - \alpha^*\Delta c_{t+1}^* + \gamma_1\Delta c_t - \gamma_1^*\Delta c_t^* + \upsilon_{t+1}$$

| Austria | Short-term bond market | Long-term bond market[a] | Stock market[a] |
|---|---|---|---|
| *Constant* | −0.002 (0.004) | −0.006 (0.003)* | −0.02 (0.04) |
| $\Delta c_{t+1}$ | 0.06 (0.21) | 0.15 (0.15) | 2.32 (2.00) |
| $\Delta c_{t+1}^*$ | −0.09 (0.21) | −0.18 (0.16) | −2.60 (2.07) |
| $\Delta c_t$ | −0.35 (0.20)* | −0.32 (0.15)* | 0.58 (1.91) |
| $\Delta c_t^*$ | 0.40 (0.20)* | −0.33 (0.15)* | −0.57 (1.98) |
| $\bar{R}^2$ | 0.02 | 0.11 | −0.12 |
| $LM_{AR}(1)$ | 1.45 | 1.87 | 1.73 |
| **Belgium** | **Short-term bond market** | **Long-term bond market** | **Stock market** |
| *Constant* | 0.005 (0.006) | 0.002 (0.005) | −0.02 (0.03) |
| $\Delta c_{t+1}$ | 0.77 (0.15)* | 0.80 (0.12)* | 2.25 (0.67)* |
| $\Delta c_{t+1}^*$ | −0.73 (0.16)* | −0.78 (0.13)* | −2.48 (0.71)* |
| $\Delta c_t$ | −0.002 (0.15) | −0.04 (0.12) | −0.61 (0.66) |
| $\Delta c_t^*$ | 0.03 (0.16) | 0.09 (0.13) | 0.17 (0.71) |
| $\bar{R}^2$ | 0.48 | 0.61 | 0.25 |
| $LM_{AR}(1)$ | 14.68 | 11.47 | 0.77 |
| **Denmark** | **Short-term bond market** | **Long-term bond market** | **Stock market** |
| *Constant* | 0.01 (0.01) | 0.02 (0.01)* | 0.04 (0.04) |
| $\Delta c_{t+1}$ | 0.92 (0.28)* | 0.92 (0.23)* | 1.16 (1.23) |
| $\Delta c_{t+1}^*$ | −0.91 (0.28)* | −0.93 (0.23)* | −0.44 (1.24) |
| $\Delta c_t$ | 0.29 (0.24) | 0.10 (0.20) | −1.37 (1.07) |
| $\Delta c_t^*$ | −0.30 (0.25) | −0.19 (0.21) | 1.01 (1.12) |
| $\bar{R}^2$ | 0.32 | 0.32 | 10.03 |
| $LM_{AR}(1)$ | 11.22 | 6.69 | 0.11 |
| **Finland** | **Short-term bond market** | **Long-term bond market[a]** | **Stock market** |
| *Constant* | 0.007 (0.01) | 0.01 (0.02) | −0.08 (0.06) |
| $\Delta c_{t+1}$ | 0.71 (0.20)* | 0.70 (0.30)* | 1.16 (0.84) |
| $\Delta c_{t+1}^*$ | −0.86 (0.17)* | −0.88 (0.23)* | −1.26 (0.68)* |
| $\Delta c_t$ | −0.30 (0.19) | −0.36 (0.26) | 1.94 (0.80)* |
| $\Delta c_t^*$ | 0.36 (0.17)* | 0.44 (0.22)* | −2.10 (0.70)* |
| $\bar{R}^2$ | 0.48 | 0.48 | 0.25 |
| $LM_{AR}(1)$ | 6.48 | 5.23 | 1.82 |

| France | Short-term bond market | Long-term bond market | Stock market |
|---|---|---|---|
| *Constant* | 0.02 (0.02) | 0.03 (0.02) | 0.001 (0.07) |
| $\Delta c_{t+1}$ | −1.42 (0.85) | −1.45 (0.78)* | 0.77 (2.87) |
| $\Delta c^{*}_{t+1}$ | −0.04 (0.11) | −0.06 (0.10) | −0.25 (0.36) |
| $\Delta c_{t}$ | 1.23 (0.83) | 1.21 (0.77) | 0.02 (2.82) |
| $\Delta c^{*}_{t}$ | 0.17 (0.11) | 0.16 (0.10) | −0.35 (0.38) |
| $\bar{R}^2$ | −0.003 | 0.01 | −0.07 |
| $LM_{AR}(1)$ | 2.35 | 1.81 | 0.003 |

| Greece | Short-term bond market | Long-term bond market | Stock market |
|---|---|---|---|
| *Constant* | – | – | 0.14 (0.10) |
| $\Delta c_{t+1}$ | – | – | −1.05 (1.00) |
| $\Delta c^{*}_{t+1}$ | – | – | −0.57 (0.90) |
| $\Delta c_{t}$ | – | – | 0.08 (0.95) |
| $\Delta c^{*}_{t}$ | – | – | −0.75 (0.79) |
| $\bar{R}^2$ | – | – | 0.24 |
| $LM_{AR}(1)$ | – | – | 1.98 |

| Ireland | Short-term bond market[a] | Long-term bond market[a] | Stock market |
|---|---|---|---|
| *Constant* | 0.03 (0.15) | 0.01 (0.01) | 0.07 (0.04) |
| $\Delta c_{t+1}$ | 0.60 (0.19)* | 0.63 (0.14)* | 0.83 (0.60) |
| $\Delta c^{*}_{t+1}$ | −0.71 (0.19)* | −0.70 (0.14)* | −1.25 (0.62)* |
| $\Delta c_{t}$ | −0.15 (0.19) | −0.04 (0.14) | −1.19 (0.59)* |
| $\Delta c^{*}_{t}$ | 0.22 (0.19)* | 0.09 (0.14) | 0.51 (0.61) |
| $\bar{R}^2$ | 0.37 | 0.56 | 0.19 |
| $LM_{AR}(1)$ | 1.73 | 1.28 | 1.20 |

| Italy | Short-term bond market | Long-term bond market | Stock market |
|---|---|---|---|
| *Constant* | −0.01 (0.01) | 0.005 (0.009) | −0.04 (0.07) |
| $\Delta c_{t+1}$ | 0.66 (0.12)* | 0.62 (0.10)* | 1.58 (0.69)* |
| $\Delta c^{*}_{t+1}$ | −0.65 (0.14)* | −0.60 (0.11)* | −1.80 (0.75)* |
| $\Delta c_{t}$ | 0.04 (0.12) | −0.10 (0.10) | −1.49 (0.69)* |
| $\Delta c^{*}_{t}$ | 0.01 (0.14) | 0.18 (0.11) | 1.21 (0.75) |
| $\bar{R}^2$ | 0.48 | 0.55 | 0.15 |
| $LM_{AR}(1)$ | 5.37 | 4.34 | 2.05 |

| The Netherlands | Short-term bond market | Long-term bond market[a] | Stock market |
|---|---|---|---|
| *Constant* | −0.004 (0.005) | 0.007 (0.004)[*] | 0.02 (0.02) |
| $\Delta c_{t+1}$ | 0.18 (0.25) | 0.12 (0.22) | 0.20 (0.91) |
| $\Delta c_{t+1}^{*}$ | −0.15 (0.25) | −0.07 (0.22) | 0.11 (0.93) |
| $\Delta c_{t}$ | −0.43 (0.25)[*] | −0.53 (0.23)[*] | −2.22 (0.90)[*] |
| $\Delta c_{t}^{*}$ | 0.41 (0.25) | 0.54 (0.23)[*] | 1.95 (0.93)[*] |
| $\bar{R}^{2}$ | −0.03 | 0.26 | 0.18 |
| $LM_{AR}(1)$ | 5.54 | 3.40 | 0.51 |
| Spain | Short-term bond market[a] | Long-term bond market | Stock market |
| *Constant* | −0.02 (0.02) | – | 0.01 (0.07) |
| $\Delta c_{t+1}$ | 0.83 (0.24)[*] | – | 0.20 (0.77) |
| $\Delta c_{t+1}^{*}$ | −0.75 (0.24)[*] | – | −0.17 (0.78) |
| $\Delta c_{t}$ | 0.10 (0.23) | – | −0.21 (0.74) |
| $\Delta c_{t}^{*}$ | 0.03 (0.24) | – | −0.54 (0.78) |
| $\bar{R}^{2}$ | 0.41 | – | −0.06 |
| $LM_{AR}(1)$ | 2.96 | – | 7.46 |
| Sweden | Short-term bond market | Long-term bond market | Stock market |
| *Constant* | −0.009 (0.006) | −0.005 (0.005) | 0.001 (0.03) |
| $\Delta c_{t+1}$ | 0.72 (0.13)[*] | 0.74 (0.11)[*] | 2.22 (0.69)[*] |
| $\Delta c_{t+1}^{*}$ | −0.83 (0.10)[*] | −0.85 (0.08)[*] | −1.38 (0.53)[*] |
| $\Delta c_{t}$ | 0.21 (0.13) | 0.14 (0.11) | −0.02 (0.67) |
| $\Delta c_{t}^{*}$ | 0.03 (0.10) | 0.01 (0.08) | −0.89 (0.51)[*] |
| $\bar{R}^{2}$ | 0.76 | 0.81 | 0.29 |
| $LM_{AR}(1)$ | 5.43 | 5.16 | 0.02 |
| United Kingdom | Short-term bond market | Long-term bond market | Stock market |
| *Constant* | −0.005 (0.006) | −0.007 (0.006) | 0.06 (0.04) |
| $\Delta c_{t+1}$ | 0.93 (0.09)[*] | 0.93 (0.08)[*] | 0.94 (0.51)[*] |
| $\Delta c_{t+1}^{*}$ | −0.88 (0.07)[*] | −0.88 (0.07)[*] | −0.78 (0.43) |
| $\Delta c_{t}$ | 0.03 (0.08) | 0.05 (0.08) | −1.10 (0.49)[*] |
| $\Delta c_{t}^{*}$ | 0.02 (0.07) | 0.01 (0.07) | 0.58 (0.43) |
| $\bar{R}^{2}$ | 0.86 | 0.88 | 0.09 |
| $LM_{AR}(1)$ | 1.29 | 0.70 | 0.34 |

*Notes:*

[a]   Estimated over the period 1973–1992 due to data availability.
[*]   Significantly different from zero for $\alpha=5$ per cent (one-tailed test).

Standard errors are indicated between parentheses. The estimation method for the results in the table was OLS. $\bar{R}^{2}$ is the coefficient of determination adjusted for degrees of freedom. $LM_{AR}(1)$ is the Lagrange Multiplier test for first-order serial correlation. The critical value for the Lagrange Multiplier test for first-order serial correlation is $\chi^{2}(1)=3.84$.

*Sources:* Penn World Table, *Mark 6* and OECD *Main Economic Indicators.*

of test III is low. This probably means that for some pairs of countries, the assumption of CRRA utility function is not correct.[24] Furthermore, since rates of return and consumption growth are expressed in national currency units, real exchange rate fluctuations, that is, deviations from *ex ante* relative PPP may frustrate the results. To solve for this problem one might be willing to express consumption growth and rates of return in a common currency. Hence, the variance of the rates of return may decline with the variance of exchange rate fluctuations. However, since complete hedging of exchange rate risk is not possible – partly due to the incomplete availability of hedge instruments (for example, forward markets for long-term bond instruments) – the whole problem cannot be solved. Perhaps subsets of countries in which PPP is thought to hold could be examined separately from those in which PPP is less likely to be valid.

## 4.4 An Evaluation of Euler Equation Tests of Financial Integration

Despite the fact that several papers have tested consumption risk sharing with international aggregate data (Bayoumi and MacDonald, 1995, Canova and Ravn, 1994, Kollmann, 1995 and Ubide, 1995, among others), we are rather sceptical that this is a fruitful approach to measure the degree of financial integration. Rejection of the null hypothesis of perfect financial integration can be attributed to any of the assumptions above (complete markets, aggregation, lack of economic integration), not to mention econometric issues (lognormality assumption, endogeneity, and so on), and not just the integration of financial markets. Suppose there are common shocks hitting Europe as a whole at the same time but financial markets are autarkic. Then, consumption correlations may be different from zero even if no risk sharing takes place (Canova and Ravn, 1994). With other factors affecting the utility function (for example, non-traded goods), correlations may be low even when there is perfect risk sharing in tradable goods.

At the very best, Euler equation tests offer some additional information to the other tests of financial integration derived from interest parity conditions and savings-investment correlations. We agree with Bayoumi and MacDonald (1995, pp. 555–6) who argue: 'Focusing on consumption has several attractive features. The underlying theory is stronger than that for savings-investment correlations. In addition, since consumption is the ultimate goal of economic activity, it is a more fundamental test of the effects of financial integration on economic welfare than either the savings-investment correlations or interest rate comparisons. Also, it appears unlikely that macroeconomic policy is directed at private nondurable consumption patterns in the way it may be at the current account'.[25] In addition, unlike arbitrage tests based upon closed, covered or uncovered interest parity, Obstfeld's (1986, 1989, 1994a, 1994b) Euler equation tests do not require comparisons between rates of return on what might be dissimilar assets – since it uses non-financial (real per capita private consumption) data. Thus, tests I and II avoid methodological problems related to the definition and measurement of interest rates. In addition, test I implicitly incorporates a test of *ex ante* UIP which does not require the assumption of a zero exchange risk premium. The derivation of Test I is based on *ex ante* PPP which is often violated. Tests II and III implicitly incorporate tests of *ex ante* RIP which does not require *ex ante* relative PPP is expected to hold (Bayoumi and MacDonald, 1995, p. 556).

This chapter (and much of the economic literature) has focused on statistical rejections of Euler equations. Future research may want to offer a more positive response by calculating the *economic* significance of departures from perfect financial market integration. Such calculations would be very interesting, and would represent a step forward in this literature.

## 4.5  Conclusions

Chapter 4 tested for the degree of financial integration using three Euler equation-based tests. Since there is no single widely accepted empirical measure for the degree of financial integration, Euler equation tests may shed some light on the integration between European financial markets. Two tests suggested by Obstfeld are applied and in addition we propose one new test. One of the benefits expected to result from cross-border capital mobility is an improvement in international risk sharing, specifically, improvements in consumption smoothing and risk diversification. What do we learn from undertaking these tests?

1.   Euler equation tests of financial integration essentially are benchmark tests of *perfect* financial integration. In Chapter 1 we argued that financial integration is a matter of degree, and the extreme cases (perfect or no financial integration) are only of theoretical interest. We are pretty sure in advance that the hypotheses that are tested do not hold. There is not perfect financial integration with respect to a risk-free asset (test I), and there is certainly not perfect financial integration combined with a complete set of markets in Arrow–Debreu securities (test II). The tests will reject the hypotheses if they have sufficiently high power. However, if the tests have low power, they may fail to reject the hypotheses. Moreover, the degrees of freedom for the empirical analysis are limited. In either case, the information we obtain is about the power of the tests, and not about the validity of the hypotheses. Nowadays, one may argue that financial

markets are integrated as an approximation. A good test will not reject the null hypothesis of perfect financial integration. Clearly, to improve upon the estimation results, future research should pool the data across countries using dummies to control for country-specific effects (panel data analysis).

2.  The information content of macro-consumption data with respect to financial market integration is low. The positive correlation of consumer growth may, as the tests presume, follow from financial integration. It may, however, also follow from countries being subject to common shocks (for example, technology, oil price and policy shocks). Common shocks could be tested for if the calculations were performed as a system. Furthermore, the EU countries are to a large extent integrated via trade, which imply large spillovers of shocks among the countries. The effects of trade might be examined by comparing countries with close and distant trade relations. Similarly, one may also want to adjust for income levels.

3.  Cross-country consumption correlations have typically been larger during the 1979–1992 period than during the 1961–1978 period, which might be viewed as an *indication* of closer financial integration in the second half of the sample period. Clearly, this result may point at increased risk sharing through the European financial markets. However, all correlation coefficients are substantially below unity and differ considerably. Low correlation coefficients may indicate imperfect financial market integration and/or market incompleteness. Concluding, the simple correlations coefficients in Table 4.2 indicate that there is still significant room for risk diversification among EU countries.

The strong assumptions needed for the Euler equation tests suggest that the most suitable way to test for the degree of financial market integration is to use covered and closed interest parity conditions which do need less severe assumptions. Consequently, research in Chapters 5 and 6 is based on these interest parity conditions.

# Notes

1. We assume that there exists only one consumption good in the world, although the analysis could equally well be performed with a vector of consumption goods.

2. A key characteristic of the Lucas (1978) asset-pricing model is that it assumes *complete frictionless* markets.

3. For simplicity, this chapter assumes that the information sets used in the domestic and foreign countries are the same.

4. The virtue of this constant relative risk aversion (CRRA) utility function is its simplicity, and therefore it is well suited for our benchmark test of financial integration.

5. Since for this utility function marginal utility is given by $C^{-\alpha}$.

6. Of course, the information set could be expanded beyond just lags of the variables that appear in the Euler equation. Perhaps variables can be chosen that are likely to be correlated with $\eta_t$ under certain alternative hypotheses.

7. Assets are characterized by non-negative payoffs they generate in different states. The payoff is in terms of a consumption good. See, for example, Eichberger and Harper (1993, Chapter 3) and Aiyagari (1993).

8. Individuals do not face transaction costs, borrowing or short-sale constraints and all claims are always fulfilled, that is, there is neither default nor bankruptcy (Aiyagari, 1993, p. 19).

9. A set of Arrow–Debreu securities is said to be complete if there are exactly as many securities as there are states of nature.

10. Representative consumers from different countries need not consume the same basket of goods, nor does the law-of-one-price necessarily hold for each good. The existence of restrictions on trade between countries will generally not lead to the segmentation of international asset markets. If no goods can ever be traded, however, asset markets will be completely segmented internationally (see Wheatley, 1988, p. 184).

11. Subtracting the fundamental equation of the Permanent Income Hypothesis (PIH) for the foreign country from that of the home country, and assuming CRRA utility, jointly lognormal distribution of consumption growth and rates of return also yields equation (4.22) (see Mankiw, 1981, 1985, Koedijk and Smant, 1994).

12. Since the interest rates paid on straight bonds are non-stochastic, contrary to equity returns, they may be placed outside the conditional expectations operator.

13. One may want to conduct two tests. First, test the orthogonality conditions separately for each country and then perform the differential test. It is possible and potentially quite interesting to see if the orthogonality conditions fail individually (perhaps due to a common factor or misspecification) but not in differences (perhaps because the common factor cancels in differences).

14. Note that since the constant includes variances terms, it does not have to be zero for perfect financial integration to hold.

15. This chapter mainly tests for private capital flows. During the 1980s private capital flows became increasingly more important as opposed to public capital flows.

16. Quarterly consumption data are not available for a sufficient number of EU countries.

17. That is, we exclude Luxemburg. Data for Germany refer to the Federal Republic of Germany before unification.

18. Test III relaxes these assumptions.

19. Ideally, one would want to estimate $\alpha$ and $\alpha^*$. The estimation of $\alpha$ and $\alpha^*$ is taken up in our new Euler equation test of financial integration. Obstfeld (1989) uses the following values for the parameter $\alpha$ to construct quarterly times series of $\eta_t$ over the period 1962:II–1985:II using Japan and Germany as the foreign countries and the US as the domestic country: $\alpha=0.5$, 0.75, 1, 1.5, 2, 3, 5, 7, 12, 25. Note that since $\alpha$ is assumed to be constant, $\alpha=0.75$, $\alpha=1$ and $\alpha=2$ imply a constant risk premium.

20. However, Obstfeld emphasizes the dramatically increasing correlation between German consumption growth and world consumption growth. Therefore, one may argue that Germany does not appear to be a very representative reference country to test for financial integration in Europe.

21. Alternatively, one may also want to test the null hypothesis that the correlation coefficient is unity.

22. With full international portfolio diversification, we expect portfolio positions to reflect the countries' size of the economy relative to the rest of the world (Krugman and Obstfeld, 1994, p. 596).

23. It might be interesting to see if the orthogonality conditions fail individually (perhaps to a common factor of misspecification) but not in differences (perhaps because the common factor cancels in differences).

24. Would the CRRA utility function be more likely to fail in countries with a certain characteristic (for example, less homogeneous or older population, differences in wealth and consumption taxes, and so on)? Can such characteristic be used to help us understand why the model is failing? Is the specification of the Euler equations independent of these differences?

25. Note that all these Euler equations are appropriate for the *flow* of consumption services. So for nondurable consumption, expenditures equal service flows, and no problem arises. However, this equality does not hold for durables. Since rich countries consume proportionately more durables than poorer countries, some account of durables consumption must be taken. Either focus on nondurables or replace durable consumption expenditures with a constructed series of the service flow from the stock of durables.

## Appendix 4A1: Data Sources

We apply data from the latest Penn World Table, *Mark 6*. We use variable 3, RGDPL, real GDP per capita, 1985 international prices; variable 4, C, real private consumption share of GDP, 1985 international prices; variable 14, PC, price level of private consumption; and variable XR, exchange rate with US dollar (Penn World Table, *Mark 6* and Summers and Heston, 1991). Per capita consumption was used to reduce the effect of differences in population growth on consumption. All per capita private consumption data are in real terms and expressed in US dollars.

Representative short-term rates were obtained from the OECD *Main Economic Indicators* via DATASTREAM (Austria, three-month vibor (monthly average), Belgium, three-month Treasury certificates (monthly average), Denmark, three-month interbank rate, Finland, three-month helibor (monthly average), France, three-month pibor (monthly average), Germany, three-month fibor (monthly average), Ireland, three-month Treasury (Excheq.) bills (end period), Italy, interbank sight deposits (ten-day average), The Netherlands, three-month loans to local authorities (monthly average), Spain, three-month interbank loans (monthly average), Sweden, three-month Treasury discount note (monthly average), the United Kingdom, three-month interbank loans (monthly average)).

Representative long-term interest rates were obtained from the OECD *Main Economic Indicators* via DATASTREAM (Austria, one-year public sector bonds (monthly average), Belgium, five-year central government bonds, Denmark, yield on ten-year government bonds (end period), Finland, three to six years yield on taxable public bonds, France, public and semi-public sector bonds (end period), Germany, seven to fifteen-year public sector bonds (monthly average), Ireland, five-year central government bonds (end period), Italy, six-year average maturity Treasury bonds, The Netherlands, five-year longest running central government bonds (monthly average), Sweden, ten-year central government bonds (monthly average), the United Kingdom, twenty-year central government bonds (monthly average)).

Representative stock market indices to calculate rate of returns were also obtained from the OECD *Main Economic Indicators* via DATASTREAM (Austria, share prices (Vienna stock exchange), Belgium, share prices – industrials, Denmark, share prices – industrials, Finland, share prices – industrials (Helsinki exchange), France, share prices – industrials (INSEE), Greece, share prices – industrials (Athens exchange), Ireland, share prices – common stocks (Irish stock exchange), Italy, share prices (Milan stock exchange), The Netherlands, share prices – industrials, commercial shares (Amsterdam stock exchange), Spain, share prices (Madrid stock exchange), Sweden, share prices (Stockholm stock exchange), the United Kingdom, share prices – FT financial actuaries (500 shares)).

# PART II

# THE DETERMINATION OF FINANCIAL INTEGRATION

# 5. The Fundamental Determinants of Financial Integration in the European Union

## 5.1 Introduction

This chapter focuses on the fundamental determinants of the degree of financial integration – or more precisely of the intensity of capital controls – in the EU over the period 1974–1993.[1] The sample period starts with the fall of the Bretton Woods system of fixed exchange rates. Macroeconomic evidence seems to support the view that the integration between European financial markets has increased in recent years (see Lemmen and Eijffinger, 1993, Frankel, Phillips and Chinn, 1993 and Lemmen and Eijffinger, 1996a). It fosters the impression that remaining differences in national economic and financial structures are unimportant. Moreover, it may tend to overstate the pressure towards, and hence the speed of integration. An obvious question, then, is what are the main determinants of financial integration? A thorough understanding of the determinants of the intensity of capital controls may provide an important insight into the process of financial and monetary integration in Europe and may help in policy formulation.[2]

We improve analysis started by Epstein and Schor (1992) and Alesina, Grilli and Milesi-Ferretti (1994) in a number of aspects. First, previous investigations of the determinants of capital controls (Epstein and Schor, 1992, Alesina et al., 1994, Gruijters, 1995, Milesi-Ferretti, 1995 and Grilli and Milesi-Ferretti, 1995) typically constructed dummy variables or capital control indices to measure the degree of financial integration. As we shall argue, these measures are problematic because they do not account for different intensities of capital controls. We compute deviations from closed interest parity to measure the intensity of capital controls. Resulting negative (positive) deviations from closed interest parity are associated with capital export (import) restrictions. Second, Alesina et al. (1994) apply their analysis to the financial markets of 20 OECD countries. Grilli and Milesi-Ferretti (1995) apply their analysis to 61 developed and less-developed countries. In practice, integration attempts across the world are more of a geographical nature. The EU financial markets can be seen as

133

an excellent sample to test for the fundamental determinants of financial integration because they are in the process of institutional integration. Most legal barriers either have been removed or are scheduled to be removed. Furthermore, the EU has adopted a stronger form of harmonization for its financial services – a policy of mutual recognition whereby member states within the EU have agreed to allow financial intermediaries from other states to operate under home country rules and supervision. Third, Alesina et al. (1994) apply Maximum Likelihood Estimation to estimate various logit/probit models. We innovatively apply a pooled cross-section time-series approach to identify the fundamental determinants of capital controls. The pooled cross-section time-series model allows us to include those authors' political variables along with other explanatory variables. Furthermore, several new explanatory variables are included in our analysis: the unemployment rate, the productivity in the business sector, the ratios of general government deficit, domestic credit, broad money and gross fixed capital formation over gross domestic product and the ratio of broad money over narrow money. We find that realized inflation, government instability and gross fixed capital formation are the fundamental determinants of financial integration in the EU.

Chapter 5 is organized as follows. Section 5.2 provides a meaningful measure of financial integration, which is the dependent variable in our empirical analysis. As we shall argue, the price measure – that is, the closed interest rate differential – is particularly suited to measure the intensity of capital controls (lack of offshore interest rates in a number of countries forces us to construct a synthetic approximation of closed interest differentials using forward exchange rates). Section 5.3 identifies the fundamental determinants of capital controls. First, we briefly summarize the rationales for capital controls. Subsequently, we link these rationales to several analytical indicators. The empirical analysis is carried out for 11 EU countries over the period 1974–1993 for which relevant data are available. Finally, Section 5.4 concludes.

## 5.2   Alternative Measures of the Degree of Financial Integration

This section addresses the definition and measurement of the dependent variable: the degree of financial integration. First, we argue that the *price* measure is to be preferred to concentrating on the *volume* of capital flows themselves. As markets become more integrated, asset prices often adjust in anticipation of capital flows that would otherwise occur. Consequently, the volume of capital flows is less suited to measure the degree of financial integration.[3] In addition, the price measure is also to be preferred to more *legal* oriented approaches of capital controls. Since financial integration is essentially a legal concept, previous research on the determinants of financial integration (Epstein and Schor, 1992, Alesina et al., 1994, Gruijters, 1995, Milesi-Ferretti, 1995 and Grilli and Milesi-Ferretti, 1995) typically constructed dummy variables or capital control indices to measure the degree of financial integration. For example, Alesina et al. (1994) use dummy variables – taking the value 1 when capital controls are in place and 0 otherwise – to measure capital controls. Unfortunately, dummy variables cannot explain different degrees of intensity of capital controls over time (Epstein and Schor, 1992, p. 143). The binary nature of dummy variables is not capable of capturing the actual intensity of capital controls. Epstein and Schor construct an annual capital control index compiled from the summary table at the end of the International Monetary Fund's (IMF's) *Annual Reports on Exchange Arrangements and Exchange Restrictions*. This index is composed of restrictions on payments for capital transactions (that is, capital controls) and the use of separate exchange rate(s) for some or all capital transactions and/or some or all invisibles (that is, exchange controls). Both types of restrictions are given equal weight. If both restrictions are in place, the index takes the value of 2, if one restriction is in place the index takes the value of 1, and 0 otherwise. Appendix 5A2 at the end of this chapter gives an idea of what this means for our 11 EU countries. Capital control indices are already more capable of explaining different degrees of intensity of capital controls than dummy variables. Epstein and Schor (1992, p. 141), however, argue that the IMF definitions do not include some indirect measures against capital flows which might reasonably be considered capital controls (for example, the interest equalization tax). Furthermore, the IMF does not distinguish between restrictions to limit capital outflows and restrictions to limit capital inflows (that is, the direction of capital flows), and between restrictions on short-term and restrictions on long-term capital flows (that is, the maturity of capital flows). In our opinion, these aspects are of crucial importance for policy analysis.

Gruijters (1995, pp. 198–213) tries to overcome these weaknesses and constructs two capital control indices to explain the intensity of capital import restrictions and the intensity of capital export restrictions, respectively. The indices are based upon a historical survey of direct and indirect capital control measures in 11 OECD countries. The measure implicitly embodies numerous types of restrictions, with some being more important than others across different countries. However, the major shortcoming endemic to all legal measures is the subjective element needed to construct them. Ample historical evidence suggests that there have been significant discrepancies between the legal and actual intensity of controls. Restrictions are not always binding (that is, effective) or some indirect restrictions are simply not taken into account.[4] As a result it may be a mistake to conclude that the market is segmented. The private sector is extremely creative in finding ways to move capital internationally.[5] In countries with restrictions on capital mobility, the private sector has typically resorted to leads and lags in average payments terms for exports and imports to evade legal controls on capital flows.[6] Moreover, the Euro currency market has played an important role in evading capital controls. So, one needs to go beyond legal restrictions in assessing the extent of capital mobility.

The measure we use takes account of *short-term* financial integration because forward exchange rates exist only for short horizons generally not exceeding one year.[7] Our measure can be seen as a somewhat more continuous (and obviously more time-varying) measure for capital control intensity than dummy variables and capital control indices. In the investigation design, the underlying financial assets differ only with respect to currency of denomination and country-specific regulation (for example, capital controls and tax treatment), rather than with respect to asset-specific types of risk (for example, default risk and liquidity risk) or other risk characteristics.[8]

We argue that closed nominal interest rate differentials are most suited to capture differences in the intensity of capital controls. Regulations vary in intensity and effect. The continuous nature of our measure captures the actual intensity of capital controls. Our argument follows from the decomposition of *onshore* covered nominal interest rate parity in Table 5.1. This may be demonstrated by distinguishing between covered nominal interest parity in *onshore* markets (for comparable assets in different political jurisdictions and restrictions on cross-border capital flows) and covered nominal interest parity in *offshore* markets (for comparable assets in the same political jurisdiction and no restrictions on cross-border capital flows). Each of the components $\phi_{Domestic}$, $\phi_{Foreign}$ and $\phi_{Euro}$ provides information on the source of the onshore covered nominal interest rate differential. $\phi_{Domestic}$ measures the extent to which *domestic* controls are the cause of a nonzero onshore covered nominal interest rate differential. Similarly, $\phi_{Foreign}$ measures the extent to which *foreign* controls contribute to a nonzero onshore covered nominal interest rate differential. Finally, $\phi_{Euro}$ measures deviations from covered interest arbitrage in offshore markets. We assume that interest arbitrage ensures that differences from covered interest rate parity in offshore markets $\phi_{Euro}$ are negligible. Since banks in Euro markets set Euro interest rates of the domestic country (say the Euro British pound sterling rate) equal to foreign Euro interest rates (say the Euro Deutsche mark rate) adjusted for the forward premium (discount) on the foreign currency, *offshore* covered nominal interest parity will always hold in Euro markets. Deviations in the Euro market are largely due to technical factors and/or transactions costs (see Giavazzi and Giovannini, 1989, p. 172). Under this assumption, the domestic onshore-offshore interest rate differential may be approximated by the adjusted domestic covered nominal interest rate differential. Consequently, the domestic intensity of capital controls may either be measured

*Table 5.1 The decomposition of the onshore covered nominal interest rate differential*

---

**(1) Offshore covered nominal interest rate differential**

$$\phi_{Euro} = i_{t,t+k}^{Euro} - i_{t,t+k}^{*Euro} - (f_t^{t+k} - s_t)$$

**(2) Domestic onshore–offshore closed nominal interest rate differential**

$$\phi_{Domestic} = i_{t,t+k} - i_{t,t+k}^{Euro}$$

**(3) Foreign offshore–onshore closed nominal interest rate differential**

$$\phi_{Foreign} = i_{t,t+k}^{*Euro} - i_{t,t+k}^{*}$$

**(4)=(1)+(2)+(3) Onshore covered nominal interest rate differential**

$$\phi = \phi_{Domestic} + \phi_{Foreign} + \phi_{Euro} =$$

$$i_{t,t+k} - i_{t,t+k}^{*} - (f_t^{t+k} - s_t) =$$

$$(i_{t,t+k} - i_{t,t+k}^{Euro}) + (i_{t,t+k}^{*Euro} - i_{t,t+k}^{*}) + (i_{t,t+k}^{Euro} - i_{t,t+k}^{*Euro} - (f_t^{t+k} - s_t))$$

---

Now, we may derive our measure for the intensity of capital controls. The domestic intensity of capital controls may be approximated by the adjusted domestic covered nominal interest rate differential

$$\xi_{Domestic} = \phi - \phi_{Foreign} = \phi_{Domestic} + \phi_{Euro} = i_{t,t+k} - i_{t,t+k}^{*Euro} - (f_t^{t+k} - s_t)$$

while the foreign intensity of capital controls may be approximated by the adjusted foreign covered nominal interest rate differential

$$\xi_{Foreign} = \phi - \phi_{Domestic} = \phi_{Foreign} + \phi_{Euro} = i_{t,t+k}^{Euro} - i_{t,t+k}^{*} - (f_t^{t+k} - s_t)$$

where banks ensure that offshore covered nominal interest rate parity holds continuously. That is, we may write

$$i_{t,t+k}^{Euro} = i_{t,t+k}^{*Euro} + (f_t^{t+k} - s_t)$$

and

$$i_{t,t+k}^{*Euro} = i_{t,t+k}^{Euro} - (f_t^{t+k} - s_t)$$

**Symbols:**

| | | |
|---|---|---|
| $i_{t,t+k}$ | = | domestic onshore nominal interest rate at time $t$ on a $k$-period bond held between time $t$ and $t+k$ |
| $i_{t,t+k}^{Euro}$ | = | domestic offshore nominal interest rate at time $t$ on a $k$-period bond held between time $t$ and $t+k$ |
| $f_t^{t+k}$ | = | forward exchange rate at time $t$ for the delivery of foreign currency at time $t+k$ |
| $s_t$ | = | spot exchange rate at time $t$ (defined as units of domestic currency per unit of foreign currency) |
| $k$ | = | holding period of the underlying financial instrument |
| $*$ | = | denotes a foreign variable |
| $t$ | = | denotes time $t$ |

*Sources:* Goldsbrough and Teja (1991) and author's own summary of the literature.


by the domestic onshore–offshore closed nominal interest rate differential or

$$\phi_{Domestic} = i_{t,t+k} - i_{t,t+k}^{Euro} \tag{5.1}$$

by the adjusted domestic covered nominal interest rate differential

$$\xi_{Domestic} = i_{t,t+k} - i_{t,t+k}^{*Euro} - (f_t^{t+k} - s_t) \tag{5.2}$$

Domestic capital controls will be an important reason for significant deviations from onshore closed interest parity.[9] Since offshore covered nominal interest rate parity is zero by assumption, it follows that any differential between the domestic rate and the Euro rate on a comparable asset is likely to reflect domestic capital controls.[10] Closed and adjusted covered nominal interest rate differentials have been widely used to measure the intensity of capital controls. The closed and adjusted covered nominal interest differentials – which we shall refer to as country risk premia – primarily reflect the joint influence of existing and expected capital controls (that is, political risks) (Aliber, 1973, p. 1453). They indicate agents' ability to move financial assets across national borders. Nevertheless, care must be exercised in taking the closed interest rate differentials as an indication of the intensity of capital controls, since differences in asset-specific types of risk cannot be completely excluded.[11]

Annual series of closed interest rate parity for Germany, France, The Netherlands and the United Kingdom may be derived as follows (see Appendix 5A1)[12]

$$\phi_{Domestic}^{Year} = \frac{\sum\limits_{j=1}^{j=12} [i_{t,t+3} - i_{t,t+3}^{Euro}]_j}{12} \tag{5.3}$$

Unfortunately, Euro interest rates are not available for Austria, Belgium, Denmark, Finland, Italy, Spain and Sweden. Therefore, for these countries we calculate annual series of adjusted domestic covered nominal interest rate differentials (see Appendix 5A1)

$$\xi_{Domestic}^{Year} = \frac{\sum\limits_{j=1}^{j=12}[i_{t,t+3} - i_{t,t+3}^{*Euro} - (f_t^{t+3} - s_t)]_j}{12} \qquad (5.4)$$

which is equivalent to the closed interest rate differential under the assumption of covered interest rate parity in offshore markets. Three-month Euro DM interest rates are used to calculate the adjusted domestic covered nominal interest rate differentials. Furthermore, we use own cross-rate calculations of spot and forward exchange rates of EU countries *vis-à-vis* the DM based upon end-of-period spot and forward exchange rates *vis-à-vis* the US dollar. Henceforth, when we speak about closed interest differentials we also mean adjusted covered interest rate differentials.

Appendix 5A3 plots the year-by-year average deviations from the price measure over the period 1974–1993. Unfortunately, we had to take a shorter sample period for Italy (1977–1993) due to the lack of forward exchange rate data. Clearly, Appendix 5A3 shows a declining pattern of closed interest differentials, with alternating periods of relatively high and low capital control intensity. Why do governments regulate financial markets? The next section identifies the main determinants of capital controls.

## 5.3   Empirical Results and Interpretation

This section identifies empirically the fundamental determinants of financial integration in the EU. Furthermore, we take an eclectic approach to identify the fundamental determinants of financial integration in the EU. Before turning to the estimation results, we shall briefly describe the main rationales for capital controls. In addition, we offer some analytical indicators for the relevant determinants of capital controls.[13] The following explanations for the introduction of capital controls have been given in the literature:[14]

### (1) Monetary determinants of capital controls
Possible candidate determinants of capital controls with respect to monetary policy are realized inflation (*INF*), domestic credit (*CRED*) and broad money (*M2*).[15] In integrated financial markets monetary policy cannot control interest rates and exchange rates simultaneously, without the use of another instrument

– capital controls. Controls on capital inflows are intended to keep a strong currency from becoming stronger. Controls on capital outflows are intended to support a weak currency. The imposition of capital controls allows the authorities to pursue 'inconsistent' monetary policies for a while.[16] Consequently, high (low) levels of *INF*, *CRED* and *M2* may indicate the increased presence of capital export (import) controls.

## (2) Fiscal determinants of capital controls
We conjecture that the ratio of general government deficits to gross domestic product (*DEF*) may be a relevant indicator for the intensity of capital controls. Capital controls may help to smooth and/or delay necessary internal adjustments to outside pressures. Governments with large budget deficits relative to gross domestic product are expected to impose more capital export restrictions to preserve the tax base.

## (3) Political determinants of capital controls
Possible political determinants of capital controls are the proxy for the political leaning of the government (*LEFT*) and the proxy for the political instability of countries (*SIGGOV*). Left-wing governments are hypothesized to favour the taxation of capital income over that of labour income. They are tempted to introduce capital controls to prevent capital export to maintain a large domestic tax base for capital levies (Alesina et al., 1994). We introduce the dummy variable *LEFT*, taking the value 1 when a left-wing government is in place and the value 0 otherwise (see Appendix 5A1). Our dummy variable *LEFT* corresponds to the one constructed by Milesi-Ferretti (1995) and Grilli and Milesi-Ferretti (1995).[17] However, note that left-wing governments may conduct perfectly right-wing policies. Further, note that the dummy variable *LEFT* does not distinguish between weakly and strongly left governments. Both weakly and strongly left governments take the value 1 in the dummy variable *LEFT*. The construction of a strongly *LEFT* dummy variable would have led to too many zero entries. Of course, future research should construct an index variable to account for different intensities of left-wing governments. Furthermore, we expect political unstable countries to have more capital export restrictions. We proxy the political instability of countries with the frequency of significant government changes (*SIGGOV*) as constructed by De Haan and Van 't Hag (1995) (see Appendix 5A1).[18] Inflation tax and seigniorage revenue are positively related to the instability of the government. Countries with more unstable governments rely more on inflation tax and seigniorage revenue as opposed to income taxation as source of revenue (Grilli, Masciandaro and Tabellini, 1991 and Cukierman, Edwards and Tabellini, 1992). Consequently, the inflation tax and seigniorage revenue argument for capital export controls is also captured by the political instability variable.[19]

## (4) Institutional determinants of capital controls

Possible institutional determinants of capital controls are the proxy for the independence of the central bank ($ES$) and the proxy for the flexibility of the exchange rate arrangement ($EXR$). The incentive of the government to impose capital controls depends on the degree of control the government has over monetary policy. The control the government acquires over monetary policy depends (among other things) on the degree of independence of the central bank. We employ the Eijffinger–Schaling index ($ES$) of central bank independence, since it is available for all EU countries considered (see Appendix 5A1).[20] For the Eijffinger–Schaling index, the following rule applies: the higher the score ranging from 1 to 5, the more independent the central bank. Thus, we hypothesize the less independent the central bank the more capital export controls are expected to be in place. Ensuing, we argue that countries participating in less flexible exchange rate arrangements are more inclined to use either capital import or capital export controls. Of course, the ultimate objective of capital controls further depends on the direction of capital flows. To that end, we construct an index variable $EXR$ of exchange rate flexibility taking the value of 2 during periods of minimal flexibility, that is the exchange rate flexibility is limited in terms of a cooperative arrangement under mutual intervention arrangements (the 'snake' or EMS), 1 during periods of intermediate flexibility, that is, the exchange rate is maintained within relatively narrow margins in terms of a single currency (DM or US dollar) or a composite of currencies (ECU)), and the value of 0 during periods of maximal flexibility (that is, more flexible arrangements) (see Appendix 5A1). Our index variable $EXR$ differs from the dummy variable $EXR$ constructed by Alesina et al. (1994) where periods of minimal and intermediate flexibility take the value 1 and periods with maximal flexibility take the value 0.

## (5) Structural determinants of capital controls

Relevant *financial* structure arguments for capital controls are the ratio of general government debt to gross domestic product ($DEBT$) and the ratio of broad money ($M2$) over narrow money ($M1$) ($M2M1$). Relevant *economic* structure arguments for capital controls are the ratio of current account balance to gross domestic product ($CA$), the unemployment rate ($UN$), the productivity in the business sector ($PROD$), the ratio of gross fixed capital formation to gross domestic product ($GCF$) and the openness of the economy ($OPEN$). Some structural determinants of capital controls may actually apply more to long-term capital flows. So, in the empirical analysis we should find them to be less significant. The structure and regulation of the domestic financial system is at the heart of the use of capital controls. The rationale for capital controls and regulation of domestic financial markets basically results from the desire to avoid systemic risk. Governments with large proportions of gross debt relative to gross domestic product (*DEBT*) are expected to impose more capital export controls. In addition, we hypothesize that countries with less-developed financial markets typically impose more capital export controls. Less-developed financial markets are characterized by relatively low ratios of broad money (*M2*) over narrow money (*M1*) (*M2M1*). That is, the development of more sophisticated deposit instruments is relatively low.[21] Countries typically have implemented capital controls measures to facilitate the financing of current account deficits (*CA*). We expect countries with large current account deficits (surpluses) to impose capital export (import) restrictions. Note however, that countries generally show asymmetric behaviour with respect to targeting the current account: capital export restrictions with current account deficits, no capital import restrictions with current account surpluses. Another argument for capital controls is derived from possible differences between private and social returns. This argument has been used particularly in relation to direct foreign investment. The OECD (1990b, p. 26) argues: 'Whereas a private investor will invest abroad if the after-tax return from foreign assets is higher than the domestic return, the social return to the home country of the investment may be less than that of a domestic investment since the employment, production and tax-revenue benefits accrue to the host country'. Capital controls can be used to retain domestic savings at home by reducing the return on foreign assets and by limiting access to foreign assets. Thus, capital export controls may help to raise investment in the domestic economy and, hence, economic growth. A relevant indicator for the private return is the productivity in the business sector (*PROD*). The productivity in the business sector reflects the attractiveness of domestic financial markets as the potential location of foreign capital. It provides an indication of the direction of capital flows and, hence, for the objective of capital controls. Low productivity of the business sector may be an influential argument for restricting capital exports. A relevant indicator for investment is the ratio of gross fixed capital formation over gross domestic product (*GCF*). The lower (higher) *GCF*, the lower (higher) collateral for the loan, the higher (lower) the interest rate, the less (more) capital export restrictions are expected to be in place. With relatively closed financial markets, domestic investors are obliged to invest in the domestic economy. The unemployment rate (*UN*) may be a relevant indicator of social costs. With relatively high unemployment rates more capital export restrictions are expected to be in place. Another relevant indicator of capital controls may follow from the openness of the economy (*OPEN*). With high openness capital controls are less effective, so they are less likely imposed. On the other hand, one may argue, with high openness capital controls may shield the economy from foreign competition, so they are more likely imposed. The correct argument still has to be decided upon.

Now, we turn to the estimation of the model. Using a pooled cross-section time-series regression model, the following general specification for closed interest differentials can be postulated. The expected signs of the parameters are shown in parentheses under the variables. The subscript $i$ represents the countries in our sample $(i = 1, \ldots, N)$ and the subscript $t$ is the time subscript $(t = 1, \ldots, T)$.

$$(i - i^{Euro})_{i,t} = f\,[\,C, INF, CRED, M2, DEF, LEFT, SIGGOV, ES, EXR, \ldots,$$
$$\phantom{(i - i^{Euro})_{i,t} = f\,[\,} (-)\ (-)\ (-)\ (-)\ (-)\ \quad (-)\ \quad (+)\ (?)$$

$$DEBT, M2M1, CA, UN, PROD, GCF, OPEN\,]_{i,t} + \varepsilon_{i,t} \qquad (5.5)$$
$$(-)\ \ (+)\ \ (+)(-)\ \ (+)\ \ (-)\ \ (?)$$

Symbols:

| | | |
|---|---|---|
| $(i - i^{Euro})$ | = | closed nominal interest rate differential |
| $C$ | = | constant term |
| $INF$ | = | inflation rate |
| $CRED$ | = | total domestic credit to the economy as percentage of gross domestic product |
| $M2$ | = | broad money as percentage of gross domestic product |
| $DEF$ | = | general government deficit as percentage of gross domestic product |
| $LEFT$ | = | proxy for the political leaning of the government |
| $SIGGOV$ | = | proxy for government instability |
| $ES$ | = | Eijffinger–Schaling index of central bank independence |
| $EXR$ | = | proxy for the flexibility of the exchange rate arrangement |
| $DEBT$ | = | general government gross debt as percentage of gross domestic product |
| $M2M1$ | = | ratio of broad money over narrow money |
| $CA$ | = | current account balance as percentage of gross domestic product |
| $UN$ | = | unemployment rate |
| $PROD$ | = | productivity in the business sector |
| $GCF$ | = | gross fixed capital formation as percentage of gross domestic product |
| $OPEN$ | = | openness of the economy |
| $\varepsilon$ | = | a normally distributed error term with zero mean and constant variance $(\varepsilon \sim N(0, \sigma_\varepsilon^2))$ and the regressors are completely independent of the error term. |

The intention was to use publicly available data sources (see Appendix 5A1).

The frequency of the data was dictated by the absence of higher frequency data on important macroeconomic determinants of financial integration and by the fact that we want to evaluate long-term trends in financial integration. To overcome problems of multicollinearity, we apply a 'bottom-up' approach. First, we start with the inclusion of monetary policy determinants of capital controls. Then, we add fiscal policy determinants and test whether the explanatory power of the regression improves significantly (Wald test), and so forth. We average the country time-series for five-year periods (1974–1978, 1979–1983, 1984–1988, 1989–1993) to avoid multicollinearity problems endemic to such time-series. Furthermore, it removes the problem of cyclical biases in some of the right-hand variables (for example, the cyclical variations in government deficits). The sample contains 43 observations (one observation is lost due to the lack of forward exchange rate data for Italy over the period 1974–1976). The OLS results are reported in Table 5.2. Furthermore, Table 5.2 also reports various diagnostic tests. In each case the models pass the diagnostic tests.

Which determinants do best in explaining closed interest differentials? From Table 5.2 it can immediately be seen that only three variables are significantly related to the intensity of capital controls: the realized inflation rate (*INF*), the frequency of significant government changes (*SIGGOV*) and gross fixed capital formation (*GCF*). The other variables are not found to be significant.

The regressions show that the realized inflation rate (*INF*) significantly explains the presence of capital export restriction in the EU (regression (1)). By now, considerable agreement exists across studies (Alesina et al., 1994 and Milesi-Ferretti, 1995) that inflation critically rationalizes the presence of capital export controls (compare the magnitude of the estimated coefficients). Giavazzi and Giovannini (1989) have argued that in the beginning of the EMS the maintenance of capital controls was an essential feature of the functioning of the EMS. In integrated financial markets monetary policy cannot control interest rates and exchange rates simultaneously, without the use of another instrument – capital controls. If the authorities of weak currency countries wish to avoid or delay the realignment they will be obliged to raise the domestic interest rates to make investors indifferent to the choice between holding domestic and foreign assets. However, high interest rates are frequently undesirable for domestic reasons (economic growth, debt burden). Restrictions on capital export, then, may (temporarily) sustain the pressure for the domestic interest rate to rise. Capital controls (temporarily) prevent or discourage speculative capital outflows. Foreigners engaged in speculative transactions will now turn to the offshore markets, creating large offshore–onshore interest rate differentials (see Wyplosz, 1988, p. 95).

In regression (6) strong evidence is found for the intensity capital controls to depend negatively (that is, capital export controls are more likely) on the instability of the government as measured by the frequency of significant government changes (*SIGGOV*). In the years 1992 and 1993 relatively large closed interest differentials occurred in Denmark, Italy, Spain, Sweden and the United Kingdom despite complete removal of capital controls in the EMS countries as from 1 July 1990. With respect to Spain these deviations probably reflected the temporary reintroduction of capital controls while with respect to the other countries political risks such as fear of renewed introduction of capital controls have contributed to such deviations.

Left-wing governments (*LEFT*) are found to impose more capital export controls (regression (5)). However, analogous to Alesina et al. (1994) and Milesi-Ferretti (1995) the relationship between *LEFT* and the proxy for the intensity of capital controls is not significant. No evidence is found for justifying an important role for fiscal (*DEF*) and institutional determinants (*ES* and *EXR*) of capital controls. Probably, realized inflation and government instability may perfectly account for this result. Countries with high inflation rates and unstable governments are often associated with high government deficit and debt ratios. Furthermore, countries with high inflation rates and unstable governments are known to have less independent central banks, and to have more frequent exchange rate changes (devaluations).

Regression (14) in Table 5.2 gives a satisfactory explanation of closed interest differentials in the EU. In particular, realized inflation, government instability and gross fixed capital formation (a proxy for investment) are shown to have a strong and significant influence on closed interest differentials in the EU. The coefficient with respect to gross fixed capital formation (*GCF*) is correctly signed and moderately significant. Importantly, this variable was not included in previous research by Alesina et al. (1994). Capital export controls increase the domestic supply of capital and consequently lower the domestic interest rate.

Finally, we should mention some critical measurement issues. First, the relationship between the intensity of capital controls and its explanatory variables is often subject to uncertainty. The finding of no significant association with the intensity of capital controls may simply reflect the crudeness of the measured dependent and independent variables and/or the loss of information due to the use of five-year averages. Second, controls on capital outflows may also reduce capital inflows, as foreign investors worry about their ability to transfer income outside the country. Furthermore, a country may impose both capital import as well as capital export restrictions. These aspects of capital controls are difficult to grasp. Lastly, future research may want to consider closed interest parity for long-term bonds (calculated with the help of interest rate swaps) as it is unclear if the results go through in financial assets with maturities of say more than one year (see Chapter 6).

Table 5.2  The fundamental determinants of capital controls in the EU: empirical results

$$(i - i^{Euro})_{i,t} = f[C, INF, CRED, M2, DEF, LEFT, SIGGOV, ES, EXR, DEBT, M2M1, CA, UN, PROD, GCF, OPEN]_{i,t} + \varepsilon_{i,t}$$

| | (1) | (2) | (3) | (4) | (5) | (6) | (7) | (8) | (9) | (10) | (11) | (12) | (13) | (14) | (15) |
|---|---|---|---|---|---|---|---|---|---|---|---|---|---|---|---|
| C | 1.42 (3.76) | 1.76 (1.72) | 1.27 (1.32) | 1.19 (2.80) | 1.52 (3.35) | 2.00 (4.38) | 2.08 (2.33) | 2.00 (3.25) | 1.46 (2.40) | 2.89 (3.96) | 2.06 (4.51) | 1.62 (0.48) | -1.87 (0.59) | 4.31 (3.07) | 4.70 (2.87) |
| INF | -0.31* (6.48) | -0.32* (5.79) | -0.31* (6.25) | -0.31* (6.45) | -0.31* (6.38) | -0.31* (6.79) | -0.31* (5.87) | -0.31* (6.29) | -0.29* (5.77) | -0.33* (7.07) | -0.34* (6.62) | -0.30* (6.02) | -0.24* (3.27) | -0.28* (5.99) | -0.29* (5.79) |
| CRED | | -0.003 (0.35) | | | | | | | | | | | | | |
| M2 | | | 0.002 (0.18) | | | | | | | | | | | | |
| DEF | | | | -0.07 (1.23) | | | | | | | | | | | |
| LEFT | | | | | -0.18 (0.40) | | | | | | | | | | |
| SIGGOV | | | | | | -0.24* (2.10) | -0.24* (2.06) | -0.24* (1.82) | -0.30* (2.47) | -0.27* (2.35) | -0.22* (1.93) | -0.25* (2.53) | -0.26* (2.66) | -0.21* (1.84) | -0.19 (1.62) |
| ES | | | | | | | -0.02 (0.11) | | | | | | | | |
| EXR | | | | | | | | -0.00003 (0.0001) | | | | | | | |
| DEBT | | | | | | | | | 0.01 (1.31) | | | | | | |
| M2M1 | | | | | | | | | | -0.22 (1.55) | | | | | |

| | (1) | (2) | (3) | (4) | (5) | (6) | (7) | (8) | (9) | (10) | (11) | (12) | (13) | (14) | (15) |
|---|---|---|---|---|---|---|---|---|---|---|---|---|---|---|---|
| CA | | | | | | | | | | | 0.12 (1.15) | | | | |
| UN | | | | | | | | | | | | 0.05 (1.06) | | | |
| PROD | | | | | | | | | | | | | 0.04 (1.23) | | |
| GCF | | | | | | | | | | | | | | −0.12* (1.74) | −0.13* (1.78) |
| OPEN | | | | | | | | | | | | | | | −0.004 (0.48) |
| S.E. | 1.24 | 1.25 | 1.25 | 1.23 | 1.25 | 1.19 | 1.20 | 1.20 | 1.18 | 1.17 | 1.18 | 1.19 | 1.18 | 1.16 | 1.17 |
| ARCH(1) | 0.02 (0.87) | 0.006 (0.93) | 0.04 (0.85) | 0.19 (0.67) | 0.02 (0.89) | 0.007 (0.93) | 0.01 (0.92) | 0.007 (0.93) | 0.03 (0.86) | 0.09 (0.76) | 0.11 (0.74) | 0.0004 (0.98) | 0.0004 (0.98) | 0.30 (0.58) | 0.38 (0.54) |
| $\bar{R}^2$ | 0.49 | 0.48 | 0.48 | 0.50 | 0.48 | 0.53 | 0.52 | 0.52 | 0.54 | 0.55 | 0.54 | 0.53 | 0.54 | 0.55 | 0.55 |
| N | 43 | 43 | 43 | 43 | 43 | 43 | 43 | 43 | 43 | 43 | 43 | 43 | 43 | 43 | 43 |

*Notes:* S.E. is the standard error of the regression, $ARCH(1)$ is the Engle (1982) Lagrange Multiplier test for first order Autoregressive Conditional Heteroscedasticity ($\chi^2(1)$ distribution, probability values between parentheses), $\bar{R}^2$ is the coefficient of determination adjusted for degrees of freedom, $N$ is the number of usable observations and * indicates that the coefficient is significantly different from zero at the 95 per cent level of confidence (one-tailed test).

Absolute t-statistics are indicated between parentheses.

*Source:* See Appendix 5A1.

## 5.4    Conclusions

The estimates show that realized inflation, government instability and gross fixed capital formation can provide a reasonable explanation of closed interest differentials in the EU. Realized inflation clearly tends to exert the strongest influence on closed interest differentials, followed by government instability and gross fixed capital formation. Apparently, the most important implication of increased financial integration is that it forces a greater degree of interest rate parity across countries, and that it reduces the scope for independent monetary policy. After allowing for realized inflation, remaining differentials from closed interest parity may be explained by political risks imposed by the international financial community on particular countries. These political risks are basically attributed to political instability approximated by the number of significant government changes.

Furthermore, we would like to emphasize that government deficits, current account deficits and the productivity in the business sector are correctly signed but insignificantly related to closed interest differentials. Therefore, the adverse effect of inconsistent monetary and fiscal policies with concomitant large government deficits, current account deficits and low productivity in the business sector may be of some importance in explaining the intensity of capital controls in the long run.

In accordance with Alesina et al. (1994), we find capital export controls to be more likely in countries with high inflation rates and significant government changes. In contrast with them, we also find gross fixed capital formation to be a relevant determinant of capital control intensity. Capital export controls increase the domestic supply of capital and consequently lower the domestic interest rate. Furthermore, this chapter emphasizes the importance of closed interest differentials to measure the intensity of capital controls which enables us to distinguish between restrictions to limit capital outflows and restrictions to limit capital inflows (that is, the direction of capital flows). Finally, we want to highlight the impact of (differences in) national economic and financial structures on financial integration. With capital controls increasingly being eliminated, we expect the underlying characteristics of economic and especially financial market structure to become increasingly important for the determination of closed interest rate differentials in the future. Monetary and fiscal policy in the EU are expected to become increasingly dependent on varying economic and financial structures, rather than on financial integration.

# Notes

1. The concepts of 'financial integration' and 'intensity of capital controls' are used interchangeably.

2. Lamfalussy (1990, p. 20) argues: '(...) in order to prevent the emergence of major exchange rate misalignments policy action has to be directed towards the causes of capital movements or, more precisely, towards what market participants believe to be fundamentals'. This argument is also demonstrated by the events during the exchange crises in the EMS.

3. Besides, long time-series data on the volume of gross capital flows are not available (see Kouri and Porter, 1974).

4. Clearly, evasion of controls increases over time as agents learn to set up escape routes, so the intensity of capital controls may decline over time.

5. Jorion and Schwartz (1986, p. 604) argue: 'Documenting barriers to investment is not sufficient to prove segmentation, since prices are determined by marginal investors who may find innovative ways to get around controls'.

6. Therefore, Milesi-Ferretti (1995) and Grilli and Milesi-Ferretti (1995) use a current account restrictions dummy variable to proxy for the intensity of capital controls.

7. Although currency swaps allow us to calculate deviations from covered interest rate parity for longer horizons, they are not available over a sufficiently long time horizon (see Popper, 1993).

8. Preferably, one might also want to disentangle the effect of nonresident interest rate withholding taxation. Interest withholding taxes importantly affect the pre-tax gross return demanded by international investors. Huizinga (1994) adjusts the interest rate parity condition for the effect of nonresident interest withholding taxation. Since the effects of interest rate withholding taxation are difficult to grasp, we discuss this aspect in Chapter 6.

9. More precisely, capital controls that are economically significant – thus lying outside a small band of differentials created by transaction costs.

10. This reasoning applies to both direct or quantitative measures (consisting of outright restrictions or prohibitions of certain capital transactions) and indirect or cost measures (affecting the operations of the banking and nonbanking sector). Of course, with indirect capital controls cross-border capital flows are still possible. Numerous qualitative studies exist that describe the introduction and workings of capital control measures.

11. The price measure may be more informative about country-specific regulation using Treasury bill rates with the same default risks. Unfortunately, Treasury bill rates are unavailable for all EU countries considered, or the depth of the Treasury bill market is low (see Cumby and Obstfeld, 1984, p. 132 and Appendix 5A1).

12. Data for Germany refer to the Federal Republic of Germany before the unification of Germany.

13. These analytical indicators are partly justified by previous findings of Alesina et al. (1994).

14. Several authors have dealt with the issue of the rationales for capital controls (see, for example, Cairncross, 1973, OECD, 1980, 1990b, Bank for International Settlements, 1990, 1994, Goldstein, Mathieson and Lane, 1991, Bacchetta, 1993 and Mathieson and Rojas-Suarez, 1993, 1994). See also Knot (1996) on the issue of the fundamental determinants of interest differentials in the EMS.

15. Since related attributes such as the inflation tax and seigniorage revenue are strongly positively correlated with the inflation rate, they are not included in the analysis. Similarly, the depreciation of the exchange rate is not included in the analysis since it is highly positively correlated with the inflation rate. In addition, the depreciation of the exchange rate is less well suited since it also involves foreign policy behaviour.

16. The OECD (1990a, p. 23) argues: 'Thus, exchange controls have been often viewed as a means whereby the authorities may seek to insulate, at least temporarily, domestic credit expansion from monetary developments abroad and increase the autonomy with which the supply of money can be steered to influence domestic objectives'. See also the articles of Eichengreen, Tobin and Wyplosz (1995, pp. 162–72), Garber and Taylor (1995, pp. 173–80) and Kenen (1995, pp. 181–92) written for the January 1995 *Economic Journal* Policy Forum on 'Sand in the Wheels of International Finance'.

17. Alesina et al. (1994) construct an index variable taking the value −1 when a left-wing government is in power and +1 when a right-wing government is in power.

18. Of course, future research may want to address other indicators for political instability such as *MAJOR* (that is, a majority government is in power) and *DURA* (that is, the average number of years in power of the executive during the sample period) (see Alesina et al., 1994). Other political instability variables proposed by Milesi-Ferretti (1995) such as *COUP* (that is, the number of successful coups during the sample period) and *NODEM* (that is, the government is non-democratic) are less relevant in the EU. Siermann (1996) constructs an excellent data-set of indicators to proxy for the democratic character of a country and its level of political instability.

19. The Grilli, Masciandaro and Tabellini (1991) index of significant government changes gives similar results. However, this index is not available for Finland and Sweden.

20. Cukierman's legal index (*LVAU*) of central bank independence which is also available for all EU countries in our sample gives similar results. The Grilli, Masciandaro and Tabellini (1991) total (economic and political) index of central bank independence also gives similar results. However, this index is not available for all EU countries. The same holds for the Alesina (1988, 1989) legal indices of central bank independence.

21. Unfortunately, it is rather difficult to find relevant indicators of financial market structure. Due to data availability, we had to employ rather crude measures of financial market structure. Of course, there are more relevant indicators such as the market share of the five largest banks, or the number of bank branches per 100,000 inhabitants. Goodhart (1993), King and Levine (1993), Mooslechner (1994) and Cottarelli and Kourelis (1994) examine many other aspects of financial market structure.

# Appendix 5A1: Data Sources

*The dependent variable*

| Variable | Countries |
|---|---|
| $\phi_{Domestic}^{Year} = \dfrac{\displaystyle\sum_{j=1}^{j=12} [i_{t,t+3} - i_{t,t+3}^{Euro}]_j}{12}$ | Germany, France, The Netherlands, United Kingdom. |
| $\xi_{Domestic}^{Year} = \dfrac{\displaystyle\sum_{j=1}^{j=12} [i_{t,t+3} - i_{t,t+3}^{*Euro} - (f_t^{t+3} - s_t)]_j}{12}$ | Austria, Belgium, Denmark, Finland, Italy, Spain, Sweden. |

---

### Representative three-month Euro money market interest rates

Representative three-month Euro money market interest rates are available for the following EU countries: Germany, France, The Netherlands and the United Kingdom (monthly series). Three-month Euro DM interest rates are used to calculate the adjusted domestic covered nominal interest rate differentials.

*Source:* OECD, *Financial Statistics Monthly*, Part I.

---

### Representative three-month domestic money market interest rates

Finding consistent comparable interest rate data for the EU countries under consideration is far from easy. To the extent possible, given data availability over long sample periods, we tried to use publicly available representative three-month money market interest rates (monthly series). The integration of one segment of the money market, that is taking one asset among many, may give a misleading impression of the overall short-term mobility of capital. This problem may partly be overcome by the use of representative short-term interest rates. Quoting the OECD (1990c, p. 45): '(...) the aim has not necessarily been to take the same rate for all countries, but to choose the rates which are the most typical or the most revealing, or again, those which may be described as the "reference" rates. In drawing up the following norms, while attention has, of course, been given to ensuring as much international comparability as possible, it has nevertheless been necessary to have regard for the fact that the methods of calculation used by countries to some extent reflect the institutional features of their financial markets'.

| Country | Period | Description | Source |
|---|---|---|---|
| Austria | January 1974–December 1993 | Three-month vibor | OECD, Financial Statistics Monthly, Part I |
| Belgium | January 1974–December 1993 | Three-month Treasury bills | OECD, Financial Statistics Monthly, Part I |
| Denmark | January 1974–December 1975 | Central bank deposit certificates | OECD, Financial Statistics Monthly, Part I |
| | January 1976–December 1993 | Three-month interbank rate | OECD, Main Economic Indicators |
| Finland | January 1974–April 1987 | Average cost of central bank financing | OECD, Financial Statistics Monthly, Part I |
| | May 1987–December 1993 | Three-month helibor | OECD, Financial Statistics Monthly, Part I |
| France | January 1974–December 1993 | Three-month pibor | OECD, Financial Statistics Monthly, Part I |

| Germany | January 1974–December 1993 | Three-month fibor | OECD, Financial Statistics Monthly, Part I |
|---|---|---|---|
| Italy | January 1974–December 1993 | Three-month Treasury bills | OECD, Financial Statistics Monthly, Part I |
| The Netherlands | January 1974–December 1985 | Three-month loans to local authorities | OECD, Financial Statistics Monthly, Part I |
| | January 1986–December 1993 | Three-month aibor | OECD, Financial Statistics Monthly, Part I |
| Spain | January 1974–December 1976 | Short-term credits up to three months | OECD, Financial Statistics Monthly, Part I |
| | January 1977–December 1993 | Three-month interbank loans | OECD, Financial Statistics Monthly, Part I |
| Sweden | January 1974–December 1981 | Three-month Treasury bills | OECD, Financial Statistics Monthly, Part I |
| | January 1982–December 1993 | Three-month discount notes | OECD, Financial Statistics Monthly, Part I |
| United Kingdom | January 1974–December 1993 | Three-month interbank rate | OECD, Financial Statistics Monthly, Part I |

---

### Three-month forward exchange rates *vis-à-vis* the DM

The following are our own cross-rate calculations of forward exchange rates of EU currencies *vis-à-vis* the DM based upon end-of-period three-month forward exchange rates *vis-à-vis* the US dollar (monthly series). The forward exchange rates are expressed as premiums (+) and discounts (–) on the forward value of the currency relative to its spot price. Defining the spot rate as currency units per US dollar, the formula for the forward premium on the currency in per cent per annum is:

$$\frac{(S_t - F_t^{t+3}) \times 4 \times 100}{S_t}$$

The annualized forward premium or discount is based on a 360-day year, and the three-month forward rate is the rate for 90 days, yielding the factor 4 that is employed in the formula. Since direct DM forward (and spot) exchange rates are not available for all EU countries considered and/or over a sufficiently long period, we used cross-rate calculations of forward and spot exchange rates of EU currencies *vis-à-vis* the DM based upon forward exchange rates *vis-à-vis* the US dollar. Concerning these cross-rate calculations, we already *presume* in the investigation design perfect capital mobility. However, this is only possible on the basis of the assumption of perfect arbitrage between markets of foreign exchange. Due to transactions costs in triangular arbitrage, cross-rate calculations do not exactly correspond to direct quotations. In constructing DM forward and spot exchange rates, dollar cross-rate calculations are preferred because of the reserve currency status of the dollar, the role of the dollar as the world's major intervention currency and the scale and efficiency of the US financial markets. Forward exchange rates for Italy are only available from January 1977 onwards.

*Sources:* IMF (1985) and IMF, *International Financial Statistics*, line 60f.

---

### Spot exchange rates *vis-à-vis* the DM

Own cross-rate calculations of spot exchange rates of EU countries *vis-à-vis* the DM based upon end-of-period spot exchange rates *vis-à-vis* the US dollar (monthly series).

*Source:* IMF, International Financial Statistics, line ae.

## The independent variables

| Indica-tor | Description | Source |
|---|---|---|
| CA | Current account balance as percentage of gross domestic product | OECD, *National Accounts, Main Aggregates*, Volume I, 1960–1993 |
| CRED | Total domestic credit to the economy as percentage of gross domestic product | IMF, *IFS Yearbook 1994*, line 32 |
| DEBT | General government gross debt as percentage of gross domestic product | OECD, *Economic Outlook*, No. 55 |
| EXR | Variable indicating exchange rate flexibility, 2 minimal flexibility, 1 intermediate flexibility and 0 maximal flexibility | IMF, *Exchange Restrictions*, Annual Report, 1974–1978. IMF, *Exchange Arrangements and Exchange Restrictions*, Annual Report, 1979–1993 |
| ES | Eijffinger–Schaling index of central bank independence (ranges from 1 minimal independence to 5 maximal independence) | Eijffinger and Schaling (1993), Eijffinger and Van Keulen (1995) |
| DEF | General government financial balance (government net lending) as percentage of gross domestic product | OECD, *Economic Outlook*, No. 55 |
| GCF | Gross fixed capital formation as percentage of gross domestic product | IMF, *IFS Yearbook 1994*, line 93e |
| GDP | Gross domestic product | OECD, *National Accounts, Main Aggregates*, Volume I, 1960–1993 |
| M1 | Money as percentage of gross domestic product | IMF, *IFS Yearbook 1994*, line 34 |
| M2 | Money plus quasi-money as percentage of gross domestic product | IMF, *IFS Yearbook 1994*, lines 34 (money) and 35 (quasi-money) |
| M2M1 | Money plus quasi-money over money | IMF, *IFS Yearbook 1994*, lines 34 (money) and 35 (quasi-money) |
| INF | Rate of change in the consumer price index (1990=100) | IMF, *International Financial Statistics*, line 64 |
| LEFT | Dummy variable, taking the value 1 when a left-wing government is in place and the value 0 otherwise | Banks (1993) |
| OPEN | Openness of the economy = export of goods and services plus imports of goods and services over gross domestic product | OECD, *National Accounts, Main Aggregates*, Volume I, 1960–1993 |
| PROD | Index of productivity in the business sector (1987=100) | OECD, *Economic Outlook*, No. 55 |
| SIGGOV | Total number of significant government changes, measure for political instability | De Haan and Van 't Hag (1995) |
| UN | Unemployment rate | OECD, *Economic Outlook*, No. 55 |

## Eijffinger–Schaling index of central bank independence (ES)

| | AUS | BEL | DEN | FIN | FRA | GER | ITA | NET | SPA | SWE | UK |
|---|---|---|---|---|---|---|---|---|---|---|---|
| ES | 3 | 3 | 4 | 3 | 2 | 5 | 2 | 4 | 1 | 2 | 2 |

*Sources:* Eijffinger and Schaling (1993) and Eijffinger and Van Keulen (1995).

*The Determination of Financial Integration*

*De Haan–Van 't Hag index of significant government changes (SIGGOV)*

|        | AUS | BEL | DEN | FIN | FRA | GER | ITA | NET | SPA | SWE | UK |
|--------|-----|-----|-----|-----|-----|-----|-----|-----|-----|-----|-----|
| *SIGGOV* | 2 | 4 | 1 | 3 | 4 | 1 | 6 | 3 | 1 | 2 | 0 |

*Source:* De Haan and Van 't Hag (1995).

*Exchange Rate Arrangements (EXR): minimal flexibility (2), intermediate flexibility (1) and maximal flexibility (0)*

| EXR | AUS | BEL | DEN | FIN | FRA | GER | ITA | NET | SPA | SWE | UK | TOTAL |
|-----|-----|-----|-----|-----|-----|-----|-----|-----|-----|-----|-----|-------|
| 1974 | 1 | 2 | 2 | 1 | 0 | 2 | 0 | 2 | 2 | 2 | 0 | **14** |
| 1975 | 1 | 2 | 2 | 1 | 0 | 2 | 0 | 2 | 1 | 2 | 0 | **13** |
| 1976 | 1 | 2 | 2 | 1 | 2 | 2 | 0 | 2 | 1 | 2 | 0 | **15** |
| 1977 | 1 | 2 | 2 | 1 | 0 | 2 | 0 | 2 | 1 | 2 | 0 | **13** |
| 1978 | 1 | 2 | 2 | 1 | 2 | 2 | 0 | 2 | 1 | 1 | 0 | **14** |
| 1979 | 1 | 2 | 2 | 1 | 2 | 2 | 2 | 2 | 0 | 1 | 0 | **15** |
| 1980 | 1 | 2 | 2 | 1 | 2 | 2 | 2 | 2 | 0 | 1 | 0 | **15** |
| 1981 | 1 | 2 | 2 | 1 | 2 | 2 | 2 | 2 | 0 | 1 | 0 | **15** |
| 1982 | 1 | 2 | 2 | 1 | 2 | 2 | 2 | 2 | 0 | 1 | 0 | **15** |
| 1983 | 1 | 2 | 2 | 1 | 2 | 2 | 2 | 2 | 0 | 1 | 0 | **15** |
| 1984 | 1 | 2 | 2 | 1 | 2 | 2 | 2 | 2 | 0 | 1 | 0 | **15** |
| 1985 | 1 | 2 | 2 | 1 | 2 | 2 | 2 | 2 | 0 | 1 | 0 | **15** |
| 1986 | 1 | 2 | 2 | 1 | 2 | 2 | 2 | 2 | 0 | 1 | 0 | **15** |
| 1987 | 1 | 2 | 2 | 1 | 2 | 2 | 2 | 2 | 0 | 1 | 0 | **15** |
| 1988 | 1 | 2 | 2 | 1 | 2 | 2 | 2 | 2 | 0 | 1 | 0 | **15** |
| 1989 | 1 | 2 | 2 | 1 | 2 | 2 | 2 | 2 | 0 | 1 | 0 | **15** |
| 1990 | 1 | 2 | 2 | 1 | 2 | 2 | 2 | 2 | 1 | 1 | 0 | **16** |
| 1991 | 1 | 2 | 2 | 1 | 2 | 2 | 2 | 2 | 1 | 1 | 2 | **18** |
| 1992 | 1 | 2 | 2 | 1 | 2 | 2 | 2 | 2 | 1 | 1 | 2 | **18** |
| 1993 | 1 | 2 | 2 | 0 | 2 | 2 | 0 | 2 | 1 | 0 | 0 | **12** |
| **TOTAL** | **20** | **40** | **40** | **19** | **34** | **40** | **28** | **40** | **10** | **23** | **4** | |

*Sources:* Index constructed with the help of IMF, *Exchange Restrictions*, Annual Report, 1974–1978 and IMF, *Exchange Arrangements and Exchange Restrictions*, Annual Report, 1979–1993.

*Political leaning of the government (LEFT): left-wing government (1), right-wing government (0)*

| LEFT | AUS | BEL | DEN | FIN | FRA | GER | ITA | NET | SPA | SWE | UK | TOTAL |
|------|-----|-----|-----|-----|-----|-----|-----|-----|-----|-----|-----|-------|
| 1974 | 1 | 0 | 1 | 1 | 0 | 1 | 1 | 1 | 0 | 1 | 1 | 8 |
| 1975 | 1 | 0 | 1 | 1 | 0 | 1 | 0 | 1 | 0 | 1 | 1 | 7 |
| 1976 | 1 | 0 | 1 | 1 | 0 | 1 | 0 | 1 | 0 | 1 | 1 | 7 |
| 1977 | 1 | 0 | 1 | 1 | 0 | 1 | 0 | 1 | 0 | 0 | 1 | 6 |
| 1978 | 1 | 0 | 1 | 1 | 0 | 1 | 0 | 0 | 0 | 0 | 1 | 5 |
| 1979 | 1 | 0 | 1 | 1 | 0 | 1 | 1 | 0 | 0 | 0 | 1 | 6 |
| 1980 | 1 | 1 | 1 | 1 | 0 | 1 | 1 | 0 | 0 | 0 | 0 | 6 |
| 1981 | 1 | 1 | 1 | 1 | 1 | 1 | 0 | 1 | 0 | 0 | 0 | 7 |
| 1982 | 1 | 0 | 1 | 1 | 1 | 1 | 0 | 1 | 1 | 1 | 0 | 8 |
| 1983 | 1 | 0 | 0 | 1 | 1 | 0 | 1 | 0 | 1 | 1 | 0 | 6 |
| 1984 | 1 | 0 | 0 | 1 | 1 | 0 | 1 | 0 | 1 | 1 | 0 | 6 |
| 1985 | 1 | 0 | 0 | 1 | 1 | 0 | 1 | 0 | 1 | 1 | 0 | 6 |
| 1986 | 1 | 0 | 0 | 1 | 1 | 0 | 1 | 0 | 1 | 1 | 0 | 6 |
| 1987 | 1 | 0 | 0 | 1 | 0 | 0 | 1 | 0 | 1 | 1 | 0 | 5 |
| 1988 | 1 | 1 | 0 | 0 | 1 | 0 | 0 | 0 | 1 | 1 | 0 | 5 |
| 1989 | 1 | 1 | 0 | 0 | 1 | 0 | 0 | 1 | 1 | 1 | 0 | 6 |
| 1990 | 1 | 1 | 0 | 0 | 1 | 0 | 0 | 1 | 1 | 1 | 0 | 6 |
| 1991 | 1 | 1 | 0 | 0 | 1 | 0 | 0 | 1 | 1 | 1 | 0 | 6 |
| 1992 | 1 | 1 | 0 | 0 | 1 | 0 | 0 | 1 | 1 | 1 | 0 | 6 |
| 1993 | 1 | 1 | 0 | 0 | 1 | 0 | 0 | 1 | 1 | 1 | 0 | 6 |
| TOTAL | 20 | 8 | 9 | 14 | 12 | 9 | 8 | 11 | 12 | 15 | 6 | |

*Sources:* Dummy variable constructed with the help of Banks (1993).

## Appendix 5A2: Legal Measures of Capital Controls

*Dummy variable of separate restrictions on payments for capital transactions: if these restrictions are in place, the variable takes the value of 1, and 0 otherwise*

| CONTROL 1 | AUS | BEL | DEN | FIN | FRA | GER | ITA | NET | SPA | SWE | UK | TOTAL |
|---|---|---|---|---|---|---|---|---|---|---|---|---|
| 1974 | 1 | 0 | 1 | 1 | 1 | 0 | 1 | 1 | 1 | 1 | 1 | 9 |
| 1975 | 1 | 0 | 1 | 1 | 1 | 0 | 1 | 1 | 1 | 1 | 1 | 9 |
| 1976 | 1 | 0 | 1 | 1 | 1 | 0 | 1 | 1 | 1 | 1 | 1 | 9 |
| 1977 | 1 | 0 | 1 | 1 | 1 | 0 | 1 | 1 | 1 | 1 | 1 | 9 |
| 1978 | 1 | 0 | 1 | 1 | 1 | 0 | 1 | 1 | 1 | 1 | 1 | 8 |
| 1979 | 1 | 0 | 1 | 1 | 1 | 0 | 1 | 0 | 1 | 1 | 1 | 8 |
| 1980 | 1 | 0 | 1 | 1 | 1 | 0 | 1 | 0 | 1 | 1 | 0 | 7 |
| 1981 | 1 | 0 | 1 | 1 | 1 | 0 | 1 | 0 | 1 | 1 | 0 | 7 |
| 1982 | 1 | 0 | 1 | 1 | 1 | 0 | 1 | 0 | 1 | 1 | 0 | 7 |
| 1983 | 1 | 0 | 1 | 1 | 1 | 0 | 1 | 0 | 1 | 1 | 0 | 7 |
| 1984 | 1 | 0 | 1 | 1 | 1 | 0 | 0 | 0 | 1 | 1 | 0 | 6 |
| 1985 | 1 | 0 | 1 | 1 | 1 | 0 | 0 | 0 | 1 | 1 | 0 | 6 |
| 1986 | 1 | 0 | 1 | 1 | 1 | 0 | 0 | 0 | 1 | 1 | 0 | 6 |
| 1987 | 1 | 0 | 1 | 1 | 1 | 0 | 1 | 0 | 1 | 1 | 0 | 7 |
| 1988 | 1 | 0 | 1 | 1 | 1 | 0 | 1 | 0 | 1 | 1 | 0 | 7 |
| 1989 | 1 | 0 | 0 | 1 | 1 | 0 | 1 | 0 | 1 | 1 | 0 | 6 |
| 1990 | 1 | 0 | 0 | 1 | 1 | 0 | 1 | 0 | 1 | 1 | 0 | 6 |
| 1991 | 1 | 0 | 0 | 1 | 1 | 0 | 1 | 0 | 1 | 1 | 0 | 6 |
| 1992 | 0 | 0 | 0 | 0 | 1 | 0 | 1 | 0 | 1 | 1 | 0 | 4 |
| 1993 | 0 | 0 | 0 | 1 | 1 | 0 | 1 | 0 | 1 | 1 | 0 | 5 |
| TOTAL | 18 | 0 | 15 | 19 | 20 | 0 | 17 | 5 | 20 | 20 | 6 | |

*Sources:* International Monetary Fund, *Exchange Restrictions*, 1974–1978 and International Monetary Fund, *Exchange Arrangements and Exchange Restrictions*, Annual Reports, 1979–1993.

*Dummy variable of separate exchange rate(s) for some or all capital transactions and/or some or all invisibles: if these restrictions are in place, the variable takes the value of 1, and 0 otherwise*

| CONTROL 2 | AUS | BEL | DEN | FIN | FRA | GER | ITA | NET | SPA | SWE | UK | TOTAL |
|-----------|-----|-----|-----|-----|-----|-----|-----|-----|-----|-----|-----|-------|
| 1974 | 0 | 1 | 0 | 0 | 1 | 0 | 1 | 1 | 0 | 0 | 1 | 5 |
| 1975 | 0 | 1 | 0 | 0 | 0 | 0 | 1 | 0 | 0 | 0 | 1 | 3 |
| 1976 | 0 | 1 | 0 | 0 | 0 | 0 | 1 | 0 | 0 | 0 | 1 | 3 |
| 1977 | 0 | 1 | 0 | 0 | 0 | 0 | 1 | 0 | 0 | 0 | 1 | 3 |
| 1978 | 0 | 1 | 0 | 0 | 0 | 0 | 1 | 0 | 0 | 0 | 1 | 3 |
| 1979 | 0 | 1 | 0 | 0 | 0 | 0 | 1 | 0 | 0 | 0 | 0 | 2 |
| 1980 | 0 | 1 | 0 | 0 | 0 | 0 | 1 | 0 | 0 | 0 | 0 | 2 |
| 1981 | 0 | 1 | 0 | 0 | 0 | 0 | 1 | 0 | 0 | 0 | 0 | 2 |
| 1982 | 0 | 1 | 0 | 0 | 0 | 0 | 1 | 0 | 0 | 0 | 0 | 2 |
| 1983 | 0 | 1 | 0 | 0 | 0 | 0 | 0 | 0 | 0 | 0 | 0 | 1 |
| 1984 | 0 | 1 | 0 | 0 | 0 | 0 | 0 | 0 | 0 | 0 | 0 | 1 |
| 1985 | 0 | 1 | 0 | 0 | 0 | 0 | 0 | 0 | 0 | 0 | 0 | 1 |
| 1986 | 0 | 1 | 0 | 0 | 0 | 0 | 0 | 0 | 0 | 0 | 0 | 1 |
| 1987 | 0 | 1 | 0 | 0 | 0 | 0 | 0 | 0 | 0 | 0 | 0 | 1 |
| 1988 | 0 | 1 | 0 | 0 | 0 | 0 | 0 | 0 | 0 | 0 | 0 | 1 |
| 1989 | 0 | 1 | 0 | 0 | 0 | 0 | 0 | 0 | 0 | 0 | 0 | 1 |
| 1990 | 0 | 1 | 0 | 0 | 0 | 0 | 0 | 0 | 0 | 0 | 0 | 1 |
| 1991 | 0 | 0 | 0 | 0 | 0 | 0 | 0 | 0 | 0 | 0 | 0 | 0 |
| 1992 | 0 | 0 | 0 | 0 | 0 | 0 | 0 | 0 | 0 | 0 | 0 | 0 |
| 1993 | 0 | 0 | 0 | 0 | 0 | 0 | 0 | 0 | 0 | 0 | 0 | 0 |
| TOTAL | 0 | 17 | 0 | 0 | 1 | 0 | 9 | 1 | 0 | 0 | 5 | |

*Sources:* International Monetary Fund, *Exchange Restrictions*, 1974–1978 and International Monetary Fund, *Exchange Arrangements and Exchange Restrictions*, Annual Reports, 1979–1993.

*Index of restrictions on payments for capital transactions and separate exchange rate(s) for some or all capital transactions and/or some or all invisibles: if both restrictions are in place, the index takes the value 2, if one restriction is in place the index takes the value of 1, and 0 otherwise*

| *INDEX* | AUS | BEL | DEN | FIN | FRA | GER | ITA | NET | SPA | SWE | UK | **TOTAL** |
|---------|-----|-----|-----|-----|-----|-----|-----|-----|-----|-----|-----|-----------|
| 1974 | 1 | 1 | 1 | 1 | 2 | 0 | 2 | 2 | 1 | 1 | 2 | **14** |
| 1975 | 1 | 1 | 1 | 1 | 1 | 0 | 2 | 1 | 1 | 1 | 2 | **12** |
| 1976 | 1 | 1 | 1 | 1 | 1 | 0 | 2 | 1 | 1 | 1 | 2 | **12** |
| 1977 | 1 | 1 | 1 | 1 | 1 | 0 | 2 | 1 | 1 | 1 | 2 | **12** |
| 1978 | 1 | 1 | 1 | 1 | 1 | 0 | 2 | 1 | 1 | 1 | 2 | **11** |
| 1979 | 1 | 1 | 1 | 1 | 1 | 0 | 2 | 0 | 1 | 1 | 1 | **10** |
| 1980 | 1 | 1 | 1 | 1 | 1 | 0 | 2 | 0 | 1 | 1 | 0 | **9** |
| 1981 | 1 | 1 | 1 | 1 | 1 | 0 | 2 | 0 | 1 | 1 | 0 | **9** |
| 1982 | 1 | 1 | 1 | 1 | 1 | 0 | 2 | 0 | 1 | 1 | 0 | **9** |
| 1983 | 1 | 1 | 1 | 1 | 1 | 0 | 1 | 0 | 1 | 1 | 0 | **8** |
| 1984 | 1 | 1 | 1 | 1 | 1 | 0 | 0 | 0 | 1 | 1 | 0 | **7** |
| 1985 | 1 | 1 | 1 | 1 | 1 | 0 | 0 | 0 | 1 | 1 | 0 | **7** |
| 1986 | 1 | 1 | 1 | 1 | 1 | 0 | 0 | 0 | 1 | 1 | 0 | **7** |
| 1987 | 1 | 1 | 1 | 1 | 1 | 0 | 1 | 0 | 1 | 1 | 0 | **8** |
| 1988 | 1 | 1 | 1 | 1 | 1 | 0 | 1 | 0 | 1 | 1 | 0 | **8** |
| 1989 | 1 | 1 | 0 | 1 | 1 | 0 | 1 | 0 | 1 | 1 | 0 | **7** |
| 1990 | 1 | 1 | 0 | 1 | 1 | 0 | 1 | 0 | 1 | 1 | 0 | **7** |
| 1991 | 1 | 0 | 0 | 1 | 1 | 0 | 1 | 0 | 1 | 1 | 0 | **6** |
| 1992 | 0 | 0 | 0 | 0 | 1 | 0 | 1 | 0 | 1 | 1 | 0 | **4** |
| 1993 | 0 | 0 | 0 | 1 | 1 | 0 | 1 | 0 | 1 | 1 | 0 | **5** |
| **TOTAL** | **18** | **17** | **15** | **19** | **21** | **0** | **26** | **6** | **20** | **20** | **11** | |

## Appendix 5A3

*Figure 5A3.1: Year-by-year average deviations from closed interest parity (percentages per year)*

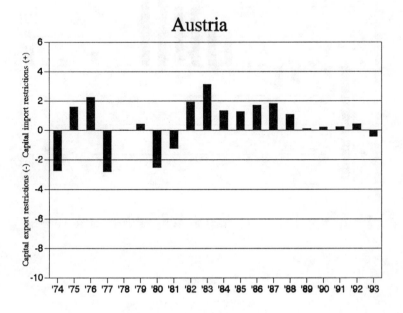

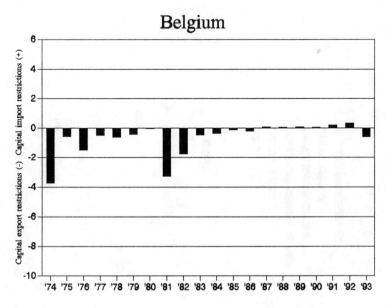

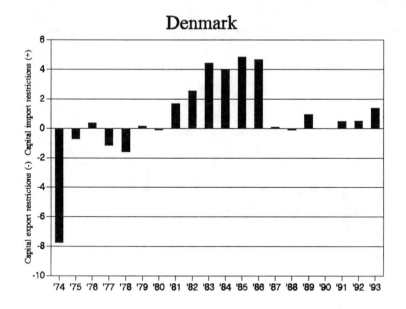

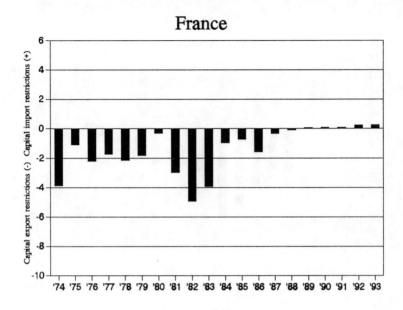

France

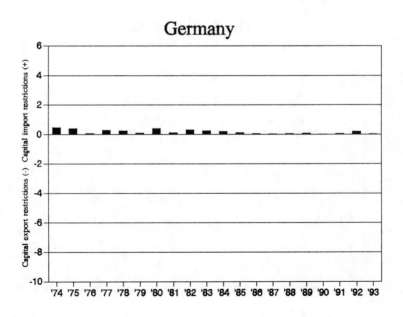

Germany

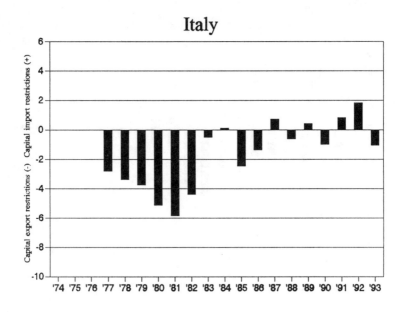

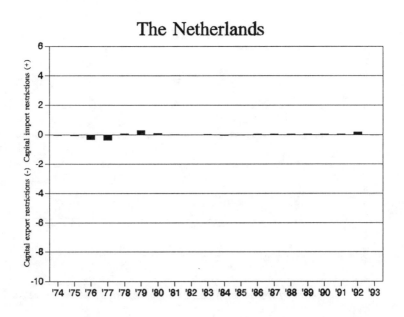

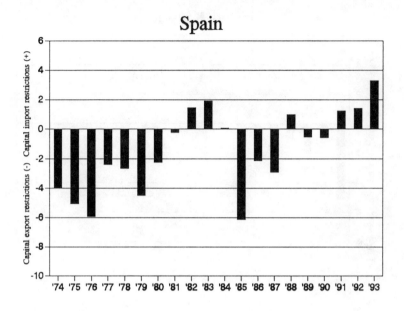

Spain

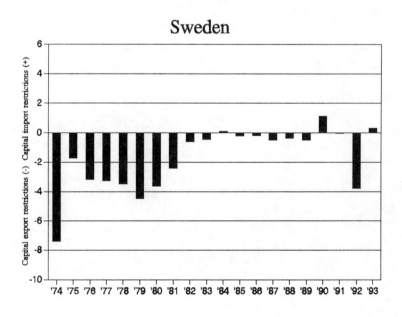

Sweden

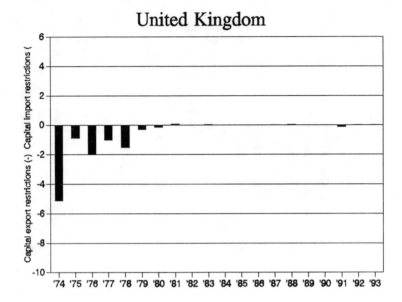

# 6. Short-term and Long-term Government Debt and Nonresident Interest Withholding Taxes

## 6.1 Introduction

In recent years, capital controls and other barriers to international capital mobility have been progressively reduced or eliminated. Many industrialized countries, however, continue to levy nonresident interest withholding taxes on interest accruing to foreign residents. The large variation in countries' withholding tax regimes in terms of rates and application suggests that countries disagree what role these taxes play or should play. To inform the debate, this chapter examines how interest withholding taxes, in so far as they apply to government debt, affect government debt yields for the industrialized countries. The basic question is to what extent a withholding tax is compounded into higher pre-tax interest rates on short-term three-month Treasury bills or T-bills and on long-term five-year government bonds. From the estimated mark-up, we can immediately infer to what extent the nonresident withholding tax is in fact borne by the debt-issuing Treasury rather than by the lender or the lender's Treasury. Nonresident withholding taxes, if compounded into higher interest rates, do not reduce the cost of international public borrowing. Higher interest rates, however, raise the cost of domestic public borrowing, to the benefit of resident holders of government debt. These issues remain important as long as most governments are heavily indebted.

A priori, the relationship between nonresident withholding taxes and interest rates can be expected to reflect, first, whether these taxes are easily evaded by way of a third country, tax-exempt financial intermediaries or by coupon washing techniques. Second, the interest rate mark-up importantly depends on whether the lender expects to receive a foreign tax-credit to offset the withholding tax. At one extreme, no mark-up should occur if a risk-neutral investor receives a fully offsetting tax-credit, while a full mark-up is consistent with the absence of any tax-credit. Given these complications, empirical estimation of the extent of mark-up is called for to provide insights into the economic working and incidence of nonresident interest withholding taxation.

The nonresident withholding tax regime tends to be a patchwork of rates and regulations. Tax treaties may stipulate different rates for different interest receiving countries, while there may be a host of exemptions based on the type of debt instrument, its maturity, and the status of interest payor or payee.[1] Many countries exempt government debt from nonresident withholding taxation altogether. Exceptions to this rule among the industrialized countries include Australia, Italy, Japan, Spain and Switzerland. This chapter focuses on government debt markets, as they are well defined, relatively liquid and as it is of prime interest to see how withholding taxes affect the tax-inclusive government cost of borrowing.

This chapter examines the link between interest rates and withholding taxes separately for three-month T-bills and five-year government bonds, while the international investors in government debt are taken to be either American or Japanese. With T-bill yields, we in fact estimate a covered interest parity relationship adjusted for the withholding-tax mark-up.[2] T-bills have the advantage that they are almost free of default risk. To check whether the results also apply to longer-term debt, we further examine a closed interest parity relationship linking the government bond yield to comparable offshore swap interest rates in the same currency – but not subject to withholding taxation. The swap rate reflects the interest rate on a benchmark bond designated by major securities houses as such, and is therefore rather liquid and trading at a premium.[3]

Previously, Brean (1984) has documented a downward effect of the 1975 elimination of interest withholding taxes on interest rates for Canadian medium- and long-term corporate borrowings from foreign sources. Along these lines, Nöhrbaß and Raab (1990) find that the yield on German corporate bonds fully reflects the 10 per cent withholding tax rate in force in early 1989.[4] In contrast, Huizinga (1996) finds that commercial bank credits to private borrowers in developing countries in the 1970s reflect significantly less than the full nonresident withholding taxes. These different results suggest that the mark-up of withholding taxes into interest rates may vary with the time period, or the nature of market participants. To add to the evidence, this chapter focuses on public debts of different maturities for a broad set of industrialized countries.[5]

The remainder of the chapter is organized as follows. Section 6.2 derives the estimating equations from underlying interest arbitrage relationships. Section 6.3 presents the empirical results for the three-month T-bill and five-year government bond markets in two separate subsections. While the evidence differs somewhat across samples and time periods, overall it is supportive of the view that withholding taxes are compounded one-for-one into higher pre-tax government yields. As indicated, this is consistent with the view that international investors (such as American and Japanese pension funds) cannot obtain any offsetting foreign tax-credits or that there is wide spread domestic tax evasion. Section 6.4 evaluates the results and concludes.

## 6.2   The Estimating Equations

Tax authorities can apply withholding taxes on interest accruing to residents and nonresidents. In the first instance, the withholding taxes are commonly credited against the residents' final income taxes. No such source-country refunding, however, occurs for nonresident withholding taxes. From a source-country perspective, a nonresident withholding tax thus is a final tax. The private creditor, however, may or may not be able to obtain a foreign tax-credit from his or her own tax authority to offset the nonresident withholding tax. The impact of nonresident withholding taxation on debt yields thus depends on the tax regimes of the foreign-source country and the investor's home country. The focus of this chapter is on nonresident withholding taxes and their impact on government debt yields. This section specifically indicates how the covered and closed interest parity conditions involving these yields can be adjusted for nonresident withholding taxes.[6]

In the later empirical work, the investors in international government debts are taken to be American or Japanese.[7] Both countries tax income on a residence basis, which means that corporations and individuals owe tax on their worldwide income, whether earned domestically or abroad. Both countries also allow foreign interest income taxes to be credited against the domestic tax liability to prevent double taxation. The allowable credit is generally limited to the amount of domestic tax on the foreign-source interest income. The investor is said to be in an excess credit position, if the foreign tax-credit limitation is binding. The precise calculation of the allowable foreign tax-credit, however, differs somewhat between the two countries. Japan, for example, allows the foreign tax-credit to be calculated on the basis of worldwide foreign-source income, and unused foreign tax-credits can be carried forward for three years. The United States has introduced an alternative basket approach to determining allowable foreign tax-credits. The 1986 Tax Reform Act specifically created nine separate income baskets or categories. The foreign tax-credit limitation is calculated separately for each of the nine baskets, thereby effectively limiting the overall size of the foreign tax-credit. One of the baskets is interest income subject to a withholding tax rate equal to or greater than 5 per cent. This basket was created specifically to limit the creditability of high nonresident withholding taxes.[8]

The top corporate and personal income tax rates in Japan and the United States exceed the withholding tax rates, if any, imposed on nonresident Japanese and US investors by the countries in this study. This suggests that it is unlikely that international portfolio investors will be in an excess credit position. This reasoning is faulty, however, as income taxes are applied to net-of-expense interest income rather than to gross interest receipts. Allowable expenses associated with a portfolio investment typically include the cost of funds necessary to finance the investment. As a result, an investor's net-of-expense foreign-source income may be very low, and the investor can be in an excess credit position. Clearly, tax-exempt institutional investors, like pension funds, are always in an excess credit position, if they pay any nonresident interest withholding taxes.

Let $\tau_{j,t}^w$ be the interest withholding tax rate imposed by government $j$ on international investors at time $t$, and let $\tau$ be the investor's marginal home country income tax rate applied to all income, including foreign exchange gains, if the investor pays any domestic tax on foreign-source income. An international investor that is in an excess credit position faces a marginal tax rate on foreign-source income of zero. Let $\gamma$ be the probability that the international investor can obtain a tax-credit *ex post*. Uncertainty regarding the availability of foreign tax-credits can, for instance, be due to the international investor's uncertain returns on financial assets other than government debt.

First, let us consider the tax-adjusted covered interest parity condition for a US (or Japanese) investor that can invest in US and non-US T-bills. Let $i_t$ and $i_{j,t}^*$ be the US and foreign country $j$'s T-bill rates at time $t$, respectively. The investor can borrow freely in dollars against the US T-bill interest rate. The costs of such borrowings are deductible from the investor's domestic taxable income. In particular, domestic interest expenses incurred to finance foreign financial assets are deductible from the investor's foreign-source taxable income. Further, any exchange risk can be eliminated by way of forward exchange contracts. Let $F_{j,t}$ and $S_{j,t}$ be the forward and spot exchange rates, defined as amounts of foreign currency $j$ per US dollar. Both US and non-US T-bills are assumed to carry some sovereign risk. In particular, let $\theta$ be the expected credit loss per dollar invested in US T-bills and $\theta_j^*$ be the expected credit loss per dollar invested in foreign T-bills issued by country $j$. In case of debt default both principal and interest are assumed to be lost, but the investor is allowed to write off the full principal investment against taxable income. A risk-neutral international investor that can freely borrow to finance any T-bill investment will then be indifferent about doing so if

$$\left[ 1 + [\gamma(1-\tau) + (1-\gamma)]i_t \right](1-\theta) + \gamma\tau\theta =$$

$$\left[ \gamma\left[ 1 + (1-\tau)[(1+i_{j,t}^*)\frac{F_{j,t}}{S_{j,t}} - 1] \right] + (1-\gamma)\left[ 1 + i_{j,t}^*(1-\tau_{j,t}^w)]\frac{F_{j,t}}{S_{j,t}} \right] \right](1-\theta_j^*) +$$

$$\gamma\tau\theta_j^* \qquad\qquad (6.1)$$

Equation (6.1) reflects that with probability $\gamma$ the investor faces a positive domestic income tax rate, $\tau$, on foreign-source income. The last terms on both sides of (6.1) are the expected values of the loss offset provision in case of debt default. In equation (6.1), we assume that the events $\theta$, $\theta^*$ and $\gamma$ are independent. Now define $p_{j,t}$ to be the percentage depreciation of the US dollar *vis-à-vis* foreign country $j$'s currency implicit in the forward exchange rate as follows,

$$p_{j,t} \equiv \frac{F_{j,t}}{S_{j,t}} - 1 \qquad (6.2)$$

Substituting for $F_{j,t}/S_{j,t}$ from (6.2) into (6.1) and setting the cross terms $i_{j,t}^* p_{j,t}$, $\theta_j^* p_{j,t}$, $\theta_i^* i_{j,t}^*$ and $\theta\, i_t$ to zero, we get after rearranging,

$$(1 - \gamma\tau)(p_{j,t} + i_{j,t}^* - i_t) = (1 - \gamma\tau)(\theta_j^* - \theta) + (1 - \gamma)\tau_{j,t}^w i_{j,t}^* \qquad (6.3)$$

After dividing by $(1 - \gamma\tau)$, we now can obtain the following tax-adjusted covered interest parity condition,

$$f_{j,t} = \theta_j + \beta\, \tau_{j,t}^w i_{j,t}^* \qquad (6.4)$$

where

$$f_{j,t} = p_{j,t} + i_{j,t}^* - i_t, \quad \theta_j = \theta_j^* - \theta, \quad \beta = \frac{1 - \gamma}{1 - \gamma\tau}$$

The variable $f_{j,t}$ in (6.4) is the part of country $j$'s T-bill yield in excess of covered interest parity. The variable $\theta_j$ simply is the expected credit loss of investment in country $j$'s T-bills relative to US T-bills. The parameter $\beta$ further indicates how much the foreign (non-US) interest rate $i_{j,t}^*$ rises if the withholding tax payment $\tau_{j,t}^w i_{j,t}^*$ is increased by unity for given values of $i_t$, $p_{j,t}$ and $\theta_j$. The parameter $\beta$, which satisfies $0 \le \beta \le 1$, thus is naturally interpreted as the share of the withholding tax borne by the foreign government itself, while $1 - \beta$ is the share of the withholding tax borne by the investor's home country Treasury.

The incidence parameter, $\beta$, is negatively related to the probability, $\gamma$, that the potential foreign tax-credit is realized *ex post* if $\tau < 1$. At the same time, the expression for $\beta$ reveals that it is positively related to the income tax rate $\tau$, if $0 < \gamma < 1$. To see why, note that the pre-tax foreign interest rate, $i_{j,t}^*$, has to rise to compensate the international investor following an increase in the withholding tax rate, $\tau_{j,t}^w$. The foreign interest payment, $i_{j,t}^*$, is subject to the investor's domestic income taxation. The foreign interest rate, $i^*_{j,t}$, thus has to rise more, the larger the income tax rate, $\tau$. The share of the incidence of the foreign withholding tax borne by the investor's national Treasury thus decreases with the income tax rate, $\tau$.

To obtain an alternative specification, we can divide both sides of equation (6.4) by the foreign interest rate, $i^*_{j,t}$, to give the following tax-inclusive covered interest parity relationship,

$$f'_{j,t} = \theta'_j + \beta \tau^w_{j,t} \tag{6.5}$$

where

$$f'_{j,t} = \frac{f_{j,t}}{i^*_{j,t}}, \quad \theta'_j = \frac{\theta_j}{i^*_{j,t}}$$

In (6.5), the interpretation of $\beta$ remains unchanged. In deriving equations (6.4) and (6.5), we have assumed that the investor reports his or her foreign-source interest income to the domestic tax authority. Alternatively, the investor evades domestic taxes on foreign investment income. In that instance, we effectively have $\gamma = \tau = 0$, which implies that $\beta$ in (6.4) and (6.5) equals 1. In case of tax evasion, the T-bill interest rate, $i^*_{j,t}$, thus rises one-for-one with the withholding tax liability, $\tau^w_{j,t} i^*_{j,t}$.

Next, let us consider the tax-adjusted closed interest parity condition for an investor who can invest in national five-year government bonds and, alternatively, in offshore five-year swap instruments in the same currency. Setting $p_{j,t} = 0$ in (6.4) and substituting the foreign-currency swap rate $i_{j,t}$ for the US T-bill rate $i_t$, we get

$$g_{j,t} = \theta_j + \beta \tau^w_{j,t} i^*_{j,t} \tag{6.6}$$

where

$$g_{j,t} = i^*_{j,t} - i_{j,t}$$

The variable $g_{j,t}$ thus is the excess of country $j$'s five-year government bond yield, $i^*_{j,t}$, over the corresponding swap interest rate, $i_{j,t}$, while the variable $\theta_j$ now reflects the expected credit loss per dollar invested in five-year government bonds relative to the corresponding swap instrument.

Analogously to equation (6.5), we can divide (6.6) by the five-year government bond yield, $i^*_{j,t}$, to obtain,

$$g'_{j,t} = \theta'_j + \beta \tau^w_{j,t} \tag{6.7}$$

where

$$g'_{j,t} = \frac{g_{j,t}}{i^*_{j,t}}$$

In practice, deviations from the tax-adjusted arbitrage relationships (6.4) and (6.6) and the tax-inclusive arbitrage relationships (6.5) and (6.7) occur for a variety of reasons, including data imperfections and transaction costs. As a result, a random component can be appended to any of these four relationships to give rise to an estimating equation.

## 6.3  Data and Empirical Results

Of the industrialized countries considered, only Australia, Germany, Italy, Japan, Spain and Switzerland have imposed interest withholding taxes on US residents. The withholding tax rate data are mostly available on an annual basis (see Appendix 6A1 for all data sources), although any within-year tax rate changes are dated as accurately as possible. Australia, specifically, has imposed a 10 per cent withholding tax applicable to American investors ever since 1980. Germany had a withholding tax of 10 per cent from January 1989 until July 1989. Italy increased its withholding tax on US investors from zero to 6.25 per cent in September 1986 and subsequently to 12.5 per cent in October 1988. Japan and Switzerland have maintained constant withholding tax rates of 5 and 10 per cent, respectively, on American investors since 1980. Spain raised its withholding tax on government debt from 20 to 25 per cent in July 1989. All of these countries apply a roughly similar withholding tax regime to nonresident Japanese investors. Of the countries in the sample, Italy and Spain and to a lesser extent Belgium, France and Sweden have imposed capital controls in the eighties. These capital controls, however, in no instance prohibited the foreign ownership of domestic government debt securities. Below we consider how the withholding tax regime has affected yields in, first, the national T-bill markets and, second, the five-year government bond markets.

### 6.3.1  Withholding taxes and three-month Treasury bills

The T-bill interest rate data set consists of monthly observations from January 1980 to December 1994 for 12 industrialized countries: Australia, Belgium, Canada, France, Germany, Italy, Japan, The Netherlands, Sweden, Switzerland, the United Kingdom and the United States.[9] The maturity of all T-bills is three months. The countries in the data set vary widely among themselves and over time in their interest withholding tax regime.

As can be seen from Garbade (1982) and OECD (1990c), national T-bill markets differ widely in, for instance, market institutions and pricing conventions. The market for US Treasury debt is arguably the deepest in the world, with a near continuum of Treasury maturities and very narrow bid-ask spreads. T-bills are issued in weekly batches by tender. In contrast to the United States, there is no active secondary market for T-bills in Germany. T-bills payable within three months are used as collateral for Lombard loans. Similarly, in Japan, a liquid secondary market in T-bills has yet to emerge. Gensaki bonds, which are repurchase agreements covering three-month transactions, are collateralized by government bonds or T-bills. Essentially, the Gensaki market is a somewhat restricted private market. The Banque Nationale de Belgique subscribes to three-month Treasury certificates at par, in practice in so far as it can transfer them on to the market. In Canada, investment dealers, the chartered banks and the Bank of Canada submit tenders to the Ministry of Finance for three-month T-bills to be issued. T-bills are sold at discount. In France, thirteen-week T-bills are an important element of the money market. T-bills are available to all economic agents and are sold in so-called Dutch auctions. T-bills in Italy are the government's most important source of short-term finance. They are issued by auction, in which the Banca d'Italia participates in the same way as other authorized dealers. Until recently, nearly all three-month Treasury paper in The Netherlands was held by monetary institutions that use it as an interest-bearing and pledgeable asset to meet the liquidity requirements imposed by De Nederlandsche Bank. The banks had practically no Treasury paper freely available for sale on the market. Secondary market dealings were rare, and secondary market rates were merely indicative.[10] T-bills in the United Kingdom are offered for tender each week. In Sweden, Treasury discount notes are the main instrument for government short-term borrowing. Switzerland possesses only the embryo of a domestic money market. The Banque Nationale Suisse may discount bills of exchange and cheques, 'rescriptions' issued by the Confederation and by the cantons and communes, though it is not obliged to. Finally, in Australia Treasury notes are issued by the Commonwealth government. They are issued at a discount by periodic tender and are redeemable at par thirteen weeks from the date of issue.

Next, we turn to the results of estimating (6.4) for the pooled cross-country, time-series data set using OLS, as reported in Table 6.1. The regressions in Table 6.1 include 11 country dummy variables, $\hat{\theta}_j$, and the nonresident withholding tax imposed on either US or Japanese investors times foreign country $j$'s interest rate, that is, $\tau^w_{US, 1980-1994} \cdot i^*_{j,t}$ or $\tau^w_{Jap, 1980-1994} \cdot i^*_{j,t}$.[11] A constant term is omitted. Newey–West (1987) standard errors are also reported to account for possible heteroscedasticity and autocorrelation resulting from overlapping three-month interest rate observations. The Newey–West standard errors differ relatively little from the OLS standard errors, with relatively minor

*Table 6.1 Tax-adjusted covered interest parity for three-month Treasury bills*

$$f_{j,t} = \hat{\theta}_j + \beta \, \tau^w_{j,t} \, i^*_{j,t}$$

| | (1) | (2) | (3) | (4) | (5) | (6) | (7) | (8) |
|---|---|---|---|---|---|---|---|---|
| $\tau^w_{US,1980-1994} \cdot i^*$ | 1.206 (4.88) [3.04] | 1.048 (3.77) [2.21] | | | | | | |
| $\tau^w_{Jap,1980-1994} \cdot i^*$ | | | | | 1.223 (4.11) [2.70] | 1.088 (3.23) [2.03] | | |
| $DEBT - DEBT_{US}$ | | 20.011 (1.46) [0.76] | | 0.006 (0.73) [0.37] | | 0.010 (1.18) [0.64] | | 0.001 (0.14) [0.08] |
| $INF - INF_{US}$ | | 0.042 (1.56) [0.78] | | 0.029 (1.02) [0.48] | | 0.041 (1.41) [0.72] | | 0.029 (0.92) [0.50] |
| $\hat{\theta}_{Australia}$ | −0.023 (6.72) [4.46] | −0.015 (2.20) [1.06] | −0.025 (7.13) [4.92] | −0.018 (2.62) [1.23] | −0.023 (5.86) [3.98] | −0.016 (2.16) [1.08] | −0.026 (6.28) [4.40] | −0.022 (2.81) [1.64] |
| $\hat{\theta}_{Belgium}$ | 0.008 (4.45) [6.79] | 0.006 (0.96) [0.73] | 0.008 (4.46) [6.78] | 0.008 (1.33) [1.01] | 0.008 (4.29) [6.79] | 0.007 (1.11) [0.86] | 0.008 (4.30) [6.78] | 0.011 (1.74) [1.23] |
| $\hat{\theta}_{Canada}$ | 0.010 (4.99) [9.15] | 0.013 (3.39) [2.34] | 0.010 (5.01) [9.14] | 0.012 (3.05) [1.95] | 0.010 (4.82) [9.15] | 0.013 (3.18) [2.16] | 0.010 (4.83) [9.14] | 0.013 (3.02) [1.68] |
| $\hat{\theta}_{France}$ | 0.007 (2.53) [2.67] | 0.014 (2.85) [1.52] | 0.007 (2.54) [2.67] | 0.011 (2.25) [1.12] | 0.007 (2.44) [2.67] | 0.013 (2.61) [1.40] | 0.007 (2.44) [2.67] | 0.011 (1.96) [1.16] |
| $\hat{\theta}_{Germany}$ | −0.007 (3.85) [4.82] | −0.0009 (0.22) [0.11] | −0.007 (3.83) [4.80] | −0.003 (0.67) [0.33] | −0.007 (3.72) [4.82] | −0.001 (0.25) [0.13] | −0.007 (3.70) [4.80] | −0.003 (0.71) [0.40] |
| $\hat{\theta}_{Italy}$ | −0.021 (8.51) [3.91] | −0.019 (4.18) [2.28] | −0.021 (8.14) [3.66] | −0.019 (4.05) [2.19] | −0.020 (7.86) [3.80] | −0.017 (3.55) [2.01] | −0.020 (7.78) [3.70] | −0.017 (3.48) [2.12] |
| $\hat{\theta}_{Japan}$ | 0.002 (0.89) [0.80] | 0.006 (1.51) [0.91] | 0.0007 (0.29) [0.28] | 0.002 (0.51) [0.30] | | | | |
| $\hat{\theta}_{The\ Netherlands}$ | 0.007 (2.96) [1.95] | 0.010 (2.49) [1.47] | 0.007 (2.97) [1.94] | 0.009 (2.22) [1.24] | 0.007 (2.86) [1.95] | 0.010 (2.36) [1.39] | 0.007 (2.86) [1.94] | 0.010 (2.25) [1.32] |
| $\hat{\theta}_{Sweden}$ | 0.008 (3.82) [2.62] | 0.013 (3.06) [1.69] | 0.008 (3.83) [2.61] | 0.011 (2.62) [1.36] | 0.008 (3.69) [2.62] | 0.013 (2.85) [1.58] | 0.008 (3.70) [2.61] | 0.012 (2.52) [1.38] |
| $\hat{\theta}_{Switzerland}$ | 0.004 (2.16) [2.79] | 0.014 (2.49) [1.17] | 0.004 (1.97) [2.64] | 0.009 (1.58) [0.71] | 0.001 (0.47) [0.46] | 0.011 (1.65) [0.80] | 0.00002 (0.008) [0.008] | 0.002 (0.32) [0.19] |
| $\hat{\theta}_{United\ Kingdom}$ | 0.004 (2.35) [1.31] | 0.010 (2.53) [1.02] | 0.004 (2.35) [1.31] | 0.008 (1.97) [0.76] | 0.004 (2.26) [1.31] | 0.010 (2.32) [0.96] | 0.004 (2.27) [1.31] | 0.008 (1.78) [0.90] |

| | | | | | | | | |
|---|---|---|---|---|---|---|---|---|
| $\tau^w_{US,1980-1982} \cdot i^*$ | | | 2.089<br>(5.85)<br>[5.21] | 2.585<br>(4.23)<br>[3.22] | | | | |
| $\tau^w_{US,1983-1985} \cdot i^*$ | | | 1.463<br>(3.70)<br>[3.32] | 1.715<br>(2.19)<br>[3.37] | | | | |
| $\tau^w_{US,1986-1988} \cdot i^*$ | | | 1.233<br>(3.56)<br>[2.84] | 1.339<br>(3.26)<br>[2.56] | | | | |
| $\tau^w_{US,1989-1991} \cdot i^*$ | | | 0.723<br>(2.55)<br>[1.84] | 0.659<br>(2.17)<br>[1.44] | | | | |
| $\tau^w_{US,1992-1994} \cdot i^*$ | | | 1.514<br>(4.06)<br>[2.65] | 1.461<br>(3.66)<br>[2.33] | | | | |
| $\tau^w_{Jap,1980-1982} \cdot i^*$ | | | | | | | 2.077<br>(4.85)<br>[4.38] | 3.117<br>(3.09)<br>[3.16] |
| $\tau^w_{Jap,1983-1985} \cdot i^*$ | | | | | | | 1.497<br>(3.24)<br>[2.82] | 1.942<br>(1.27)<br>[2.17] |
| $\tau^w_{Jap,1986-1988} \cdot i^*$ | | | | | | | 1.256<br>(3.16)<br>[2.58] | 1.496<br>(3.11)<br>[2.93] |
| $\tau^w_{Jap,1989-1991} \cdot i^*$ | | | | | | | 0.851<br>(2.58)<br>[1.97] | 0.882<br>(2.47)<br>[2.32] |
| $\tau^w_{Jap,1992-1994} \cdot i^*$ | | | | | | | 1.716<br>(3.81)<br>[2.67] | 1.820<br>(3.71)<br>[3.44] |
| $\bar{R}^2$ | 0.11 | 0.11 | 0.10 | 0.11 | 0.10 | 0.10 | 0.10 | 0.10 |
| $N$ | 1826 | 1742 | 1826 | 1742 | 1646 | 1562 | 1646 | 1562 |

*Notes:* The dependent variable $f_{j,t}$ is the return on the non-US T-bill in excess of covered interest parity. Absolute t-statistics based on OLS are in parentheses and based on Newey–West (1987) are in square brackets. $R^2$ is the coefficient of determination adjusted for degrees of freedom. $N$ is the number of usable observations.

implications for significance levels.[12]

The regressions (1) and (5) reflect the basic tax-adjusted covered interest parity condition in (6.4) for US and Japanese nonresident investors, respectively. The coefficient $\beta$ is estimated at 1.206 for US investors (in regression (1)) and at 1.233 for Japanese investors (in regression (5)). In either regressions, the $\beta$'s are statistically significantly different from zero, but not from unity. A country dummy can be interpreted as sovereign risk or country-specific transaction costs (in the form of, for instance, registration requirements) relative to the United States.[13] The estimation results suggest that there is relatively high sovereign risk for Belgian, Canadian and Swedish debts.

In regressions (2) and (6), two control variables, the ratio of non-US debt to GDP less the ratio of US debt to GDP, $DEBT - DEBT_{US}$, and the non-US inflation less US inflation, $INF - INF_{US}$, are added to the basic regressions. These control variables can be seen as somewhat more specific (and obviously more time-varying) indicators of country risk than country dummies. The coefficient $\beta$ is now estimated at 1.048 for the US investor (in regression (2)) and at 1.088 for the Japanese (in regression (6)). Again, the estimates of $\beta$ remain statistically indifferent from unity. The regressions do not explicitly control for the possible role of capital export restrictions in determining government debt yields in the absence of the requisite data.[14] The estimated positive $\beta$ coefficients thus in principle can be biased in so far as nonresident withholding tax rates are correlated with capital export restrictions. Note that a country such as Italy imposes positive nonresident withholding tax rates, and has also restricted capital exports (of course, these restrictions have been eliminated in 1990). Withholding taxes tend to increase pre-tax interest rates, while capital export restrictions have the opposite effect. A failure to control for capital export restrictions in the regressions thus cannot explain positive $\beta$ coefficients in so far as withholding taxes and capital export restrictions have been positively related.

In regressions (3) and (7), separate $\beta$ coefficients are estimated for five consecutive three-year intervals in the basic equation (6.4) for US and Japanese investors, respectively. In both regressions, the $\beta$ estimate for the 1980–1982 interval is significantly different from zero and from unity, while the $\beta$ estimates for the intervals 1983–1985, 1986–1988, 1989–1991 and 1992–1994 are significantly different from zero, but not from unity. Also note that in practice not all the estimates of $\beta$ are within the zero-one range. Regressions (4) and (8), finally, add the two debt and inflation control variables to regressions (3) and (7). Otherwise, regressions (4) and (8) correspond closely to regressions (3) and (7).

The regressions reported in Table 6.2 are based on the tax-inclusive covered interest parity specification in equation (6.5).[15] Otherwise, the regressions are fully analogous to those reported in Table 6.1. The basic regressions (1) and (5) now reveal estimates for the coefficient $\beta$ that are both not statistically different from zero and from unity. The estimated parameters for the country dummies are larger than in Table 6.1, as they now are roughly interpreted as the expected credit loss relative to the United States as a share of the foreign country $j$'s interest rate. Similar results are obtained if control variables are included in regressions (2) and (6). Regressions (3)–(7) and (4)–(8) show, however, that the $\beta$ estimates are roughly in the neighbourhood of unity for the intervals 1980–1982, 1983–1985, and 1986–1988, while they are close to zero in the subsequent intervals 1989–1991 and 1992–1994. This pattern of results is consistent with the view that key international investors did not receive offsetting foreign tax-credits in the period 1980–1988, while such tax-credits

*Table 6.2 Tax-inclusive covered interest parity for three-month Treasury bills*

$$f'_{j,t} = \theta'_j + \beta \tau^w_{j,t}$$

| | (1) | (2) | (3) | (4) | (5) | (6) | (7) | (8) |
|---|---|---|---|---|---|---|---|---|
| $\tau^w_{US,1980-1994}$ | 0.334 (0.94) [0.71] | −0.043 (0.11) [0.09] | | | | | | |
| $\tau^w_{Jap,1980-1994}$ | | | | | 0.373 (0.85) [0.64] | 0.033 (0.07) [0.05] | | |
| $DEBT-DEBT_{US}$ | | 0.266 (2.85) [2.13] | | 0.139 (1.44) [1.05] | | 0.202 (2.13) [1.60] | | 0.055 (0.53) [0.38] |
| $INF-INF_{US}$ | | 0.359 (1.16) [0.87] | | 0.117 (0.35) [0.24] | | 0.383 (1.16) [0.85] | | 0.083 (0.23) [0.16] |
| $\theta'_{Australia}$ | −0.138 (3.26) [2.52] | −0.033 (0.40) [0.28] | −0.222 (5.07) [3.69] | −0.136 (1.60) [1.06] | −0.141 (2.88) [2.18] | −0.057 (0.64) [0.44] | −0.213 (4.19) [3.08] | −0.176 (1.87) [1.22] |
| $\theta'_{Belgium}$ | 0.090 (3.98) [8.58] | −0.055 (0.77) [0.77] | 0.090 (4.04) [8.57] | 0.004 (0.06) [0.06] | 0.090 (3.98) [8.58] | −0.005 (0.07) [0.08] | 0.090 (4.02) [8.57] | 0.061 (0.80) [0.81] |
| $\theta'_{Canada}$ | 0.086 (3.83) [10.03] | 0.087 (1.93) [1.94] | 0.086 (3.88) [10.02] | 0.077 (1.62) [1.49] | 0.086 (3.82) [10.03] | 0.102 (2.14) [2.07] | 0.086 (3.86) [10.02] | 0.088 (1.77) [1.60] |
| $\theta'_{France}$ | 0.077 (2.53) [2.58] | 0.160 (2.88) [2.19] | 0.077 (2.56) [2.58] | 0.111 (1.90) [1.35] | 0.077 (2.52) [2.58] | 0.154 (2.69) [1.99] | 0.077 (2.55) [2.58] | 0.096 (1.56) [1.07] |
| $\theta'_{Germany}$ | −0.151 (6.72) [5.57] | −0.081 (1.65) [1.21] | −0.150 (6.76) [5.56] | −0.123 (2.33) [1.60] | −0.151 (6.71) [5.57] | −0.084 (1.62) [1.16] | −0.151 (6.74) [5.56] | −0.135 (2.44) [1.63] |
| $\theta'_{Italy}$ | −0.130 (4.04) [2.68] | −0.162 (3.04) [2.61] | −0.138 (4.32) [2.85] | −0.164 (2.98) [2.52] | −0.128 (3.99) [2.63] | 0.139 (2.50) [2.15] | −0.133 (4.18) [2.75] | −0.139 (2.46) [2.11] |
| $\theta'_{Japan}$ | 0.122 (2.89) [2.27] | 0.161 (2.73) [2.18] | 0.037 (0.85) [0.70] | 0.051 (0.78) [0.60] | | | | |
| $\theta'_{The Netherlands}$ | 0.115 (4.39) [2.32] | 0.115 (2.42) [1.62] | 0.115 (4.45) [2.32] | 0.105 (2.11) [1.38] | 0.115 (4.39) [2.32] | 0.129 (2.60) [1.75] | 0.115 (4.43) [2.32] | 0.116 (2.26) [1.48] |
| $\theta'_{Sweden}$ | 0.066 (2.72) [2.38] | 0.091 (1.90) [1.49] | 0.066 (2.75) [2.38] | 0.069 (1.35) [1.00] | 0.066 (2.71) [2.38] | 0.101 (1.99) [1.53] | 0.066 (2.74) [2.37] | 0.072 (1.36) [0.98] |
| $\theta'_{Switzerland}$ | 0.158 (5.52) [4.36] | 0.317 (4.48) [3.05] | 0.116 (3.99) [3.38] | 0.191 (2.48) [1.63] | 0.138 (2.81) [2.13] | 0.292 (3.27) [2.22] | 0.067 (1.31) [1.05] | 0.112 (1.08) [0.71] |
| $\theta'_{United Kingdom}$ | 0.033 (1.46) [1.24] | 0.089 (1.87) [1.18] | 0.033 (1.48) [1.42] | 0.053 (1.04) [0.62] | 0.033 (1.46) [1.24] | 0.090 (1.81) [1.13] | 0.033 (1.47) [1.24] | 0.046 (0.86) [0.50] |

| | | | | | | | |
|---|---|---|---|---|---|---|---|
| $\tau^{w'}_{us,1980-1982}$ | | | 2.690 (5.14) [4.39] | 2.765 (3.88) [3.14] | | | | |
| $\tau^{w'}_{US,1983-1985}$ | | | 1.347 (2.57) [2.35] | 0.755 (1.11) [1.12] | | | | |
| $\tau^{w'}_{US,1986-1988}$ | | | 1.692 (3.72) [2.95] | 1.503 (3.02) [2.47] | | | | |
| $\tau^{w'}_{US,1989-1991}$ | | | 0.050 (0.13) [0.10] | −0.134 (0.32) [0.25] | | | | |
| $\tau^{w'}_{US,1992-1994}$ | | | 0.121 (0.30) [0.22] | −0.094 (0.21) [0.16] | | | | |
| $\tau^{w'}_{Jap,1980-1982}$ | | | | | | | 2.601 (4.36) [3.69] | 2.889 (3.35) [2.64] |
| $\tau^{w'}_{Jap,1983-1985}$ | | | | | | | 1.039 (1.74) [1.49] | 0.267 (0.34) [0.30] |
| $\tau^{w'}_{Jap,1986-1988}$ | | | | | | | 1.476 (2.76) [2.21] | 1.404 (2.39) [1.96] |
| $\tau^{w'}_{Jap,1989-1991}$ | | | | | | | 0.164 (0.35) [0.27] | 0.071 (0.14) [0.11] |
| $\tau^{w'}_{Jap,1992-1994}$ | | | | | | | 0.144 (0.29) [0.21] | 0.044 (0.08) [0.06] |
| $\bar{R}^2$ | 0.11 | 0.12 | 0.13 | 0.15 | 0.11 | 0.11 | 0.12 | 0.13 |
| $N$ | 1826 | 1742 | 1826 | 1742 | 1646 | 1562 | 1646 | 1562 |

*Notes:* The dependent variable $f'_{j,t}$ is the return on the non-US T-bill in excess of covered interest parity per dollar invested in the foreign country $j$'s asset. Absolute t-statistics based on OLS are in parentheses and based on Newey–West (1987) are in square brackets. $R^2$ is the coefficient of determination adjusted for degrees of freedom. $N$ is the number of usable observations.

were available in the latter period 1989–1994.

Overall, the evidence suggests that withholding taxes on national T-bills were fully reflected in pre-tax yields in the earlier period till 1988. A full gross-up of pre-tax interest rates is plausible, as large institutional investors such as pension funds are tax-exempt in both the United States and Japan, and thus cannot receive foreign tax-credits to offset foreign-source interest withholding taxation. As national T-bill markets differ markedly in scope and organization, it is interesting to check to what extent these conclusions continue to hold for longer-term government debt markets. To this end, we next examine the relationship between interest withholding taxation and yields in the five-year government debt markets.

### 6.3.2 Withholding taxes and five-year government bonds

Long-term government bonds are perhaps closer substitutes in investor portfolios than national T-bills, in part because national central banks are less active in long-term government debt markets than in T-bill markets. It is interesting to test the relationship between withholding taxes and yields separately for the long-term government debt market, not the least because long-term government debt markets tend to be far more liquid than, say, corporate debt markets. Also, maturity *per se* can have an independent effect on the extent to which interest withholding taxes are marked up into higher pre-tax yields. This, for instance, is shown to be case in the commercial bank credit market to developing countries in the 1970s, by Huizinga (1996). The evidence there suggests that pre-tax interest rates are marked up less for short-term bank loans than for longer term bank loans on account of foreign-source interest withholding taxes. A reason for this 'withholding tax yield-curve effect' may be that banks on short notice know whether they can realize the foreign tax-credits associated with any loans. They therefore value foreign tax-credits associated with short-term loans relatively highly giving rise to a smaller mark-up into higher pre-tax yields for short-term credits. A second reason for a 'withholding tax yield-curve effect' may be that there is always some uncertainty about domestic tax regime changes in so far as existing financial instruments are not subject to grandfather clauses in case of policy changes. Of course, the government debt market is far more liquid than the secondary market for third world debt has ever been, and a priori any maturity effect is expected to be weaker.

The data set now consists of monthly five-year government bond yields and comparable offshore swap rates in the same currency for the period from April 1987 to December 1995. The data for 13 industrialized countries: Belgium, Canada, Denmark, France, Germany, Italy, Japan, The Netherlands, Spain, Sweden, Switzerland, the United Kingdom and the United States. Again, Newey–West (1987) corrected standard errors are also reported to account for possible heteroscedasticity and autocorrelation resulting from the overlapping sample problem.[16]

Table 6.3 first reports regressions based on the tax-adjusted closed interest parity condition in equation (6.6). The basic regressions (1) and (5) yield estimates of the coefficient $\beta$ that are close to zero and statistically insignificant for the US and Japanese investor cases. In contrast, regression (2) finds a positive and slightly significant $\beta$ estimate for the US case. Next, regressions (3)–(7) and regressions (4)–(8) test whether the mark-up of withholding taxation includes separate $\beta$ estimates for three consecutive three-year intervals to see whether the $\beta$ estimate changes over time. The results suggest that the impact of nonresident withholding taxation on pre-tax yields on five-year government bonds increases somewhat over time, although most of the individual $\beta$ estimates

*Table 6.3 Tax-adjusted closed interest parity for five-year government bonds*

$$g_{j,t} = \hat{\theta}_j + \beta\,\tau^w_{j,t}\,i^*_{j,t}$$

|  | (1) | (2) | (3) | (4) | (5) | (6) | (7) | (8) |
|---|---|---|---|---|---|---|---|---|
| $\tau^w_{US,1987-1995} \cdot i^*$ | −0.024 (0.37) [0.16] | 0.136 (1.99) [0.75] |  |  |  |  |  |  |
| $\tau^w_{Jap,1987-1995} \cdot i^*$ |  |  |  |  | −0.200 (1.93) [0.53] | −0.019 (0.18) [0.06] |  |  |
| *DEBT* |  | 0.011 (6.39) [1.89] |  | 0.012 (6.25) [1.83] |  | 0.011 (5.60) [1.84] |  | 0.009 (4.43) [1.50] |
| $\hat{\theta}_{Belgium}$ | −0.002 (4.91) [2.68] | −0.018 (7.05) [2.08] | −0.002 (4.95) [2.68] | −0.018 (6.87) [2.01] | −0.002 (4.82) [2.68] | −0.016 (6.23) [2.04] | −0.002 (4.90) [2.68] | −0.015 (5.01) [1.69] |
| $\hat{\theta}_{Canada}$ | −0.004 (7.88) [19.30] | −0.015 (8.34) [2.56] | 0.004 (7.94) [19.27] | −0.015 (8.11) [2.45] | −0.004 (7.73) [19.30] | −0.014 (7.46) [2.54] | −0.004 (7.86) [19.28] | −0.013 (6.17) [2.15] |
| $\hat{\theta}_{Denmark}$ | −0.004 (9.60) [12.93] | −0.012 (9.39) [2.93] | −0.004 (9.68) [12.91] | −0.013 (9.12) [2.80] | −0.004 (9.43) [12.93] | −0.012 (8.48) [2.93] | −0.004 (9.58) [12.92] | −0.011 (7.14) [2.51] |
| $\hat{\theta}_{France}$ | −0.004 (11.29) [8.34] | −0.010 (10.10) [3.17] | −0.003 (11.38) [8.33] | −0.010 (9.80) [3.02] | −0.004 (11.08) [8.34] | −0.010 (9.15) [3.17] | −0.004 (11.27) [8.33] | −0.009 (7.76) [2.73] |
| $\hat{\theta}_{Germany}$ | −0.004 (13.60) [8.54] | −0.009 (10.10) [3.24] | −0.003 (13.00) [7.35] | −0.009 (9.62) [3.17] | −0.004 (13.01) [7.29] | −0.009 (9.04) [3.36] | −0.003 (12.82) [7.01] | −0.008 (7.55) [2.93] |
| $\hat{\theta}_{Italy}$ | 0.005 (4.80) [2.07] | −0.011 (4.02) [1.29] | 0.003 (2.31) [0.87] | −0.012 (4.34) [1.37] | 0.007 (5.42) [1.54] | −0.008 (2.59) [1.15] | 0.003 (1.73) [0.55] | −0.008 (2.79) [1.19] |
| $\hat{\theta}_{Japan}$ | −0.005 (11.01) [6.11] | −0.014 (9.28) [2.93] | −0.005 (10.98) [4.98] | −0.015 (9.33) [2.92] |  |  |  |  |
| $\hat{\theta}_{The Netherlands}$ | −0.004 (12.17) [27.23] | −0.013 (9.33) [2.85] | −0.004 (12.27) [27.19] | −0.014 (9.03) [2.72] | −0.004 (11.95) [27.23] | −0.013 (8.39) [2.84] | −0.004 (12.15) [27.20] | −0.012 (7.00) [2.43] |
| $\hat{\theta}_{Spain}$ | −0.003 (1.59) [0.69] | −0.014 (5.62) [2.10] | −0.007 (2.81) [1.03] | −0.015 (5.64) [1.94] | −0.001 (1.14) [0.33] | −0.010 (5.09) [2.55] | −0.005 (3.65) [1.17] | −0.011 (5.69) [2.57] |
| $\hat{\theta}_{Sweden}$ | −0.008 (20.68) [13.12] | −0.017 (11.82) [3.66] | −0.008 (20.84) [13.10] | −0.017 (11.40) [3.46] | −0.008 (20.29) [13.12] | −0.016 (10.74) [3.68] | −0.008 (20.63) [13.10] | −0.015 (9.14) [3.17] |
| $\hat{\theta}_{Switzerland}$ | −0.008 (24.54) [4.15] | −0.010 (21.16) [5.06] | −0.008 (23.71) [4.49] | −0.010 (21.01) [5.29] | −0.007 (11.51) [2.67] | −0.010 (12.60) [4.61] | −0.008 (12.14) [3.80] | −0.010 (12.80) [5.36] |
| $\hat{\theta}_{United Kingdom}$ | −0.005 (19.77) [5.07] | −0.010 (12.45) [3.53] | −0.005 (19.92) [5.07] | −0.010 (12.02) [3.38] | −0.005 (19.40) [5.07] | −0.010 (11.36) [3.48] | −0.005 (19.73) [5.07] | −0.009 (9.74) [3.07] |

| | (1) | (2) | (3) | (4) | (5) | (6) | (7) | (8) |
|---|---|---|---|---|---|---|---|---|
| $\theta_{United States}$ | | | | | −0.010 (33.10) [12.82] | −0.016 (13.86) [4.73] | −0.010 (33.65) [12.80] | −0.016 (11.96) [4.20] |
| $\tau^w_{US,1987-1989} \cdot i^*$ | | | −0.386 (3.02) [1.33] | −0.234 (1.84) [1.07] | | | | |
| $\tau^w_{US,1990-1992} \cdot i^*$ | | | 0.090 (1.18) [0.42] | 0.173 (2.30) [0.83] | | | | |
| $\tau^w_{US,1993-1995} \cdot i^*$ | | | 0.122 (1.35) [0.50] | 0.144 (1.63) [0.55] | | | | |
| $\tau^w_{Jap,1987-1989} \cdot i^*$ | | | | | | | −0.405 (2.99) [1.01] | −0.310 (2.29) [0.86] |
| $\tau^w_{Jap,1990-1992} \cdot i^*$ | | | | | | | 0.073 (0.63) [0.18] | 0.130 (1.13) [0.33] |
| $\tau^w_{Jap,1993-1995} \cdot i^*$ | | | | | | | 0.222 (1.59) [0.53] | 0.175 (1.26) [0.40] |
| $\bar{R}^2$ | 0.78 | 0.79 | 0.79 | 0.80 | 0.81 | 0.83 | 0.83 | 0.83 |
| $N$ | 779 | 779 | 779 | 779 | 787 | 787 | 787 | 787 |

*Notes:* The dependent variable $g_{j,t}$ is the return on the five-year benchmark government bond index in excess of the five-year swap rate. Absolute t-statistics based on OLS are in parentheses and based on Newey–West (1987) are in square brackets. $R^2$ is the coefficient of determination adjusted for degrees of freedom. $N$ is the number of usable observations.

are significantly indifferent from zero.

To conclude, Table 6.4 reports regressions based on the tax-inclusive closed interest parity specification in equation (6.7). The estimates of the $\beta$ coefficient for the regressions (1), (2), (5) and (6) are close to zero and not significantly different from zero. In regressions (3), (4), (7) and (8), however, the $\beta$ estimates are close to unity for the intervals 1990–1992 and 1993–1995, which suggests that the foreign pre-tax interest rates rise one-for-one by the interest tax withheld.

There are several possible explanations of why the estimates of $\beta$ are not significantly different from zero for the period 1987–1989 in regressions (3), (4), (7) and (8). First, during this period the swap market came into being, with possible pricing variability. Also, there are scattered data only for Germany, Japan, the United Kingdom, and the United States during this period. Second, the United Kingdom (with no withholding taxation of public interest payments) at the time maintained high interest rates, as the British pound sterling was shadowing the DM. Third, German government bond yields shot up by about 50 basis points in October 1987 when the 10 per cent withholding tax, to take effect in January 1988, was announced. During the first half year of 1988 when this withholding tax was in place, German bond yields were actually lower than

Table 6.4 Tax-inclusive closed interest parity for five-year government bonds

$$g'_{j,t} = \theta'_j + \beta\, \tau^w_{j,t}$$

| | (1) | (2) | (3) | (4) | (5) | (6) | (7) | (8) |
|---|---|---|---|---|---|---|---|---|
| $\tau^w_{US,\,1987-1995}$ | −0.003<br>(0.02)<br>[0.04] | −0.017<br>(0.10)<br>[0.20] | | | | | | |
| $\tau^w_{Jap,\,1987-1995}$ | | | | | −0.003<br>(0.02)<br>[0.04] | 0.019<br>(0.11)<br>[0.20] | | |
| DEBT | | −0.024<br>(0.92)<br>[0.25] | | −0.025<br>(0.82)<br>[0.30] | | 0.039<br>(1.51)<br>[0.45] | | −0.073<br>(2.66)<br>(1.05) |
| $\theta'_{Belgium}$ | −0.027<br>(4.83)<br>[2.66] | 0.006<br>(0.16)<br>[0.05] | −0.027<br>(5.01)<br>[2.65] | 0.007<br>(0.17)<br>[0.06] | −0.027<br>(5.22)<br>[2.66] | −0.082<br>(2.24)<br>[0.67] | −0.027<br>(5.74)<br>[2.65] | 0.073<br>(1.92)<br>[0.75] |
| $\theta'_{Canada}$ | −0.052<br>(6.89)<br>[13.43] | −0.029<br>(1.11)<br>[0.32] | −0.052<br>(7.16)<br>[13.41] | −0.029<br>(0.96)<br>[0.36] | −0.052<br>(7.45)<br>[13.43] | −0.090<br>(3.48)<br>[1.08] | −0.052<br>(8.20)<br>[13.41] | 0.017<br>(0.64)<br>[0.26] |
| $\theta'_{Denmark}$ | −0.060<br>(8.41)<br>[15.35] | −0.043<br>(2.22)<br>[0.65] | −0.060<br>(8.74)<br>[15.33] | −0.043<br>(1.96)<br>[0.74] | −0.060<br>(9.09)<br>[15.35] | −0.087<br>(4.56)<br>[1.44] | −0.060<br>(10.01)<br>[15.33] | −0.010<br>(0.50)<br>[0.20] |
| $\theta'_{France}$ | −0.055<br>(9.72)<br>[14.04] | −0.043<br>(2.83)<br>[0.83] | −0.055<br>(10.09)<br>[14.02] | −0.042<br>(2.51)<br>[0.94] | −0.055<br>(10.50)<br>[14.04] | −0.076<br>(5.17)<br>[1.64] | −0.055<br>(11.56)<br>[14.02] | −0.017<br>(1.11)<br>[0.45] |
| $\theta'_{Germany}$ | −0.053<br>(12.59)<br>[6.36] | −0.042<br>(3.05)<br>[0.89] | −0.053<br>(13.07)<br>[6.36] | −0.041<br>(2.69)<br>[1.04] | −0.053<br>(13.61)<br>[6.36] | −0.073<br>(5.45)<br>[1.76] | −0.053<br>(14.97)<br>[6.36] | −0.018<br>(1.27)<br>[0.55] |
| $\theta'_{Italy}$ | 0.038<br>(1.65)<br>[3.78] | 0.068<br>(1.70)<br>[0.57] | −0.094<br>(3.32)<br>[1.31] | −0.065<br>(1.46)<br>[0.46] | 0.038<br>(2.19)<br>[4.56] | −0.010<br>(0.29)<br>[0.10] | −0.065<br>(3.65)<br>[3.11] | 0.021<br>(0.57)<br>[0.26] |
| $\theta'_{Japan}$ | −0.124<br>(6.76)<br>[5.41] | −0.104<br>(3.68)<br>[1.31] | −0.225<br>(10.13)<br>[3.39] | −0.206<br>(6.50)<br>[2.01] | | | | |
| $\theta'_{The\,Netherlands}$ | −0.065<br>(11.45)<br>[25.74] | −0.046<br>(2.19)<br>[0.61] | −0.065<br>(11.89)<br>[25.71] | −0.046<br>(1.91)<br>[0.70] | −0.065<br>(12.37)<br>[25.74] | −0.095<br>(4.59)<br>[1.41] | −0.065<br>(13.62)<br>[25.71] | −0.009<br>(0.40)<br>[0.16] |
| $\theta'_{Spain}$ | −0.031<br>(0.70)<br>[1.48] | −0.014<br>(0.28)<br>[0.19] | −0.295<br>(5.30)<br>[2.04] | −0.281<br>(4.85)<br>[1.67] | −0.032<br>(1.86)<br>[3.62] | −0.057<br>(2.38)<br>[1.04] | −0.134<br>(7.55)<br>[6.16] | −0.090<br>(3.77)<br>[2.17] |
| $\theta'_{Sweden}$ | −0.087<br>(14.21)<br>[15.41] | 0.068<br>(3.16)<br>[0.91] | −0.087<br>(14.76)<br>[15.39] | −0.067<br>(2.78)<br>[1.05] | −0.087<br>(15.36)<br>[15.41] | −0.117<br>(5.58)<br>[1.75] | −0.087<br>(16.91)<br>[15.40] | −0.030<br>(1.36)<br>[0.55] |
| $\theta'_{Switzerland}$ | −0.152<br>(15.42)<br>[4.63] | −0.147<br>(13.12)<br>[3.78] | −0.192<br>(17.65)<br>[6.04] | −0.187<br>(15.49)<br>[4.75] | −0.152<br>(8.99)<br>[4.52] | −0.161<br>(8.99)<br>[4.19] | −0.226<br>(13.65)<br>[19.46] | −0.212<br>(12.19)<br>[15.10] |
| $\theta'_{United\,Kingdom}$ | −0.055<br>(13.34)<br>[8.33] | −0.044<br>(3.61)<br>[1.02] | −0.055<br>(13.86)<br>[8.32] | −0.044<br>(3.19)<br>[1.16] | −0.055<br>(14.42)<br>[8.33] | −0.072<br>(6.01)<br>[1.80] | −0.055<br>(15.87)<br>[8.32] | −0.023<br>(1.84)<br>[0.69] |

| | (1) | (2) | (3) | (4) | (5) | (6) | (7) | (8) |
|---|---|---|---|---|---|---|---|---|
| $\theta'_{United\,States}$ | | | | | -0.149 (34.96) [10.86] | -0.173 (10.57) [3.28] | -0.149 (38.48) [10.99] | -0.105 (6.13) [2.67] |
| $\tau^w_{US,\,1987-1989}$ | | | -0.003 (0.02) [0.04] | -0.018 (0.10) [0.23] | | | | |
| $\tau^w_{US,\,1990-1992}$ | | | 1.098 (4.94) [2.02] | 1.092 (4.91) [1.97] | | | | |
| $\tau^w_{US,\,1993-1995}$ | | | 1.017 (4.58) [1.69] | 1.029 (4.62) [1.75] | | | | |
| $\tau^w_{Jap,\,1987-1989}$ | | | | | | | -0.003 (0.23) [0.04] | -0.045 (0.30) [0.76] |
| $\tau^w_{Jap,\,1990-1992}$ | | | | | | | 0.859 (4.97) [3.65] | 0.809 (4.67) [3.77] |
| $\tau^w_{Jap,\,1993-1995}$ | | | | | | | 1.118 (6.47) [5.30] | 1.148 (6.65) [5.51] |
| $\bar{R}^2$ | 0.79 | 0.79 | 0.80 | 0.80 | 0.83 | 0.83 | 0.86 | 0.86 |
| $N$ | 779 | 779 | 779 | 779 | 787 | 787 | 787 | 787 |

*Notes:* The dependent variable $g'_{j,t}$ is the return on the five-year benchmark government bond index in excess of the five-year swap rate per dollar invested in the foreign country $j$'s asset. Absolute t-statistics based on OLS are in parentheses and based on Newey–West (1987) are in square brackets. $\bar{R}^2$ is the coefficient of determination adjusted for degrees of freedom. $N$ is the number of usable observations.

before, as it became clear that the withholding tax would be repealed. These difficulties in the early period apparently are large enough to also yield insignificant withholding tax effects for the whole sample as in regressions (1), (2), (5) and (6). For regressions (3), (4), (7) and (8), the hypotheses of equal coefficients for the three withholding tax variables are rejected at the 5 per cent level (with statistics of $F_7^{264} = 30.93$, $F_7^{263} = 30.81$, $F_7^{272} = 82.71$ and $F_7^{271} = 85.51$).

## 6.4   Evaluation and Conclusion

This chapter has tested to what extent national T-bill and five-year government bond yields reflect the nonresident withholding tax regime. In the preferred Tables 6.2 and 6.4, the incidence parameter, where significantly different from zero, is positive, and frequently statistically insignificant from unity. These results suggest that at least during certain periods both three-month T-bill and five-year bond yields fully reflect the withholding tax regime. This conclusion suggests that key international investors receive few, if any, offsetting foreign tax-credits from their domestic tax authorities. This is to be expected as the marginal international investors are generally tax-exempt institutional investors such as pension funds. As a result, the net-of-tax government cost of funds may be invariant to the withholding tax rate. Nonresident withholding taxes thus appear to have few, if any, international redistributive implications.[17] At the same time, the international tax system *de facto* appears to be source based, although most countries *de jure* tax their residents' income on a worldwide basis with offsetting tax-credits for foreign-source income taxes.

While nonresident withholding taxes may have little impact on net-of-tax interest rates, they of course increase pre-tax interest rates. This increase in interest rates also benefits domestic holders of government debt that are not subject to nonresident withholding taxes. Nonresident withholding taxes thus have potentially important national redistributive implications. To the extent that domestic owners of government debt benefit from higher interest rates, the overall effect of nonresident withholding taxes on the government budget may be negative. The domestic demand for government debt thus poses an constraint on the efficacy of nonresident withholding taxes as a tool to generate net government revenues. Important in this regard is the extent to which higher pre-tax government yields cause a shift in ownership from foreign to domestic investors in government debt. In practice, governments appear to have an incentive to separate the domestic and foreign demands for their securities. Capital controls, which are now out of vogue, are one way to achieve this. Alternatively, governments can issue debts denominated in domestic and foreign currencies in an attempt to achieve market separation.

The insight that nonresident withholding taxes on the public debt may raise little government revenue may be a stimulus for countries to agree to harmonize the international withholding tax system.[18] By acting together, countries may in fact restore the efficacy of interest withholding taxes to generate net tax revenues. In 1989, the European Commission proposed the introduction of a minimum withholding tax of 15 per cent on foreign interest income. This proposal was an essential complement to the achievement of a free movement of capital. By 1 July 1990, cross-border capital transactions were virtually free. (with the exceptions of Greece, Ireland, Portugal and Spain). The elimination of restrictions on short-term capital flows, which may be most tax sensitive, followed the earlier liberalization of long-term capital flows. The liberalization of course implies that capital now can flow freely from countries with source-level interest taxation to countries without any such taxation. Despite the obvious benefits of concerted European action, the minimum withholding tax proposal was rejected over concerns about its effects for Europe's financial centres.[19] The European Commission (1996), however, recently restated its view that introducing a minimum withholding tax along the lines of the 1989 proposal would be a valuable first step towards ensuring the effective taxation of international interest income. The European debate on withholding tax policy points out that a common withholding tax policy ideally also involves the non-European industrialized countries and financial centres.

# Notes

1. See Gustavsson (1990) and KPMG (1988) for surveys.

2. Several reasons for deviations from covered interest parity other than plain credit risk have been noted in the literature. See Officer and Willett (1970) for an early survey. Aliber (1973) specifically considers political risk, while Frenkel and Levich (1975, 1977) and Clinton (1988) focus on transaction costs. Transaction costs, specifically, create a band of deviations around covered interest parity for which no profitable arbitrage is possible. Taylor (1987, 1989) further points out the role of data imperfections, and Dooley and Isard (1980), Otani and Tiwari (1981) and Ito (1986) consider capital controls.

3. Formally, an interest swap is a contractual agreement whereby two parties exchange a series of cash flows determined by two different interest rates on the same notional principal for a defined period of time. For a description of interest rate swaps, see Hull (1993) and Smithson, Smith and Wilford (1995).

4. In January 1989 the German government introduced a withholding tax of 10 per cent for all German domestic instruments held by residents and nonresidents. The tax was first announced in October 1987 and this resulted in massive capital outflows. On 1 July 1989, just six months after its inception, the withholding tax was removed (Deutsche Bundesbank, 1994).

5. Demirgüç-Kunt and Huizinga (1995) examine the impact of dividend and capital gains withholding taxes as imposed by developing countries on their pre-tax equity returns. Only withholding taxes on capital gains appear to have a discernible impact on pre-tax equity returns. This is consistent with the rather limited creditability of nonresident capital gains withholding taxes in the United States and other capital-exporting countries. In the domestic tax area, Poterba (1986) and Feenberg and Poterba (1991) examine the implied marginal tax rates and revenue losses in the market for tax-exempt bonds in the United States.

6. The covered interest parity linking offshore interbank interest rates and forward exchange rates generally holds very well. Government debt yields with different repayment prospects and subject to different tax regimes, however, may give rise to substantive deviations from covered interest parity.

7. By 1992, Japanese and US institutional investors (pension funds, life insurance funds, non-life insurance companies, and mutual funds) held assets of 2.0 and 7.2 trillion US dollars, respectively. In contrast, institutional investors in Canada, Germany, and the United Kingdom held assets of 0.4, 0.8 and 1.4 trillion US dollars. Further, Japanese and US pension funds (life insurance companies) held 8.4 and 4.6 (11.4 and 3.7) percent of total assets abroad. For US pension funds this translates into absolute foreign holdings of around 150 billion US dollars. See International Monetary Fund (1995, Tables II.6 and II.7).

8. See Lyon and Silverstein (1995, p. 157) for a discussion of foreign tax credits and income baskets.

9. T-bills are promises of the Treasury to pay a stipulated amount on a stated maturity (Garbade, 1982).

10. Note that since 1 January 1994 so-called Dutch Treasury Certificates (DTCs) exist to finance temporary cash deficits of the government (Goudswaard, De Haan, De Haan and Oort, 1996, p. 33).

11. With country dummies included, identification of the tax variables stems from tax rate changes.

12. The Newey–West (1987) correction is based on Bartlett weights and second-order lags.

13. Broadly interpreted, sovereign risk includes credit risk and policy risk stemming from, for instance, tax policy uncertainty.

14. See Lemmen and Eijffinger (1996b) for an empirical analysis of the determinants of capital controls in member states of the EU.

15. Note that the tax-inclusive specification excludes the possibility of spurious correlation.

16. The Newey–West (1987) correction is based on Bartlett weights and fifty-nine-order lags.

17. Nonresident withholding taxes represent to some extent a direct transfer of resources from the lender's tax authority to the borrowing government.

18. While debt pricing depends on the marginal investor in government debt, the net revenue implications of nonresident withholding taxes also depend on inframarginal holders of this debt.

19. See Kopits (1992, pp. 66–71) and Huizinga (1994, p. 279) for more information.

# Appendix 6A1: Data Sources

*Description of T-bill rates*

| Country | Period | Description | Source |
|---|---|---|---|
| Australia | January 1980–December 1994 | Three-month T-bill rate in percentage per year (end-of-period) | DATASTREAM, National Government Series |
| Belgium | January 1980–December 1994 | Three-month T-bill rate in percentages per year (end-of-period) | DATASTREAM, National Government Series |
| Canada | January 1980–December 1994 | Three-month T-bill rate in percentages per year (end-of-period) | DATASTREAM, National Government Series |
| France | December 1986–December 1994 | Bons du tresor, marché secondaire, three months, last quotation (end-of-period) | Banque de France |
| Germany | January 1980–December 1994 | Three-month T-bill rate in percentages per year (end-of-period) | DATASTREAM, National Government Series |
| Italy | January 1980–December 1994 | Three-month T-bill rate in percentages per year (end-of-period) | DATASTREAM, National Government Series |
| Japan | January 1980–December 1994 | Three-month Gensaki rate in percentages per year, that is the repurchase agreement rate using long-term bonds and more recently using T-bills as collateral (end-of-period) | Bank of Japan |
| The Netherlands | January 1980–January 1991 | Three-month T-bill rate in percentages per year (end-of-period) | DATASTREAM, National Government Series |
| Sweden | January 1981–December 1994 | Three-month T-bill rate in percentages per year (end-of-period) | Sveriges Riksbank |
| Switzerland | January 1980–December 1994 | Three-month Eidgnössische Geldmarktbuchforderungen in percentages per year (yield of last issue in month) | Schweizerische National Bank |
| United Kingdom | January 1980–December 1994 | Three-month T-bill rate in percentages per year (end-of-period) | DATASTREAM, National Government Series |
| United States | January 1980–December 1994 | Three-month T-bill rate in percentages per year (end-of-period) | DATASTREAM, National Government Series |

*Description of spot exchange rates vis-à-vis the US dollar*

End-of-period spot exchange rates over the period January 1980–December 1994 *vis-à-vis* the US dollar are obtained from IMF, *International Financial Statistics*, line ae via DATASTREAM

## Description of three-month forward exchange rates vis-à-vis the US dollar

End-of-period three-month forward exchange rates *vis-à-vis* the US dollar are obtained from IMF, *International Financial Statistics*, line b. If they are not available they are calculated from the formula for the forward premium $p_{j,t}$ on foreign country $j$'s currency at time $t$ in per cent per annum as explained in IMF (1985):

$$p_{j,t} = \frac{(S_{j,t} - F_{j,t}^{(3)}) \times 4 \times 100}{S_{j,t}}$$

End-of-period forward premia (discounts) are obtained from the IMF, *International Financial Statistics*, line 60f. The annualized forward premium (discount) is based on a 360-day year, and the three-month forward exchange rate is the rate for 90 days, yielding the factor 4 that is employed in the formula. If forward exchange rates from the IMF are unavailable, end-of-period three-month forward exchange rates *vis-à-vis* the US dollar are obtained from Barclays Bank (Canada: November 1994–December 1994 and The Netherlands: November 1993–December 1994). All data are obtained via DATASTREAM.

## Interest rate swaps and corresponding government bond yields

Interest rate swaps (see floating payment reset frequency)

| | |
|---|---|
| Source of data: | Intercapital Brokers Ltd as collected by DART Ltd obtained via DATASTREAM |
| Time of day quotes: | End of UK business day, middle rate |
| Fixed business day convention: | All modified succeeding |
| Floating business day convention: | All modified succeeding |
| Floating resets: | All discrete |
| Settlement lag: | None |
| Frequency: | Monthly, end-of-month |

Benchmark five-year government bond indices – redemption yield (see fixed payment frequency)

| | |
|---|---|
| Source of data: | EFFAS (European Federation of Financial Analysts Societies) obtained via DATASTREAM |
| Time of day quotes: | End of UK business day, middle rate |
| Frequency: | Monthly, end-of-month |

Following DART's currency specifications, data are annualized,

$$\left[ 1 + \frac{annual\ yield}{100} \right] = \left[ 1 + \frac{semi - annual\ yield}{200} \right]^2$$

and converted to a 360-day year by multiplying by 360/365 if necessary (see table).

| Country | Period | Fixed payment frequency | Fixed day count basis | Floating payment reset frequency | Floating day count basis |
|---|---|---|---|---|---|
| Belgium | June 1991–December 1995 | Annual | Actual/365 | Semi-Annual | Actual/365 |
| Canada | June 1993–December 1995 | Semi-Annual | Actual/365 | Semi-Annual | Actual/360 |
| Denmark | February 1993–December 1995 | Annual | 30/360 | Semi-Annual | Actual/360 |
| France | June 1991–December 1995 | Annual | Actual/Actual | Semi-Annual | Actual/360 |
| Germany | April 1987–December 1995 | Annual | 30/360 | Semi-Annual | Actual/360 |
| Italy | March 1991–December 1995 | Annual | 30/360 | Semi-Annual | Actual/360 |
| Japan | September 1989–December 1995 | Semi-Annual | Actual/365 | Semi-Annual | Actual/360 |
| The Netherlands | June 1991–December 1995 | Annual | 30/360 | Semi-Annual | Actual/360 |
| Spain | January 1991–December 1995 | Annual | 30/360 | Semi-Annual | Actual/360 |
| Sweden | January 1992–December 1995 | Annual | 30/360 | Semi-Annual | Actual/360 |
| Switzerland | January 1988–December 1995 | Annual | 30/360 | Semi-Annual | Actual/360 |
| United Kingdom | April 1987–December 1995 | Semi-Annual | Actual/365 | Semi-Annual | Actual/365 |
| United States | January 1989–December 1995 | Annual | Actual/360 | Semi-Annual | Actual/360 |

*Source:* Data Analysis Risk Technology Limited, Park House, 16 Finsbury Circus, London.

## Withholding tax rates

Coopers and Lybrand, *International Tax Summaries*, 1980–1995 Issues.

Interfisc, loose-leaf.

International Bureau of Fiscal Documentation, The Taxation of Private Investment Income, *Guides to European Taxation*, Vol. 3, Amsterdam.

KPMG (1988), *Withholding Taxes on Interest*, 2nd Edition, Frankfurt, July.

## Control variables

INF   =   Realized change in the consumer price index (1990=100). *Source:* IMF, *International Financial Statistics*, line 64.

DEBT   =   General government gross debt over gross domestic product. *Sources:* OECD (1995), *Economic Outlook*, No. 57, except for Switzerland, IMF, *International Financial Statistics*. Debt ratios of Australia are only available from 1987 onwards.

# PART III

# CONCLUSION

# 7. Summary and Conclusions

This study examined the measurement and determination of financial integration in the EU. Chapter 1 argued that the concept of financial integration is difficult to define. Financial integration is associated with the equalization of returns of similar financial assets across markets so that the law of one price holds. Although the law of one price definition of financial integration is theoretically preferable, the measurement of financial integration often relied on broader concepts. We briefly summarize the results of the three most influential methods to measure the degree of financial integration.

## (a) What can we learn from interest parity conditions?

Our results for CIP in Chapter 2 indicate an increasing degree of money market integration in Europe as measured by the CIP condition. The size and variability of mean (absolute) country premia declined significantly after the Basle–Nyborg agreement of September 1987. Perfect capital mobility of type I (CIP integration) can be said to exist between eight European countries and Germany. Portugal and Greece are the exceptions to the rule and are not (yet) completely integrated with Germany. In addition, the initial low degree of CIP integration urged countries like France, Greece, Italy, Portugal and Spain to catch up with the rest of the European countries during the 1980s. We also found that CIP deviations are much smaller than deviations from *ex post* UIP and *ex post* RIP. *Ex post* UIP and RIP generally do not hold, although uncovered and real interest differentials fell in the countries participating in the ERM before the first EMS crisis. Subsequently, we concluded that it is rather difficult to draw firm conclusions regarding the integration of money markets with the help of the *ex ante* UIP and the *ex ante* RIP conditions. *Ex ante* UIP incorporates expectations regarding future exchange rate changes, which are hard to predict. Tests of UIP suffer from the need to make an assumption about these unobservable expectations resulting in tests of joint hypotheses. Peso problems may also have resulted in rejection of *ex ante* UIP. Contrary to the CIP condition, the UIP condition can only give an *indirect* indication of financial integration.

Even more difficulties arise with the RIP condition as a measure for financial integration. *Ex ante* RIP only has an *indirect* impact on capital flows via its influence on exchange rate expectations. If *ex ante* PPP holds, different inflationary expectations are validated by an appropriate exchange rate adjustment. However, despite European inflation convergence and the exchange rate stabilizing effect of the ERM, exchange rate uncertainty remains. With 'incomplete goods and factor market integration, exchange rate uncertainties translate in large real exchange rate movements (deviations from *ex ante* PPP). Subsequently, this requires changes in exchange rate parities to eliminate undesirable real exchange rate movements.

In most EU countries, the greater integration of financial markets seriously reduced the ability to conduct independent monetary policy. With relatively fixed exchange rates (as in the EMS), the freedom of capital movements promotes low-risk interest arbitrage when interest rates differ across countries. In the limiting case – with perfect financial integration – movements of capital induce interest rates to be maintained at parity level across countries. This means that, for example, a reduction of domestic interest rates resulting from an expansionary monetary policy induces capital to flow out of the country, thereby offsetting the monetary expansion and provoking a rise in domestic interest rates back to the parity level.

The reason for which interest parity conditions may not hold may also result from the great diversity of assets. Such diversity in terms of quality of debtor, size, depth and segmentation of markets makes it more difficult to find really comparable assets. The concept of financial integration is less meaningful when applied at a level of aggregation that includes *all* categories of capital. Capital mobility may be short-term financial instruments such as Treasury bills, time deposits, certificates of deposits and commercial papers or long-term financial assets such as government and corporate bonds, or it may be portfolio equity investment and direct investment. Capital mobility is best viewed, at least empirically, by focusing on specific assets with similar characteristics. As we have seen in Chapter 6, concentrating on specific assets (three-month Treasury bills and five-year government bonds) may be more informative.

Research of the extent of financial integration is often confined to short-term assets since forward exchange markets for longer maturities are either unavailable or very thin. However, in Chapter 6, we innovatively apply interest rate swaps to examine closed interest parity for long-term bonds. In Chapter 6 we saw that the pricing in five-year government bond markets is highly efficient, while pricing in three-month Treasury bill markets is still inefficient. Nevertheless, we expect the breadth and depth of Treasury bill markets to increase with the transition to EMU.

### (b) What can we learn from savings-investment correlations?

Chapter 3, applying an error-correction model of savings-investment correlations, concluded that the apparent decline of short-term savings-investment correlations indicates that an increasing share of total savings and investment is held in internationally traded securities. Not only arbitrage from the wholesale markets but also from retail financial markets may have contributed to this result. Clearly, the F–H criterion is more concerned with this latter segment whereas interest parity conditions are more concerned with the former segment. Individuals and small investors, regardless of the country of origin, now have access to the same information with respect to foreign assets as a result of the tremendous improvement in computer and telecommunication technology.

### (c) What can we learn from consumption correlations?

Can countries borrow against future income? Some countries may prefer current consumption to future consumption, while other countries prefer future consumption to current consumption. Chapter 4 found that there is still significant room for risk diversification among EU countries. Per capita consumption growth correlations across European countries are far below unity and differ considerably. However, cross-country consumption correlations have typically been larger during the 1979–1992 period than during the 1961–1978 period, which might be viewed as an indication of closer financial integration in the second half of the sample period. Consumption now increasingly depends both on current and future income (the cross-country permanent income hypothesis).

The result of the above developments has been an enormous increase of expectations-driven short-term capital flows. Expectations of interest rate changes, inflationary and exchange rate expectations are important in determining the direction and extent of these capital flows and in determining the country and exchange risk premia imposed by the international financial community on particular countries.

### (d) Financial integration and country risks

Country risks may include capital controls and also include common events such as changes in taxation and changes in government. The international financial community punishes governments applying the wrong mix of macroeconomic policies. As we have seen in Chapter 5, country risk premia depend on a small number of 'fundamentals', including (realized) inflation, government instability and gross fixed capital formation. Furthermore, risks concerned with elections, government changes and bank failures may affect country risk premia. Capital flows increasingly depend on varying national economic and financial market structures.

The history of high inflation in Finland, Italy, Sweden and the United Kingdom typically have made these countries more dependent on short-term financing at variable interest rates, and thus more sensitive to shifts in short-term nominal interest rates. Also cultural and political factors have led to differences in financial structure. In this respect, the average debt maturity of the domestic sectors is of crucial importance. Large proportions of short-dated liabilities of domestic sectors (for example, government debt) are a potential threat to the viability of the financial system. The resulting short-termism of many borrowers and investors frustrates medium- and long-term oriented monetary and fiscal policies. Although, short-term oriented policies may be optimal in countries like Finland, Italy, Sweden and the United Kingdom, they are not in other EU countries (for example, Austria, Germany, France and The Netherlands). However, due to strong financial linkages, this group has become highly sensitive to events and policy actions of the previous group. Given the strong differences in national economic and financial structures, and given the fact that existing structures change gradually, and with capital controls coming down, these differences will decisively affect the direction of capital flows within the EU – the more so because not all country specific risks can be diversified away. Countries may be confronted with higher financing costs of their investments and debts. Investors simply ask compensation for holding the assets of these countries. On the other hand, countries like Finland, Italy, Sweden and the United Kingdom can benefit from the stability of the other group. More research is needed to examine the impact of differences in national economic and financial market structure on cross-border capital flows.

### (e) Financial integration and exchange rate risk

Exchange rate risks (unexpected exchange rate changes) provide an important obstacle to deeper financial integration in the EU since not all exchange risk can be hedged. The risk of an appreciation of the home currency relative to all other foreign currencies would be a risk common to all foreign investment and cannot be diversified away. Moreover, with markets being more integrated, the scope for further risk diversification may decline. Consequently, unhedged exchange rate risks continue to affect foreign investment decisions. We have seen in Chapter 2 that exchange rate uncertainties lead to differences in uncovered returns between markets. Exchange rate uncertainty undoubtedly will be a major determinant of European capital flows.

### (f) Financial integration and regulatory arbitrage

Financial integration will lead to regulatory arbitrage (see Chapter 6). If regulations are excessive, market participants will simply go to less restrictive jurisdictions. On the other hand, financial institutions probably also value their access to lender-of-last-resort facilities, the opportunity to be headquartered in a stable political climate, availability of qualified personnel, and so forth. Therefore, financial institutions find it in their interest to pay some regulatory tax. Future research of financial integration should focus on remaining factors which influence the free movement of capital within the EU. Research should identify these factors, and subsequently quantify their importance. In particular, fiscal factors such as withholding taxes on dividend and interest, capital gains taxes, reserve requirements, deposit insurance schemes and capital adequacy standards are important regulations which might affect the extent and direction of capital flows. Interestingly, one may want to analyze the incentives for evasion and the international redistributive implications of these fiscal regulations. Again, empirical estimation is called for to determine who precisely bears the burden of these regulations. Changes in these factors may have profound implications for the development of Europe's financial centres.

Finally, despite the worldwide trend of financial integration, we have argued that financial integration in fact is taking place regionally. The integration of countries' financial markets within a region, may well go hand in hand with discrimination of investments of countries outside the region. The recent movement towards EMU may lead to new explicit and implicit barriers for those countries which do not enter EMU.

# References

Aarle, B. van, S.C.W. Eijffinger and J.J.G. Lemmen (1995), 'Geldmarktintegratie, geloofwaardigheid van het monetair beleid en wisselkoersstabiliteit in het EMS', *Het Economisch en Sociaal Tijdschrift*, **49** (2), 257–80.

Aiyagari, S.R. (1993), 'Explaining Financial Markets Facts: The Importance of Incomplete Markets and Transaction Costs', *Federal Reserve Bank of Minneapolis Quarterly Review*, Winter, 17–31.

Akdogan, H. (1995), *The Integration of International Capital Markets: Theory and Empirical Evidence*, Edward Elgar, Aldershot.

Akhtar, M.A. and K. Weiller (1987), 'Developments in International Capital Mobility, A Perspective on the Underlying Forces and the Empirical Literature', In: Federal Reserve Bank of New York, *Research Papers on International Integration of Financial Markets and U.S. Monetary Policy*, New York, December, 13–69.

Alesina, A. (1988), 'Macroeconomics and Politics', In: S. Fischer (ed.), *NBER Macroeconomics Annual*, MIT Press, Cambridge, Mass., 13–61.

Alesina, A. (1989), 'Politics and Business Cycles in Industrial Democracies', *Economic Policy*, No. 8, 57–98.

Alesina, A., V. Grilli and G.M. Milesi-Ferretti (1994), 'The Political Economy of Capital Controls', In: L. Leiderman and A. Razin (eds.), *Capital Mobility: The Impact on Consumption, Investment and Growth*, Cambridge University Press, Cambridge, 329–47.

Aliber, R.Z. (1973), 'The Interest Rate Parity Theorem: A Reinterpretation', *Journal of Political Economy*, **81**, 1451–9.

Artis, M. and T. Bayoumi (1991), 'Global Capital Market Integration and the Current Account', In: M.P. Taylor (ed.), *Money and Financial Markets*, Basil Blackwell, Oxford, 297–307.

Bacchetta, P. (1993), 'Capital Controls and the Political Premium: The Spanish Experience in the late 1980s', Institut d'Anàlisi Econòmica and Studienzentrum Gerzensee, November.

Balassa, B. (1962), *The Theory of Economic Integration*, George Allen & Unwin, London.

Banerjee, A, J.J. Dolado, D.F. Hendry and G.W. Smith (1986), 'Exploring Equilibrium Relationships in Econometrics Through Static Models: Some Monte Carlo Evidence', *Oxford Bulletin of Economics and Statistics*, **48** (3), 253–77.

Bank for International Settlements (1990), *International Capital Flows, Exchange Rate Determination and Persistent Current-account Imbalances*, Monetary and Economic Department, C.B. 389, June, Basle.

Bank for International Settlements (1994), *64th Annual Report*, June, Basle.

Banks, A.S. (ed.) (1993), *Political Handbook of the World: 1993*, CSA Publications, State University of New York, Binghamton, New York.

Barro, R.J. and X. Sala-I-Martin (1990), 'World Real Interest Rates', *NBER Working Paper*, No. 3317, Cambridge.

Bayoumi, T. (1990), 'Saving-Investment Correlations: Immobile Capital, Government Policy, or Endogenous Behaviour?', *IMF Staff Papers*, **37** (2), 360–87.

Bayoumi, T. and R. MacDonald (1995), 'Consumption, Income and International Capital Market Integration', *IMF Staff Papers*, **42** (3), 552–76.

Bhandari, J.S. and T.H. Mayer (1990), 'A Note on Saving-Investment Correlations in the EMS', *IMF Working Paper*, No. 97, Washington.

Bisignano, J. (1994), 'The Internationalisation of Financial Markets: Measurement, Benefits and Unexpected Interdependence', In: Banque de France, Mouvements de Capitaux et Marchés des Changes, *Cahiers Économiques et Monétaires*, No. 43, 9–71.

Bleany, M. (1992), 'Does Long Run Purchasing Power Parity Hold within the European Monetary System?', *Journal of Economic Studies*, **19** (3), 66–72.

Blundell-Wignall, A. and F. Browne (1991), 'Increasing Financial Market Integration, Real Exchange Rates and Macroeconomic Adjustment', *OECD Working Papers*, No. 96, Paris.

Boothe, P., K. Clinton, A. Côté and D. Longworth (1985), *International Asset Substitutability, Theory and Evidence for Canada*, Bank of Canada, February.

Boughton, J.M. (1988), 'The Monetary Approach to Exchange Rates, What Now Remains?', *Essays in International Finance*, No. 171, Princeton University, Princeton.

Branson, W.H. (1988), 'Comments', *European Economic Review*, **32**, 1119–21.

Brean, D.J.S. (1984), 'International Portfolio Capital: The Wedge of the Withholding Tax', *National Tax Journal*, **37** (2), 239–47.

Brennan, M.J. and B. Solnik (1989), 'International Risk Sharing and Capital Mobility', *Journal of International Money and Finance*, **8** (3), 359–73.

Burda, M. and C. Wyplosz (1993), *Macroeconomics, A European Text*, Oxford University Press, Oxford.

Cairncross, A. (1973), *Control of Long-term International Capital Movements*, The Brookings Institution, Washington.

Canova, F. and M.O. Ravn (1994), 'International Consumption Risk Sharing', *CEPR Discussion Paper*, No. 1074, London.

Caramazza, F., K. Clinton, A. Côté and D. Longworth (1986), 'International Capital Mobility and Asset Substitutability, Some Theory and Evidence on Recent Structural Changes', Bank of Canada, *Technical Report*, No. 44, October.

Clinton, K. (1988), 'Transactions Costs and Covered Interest Arbitrage: Theory and Evidence', *Journal of Political Economy*, **96** (2), 358–70.

Coakley, J., F. Kulasi and R. Smith (1996), 'Current Account Solvency and the Feldstein–Horioka Puzzle', *Economic Journal*, **106** (436), 620–27.

Collins, S.M. (1988), 'Inflation and the European Monetary System', In: F. Giavazzi, S. Micossi and M. Miller (eds.), *The European Monetary System*, Cambridge University Press, Cambridge, 112–39.

Commission of the European Communities (1988), 'Creation of a European Financial Area, Liberalization of Capital Movements and Financial Integration in the Community', *European Economy*, No. 36, Luxemburg.

Commission of the European Communities (1989), *General Arrangements Applicable to Capital Movements*, Directorate–General for Economic and Financial Affairs, Document, No. CB–55–89–859–EN–C, Brussels.

Commission of the European Communities (1990), 'One Market, One Money, An Evaluation of the Potential Benefits and Costs of Forming an Economic and Monetary Union', *European Economy*, No. 44, Luxemburg.

Committee of Governors of the Central Banks of the Member States of the European Economic Community (1987), *Press Communiqué*, 18 September.

Committee of Governors of the Central Banks of the Member States of the European Economic Community (1993), *Annual Report 1992*, April.

Cooper, S. (1991), 'Cross-border Savings Flows and Capital Mobility in the G7 Economies', *Bank of England Discussion Paper*, No. 54, London.

Coopers and Lybrand, *International Tax Summaries*, 1980–1995 Issues.

Cottarelli, C. and A. Kourelis (1994), 'Financial Structure, Bank Lending Rates, and the Transmission Mechanism of Monetary Policy', *IMF Staff Papers*, **41** (4), 587–628.

Cukierman, A. (1992), *Central Bank Strategy, Credibility, and Independence*, MIT Press, Cambridge, Mass.

Cukierman, A., S. Edwards and G. Tabellini (1992), 'Seigniorage and Political Instability', *American Economic Review*, **82** (3), 537–55.

Cumby, R.E. and M. Obstfeld (1984), 'International Interest Rate and Price Level Linkages under Flexible Exchange Rates: A Review of Recent Evidence', In: J.F.O. Bilson and R. Marston, *Exchange Rate Theory in Practice*, University of Chicago Press, Chicago, 121–51.

Dean, A., M. Durand, J. Fallon and P. Hoeller (1990), 'Saving Trends and Behaviour in OECD Countries', *OECD Economic Studies*, No. 14, 7–58.

Delors Report (1989), *Report on Economic and Monetary Union in the European Community*, Committee for the Study of Economic and Monetary Union, April, Luxemburg.

Demirgüç-Kunt, A. and H.P. Huizinga (1995), 'Barriers to Portfolio Investments in Emerging Stock Markets', *Journal of Development Economics*, **47** (2), 355–74.

Deutsche Bundesbank (1985), 'Zur Freizügigkeit im Kapitalverkehr der Bundesrepublik mit dem Ausland', *Monatsbericht*, July, 13–24.

Deutsche Bundesbank (1994), 'Aufkommen und ökonomische Auswirkungen des steuerlichen Zinsabschlags', *Monatsbericht*, January, 45–58.

Dickey D.A. and W.A. Fuller (1979), 'Distribution of the Estimators for Autoregressive Time Series With a Unit Root', *Journal of the American Statistical Association*, **179** (366), 427–31.

Dooley, M., J. Frankel and D.J. Mathieson (1987), 'International Capital Mobility: What Do Saving-Investment Correlations Tell Us?', *IMF Staff Papers*, **34** (3), 503–30.

Dooley, M.P. and P. Isard (1980), 'Capital Controls, Political Risks, and Deviations from Interest-rate Parity', *Journal of Political Economy*, **88** (2), 370–84.

Dornbusch, R. (1976), 'Expectations and Exchange Rate Dynamics', *Journal of Political Economy*, **84** (6), 1161–76.

Dornbusch, R. (1980), *Open Economy Macroeconomics*, Basic Books, New York.

Dougherty, C. (1992), *Introduction to Econometrics*, Oxford University Press, Oxford.

Economist, The (1992), *Fear of Finance, A Survey of the World Economy*, 19 September, 4–48.

Edey, M. and K. Hviding (1995), 'An Assessment of Financial Reform in OECD Countries', *OECD Economic Studies*, No. 25, 7–36.

Ees, H. van, J. de Haan and D. Wansink (1989), 'Financiële integratie: De gevolgen voor het Nederlandse financiële systeem', In: J. de Haan and L.H. Hoogduin (eds.), *De gevolgen van financiële innovatie en integratie voor het monetaire beleid*, NIBE, Amsterdam, 94–118.

Eichberger, J. and I. Harper (1993), *Financial Economics*, Chapter 3, Manuscript.

Eichengreen, B., J. Tobin and C. Wyplosz (1995), 'Two Cases for Sand in the Wheels of International Finance', *Economic Journal*, **105** (428), 162–72.

Eijffinger, S.C.W. (1993), 'Convergence of Monetary Policies in Europe – Concepts, Targets and Instruments', In: K. Gretschmann (ed.), *Economic and Monetary Union, Implications for National Policy-makers*, European Institute of Public Administration, Martinus Nijhoff Publishers, Dordrecht, 169–93.

Eijffinger, S.C.W. (1994), 'Financial Integration and Monetary Convergence: The Main Challenges of EMU's Stage Two', In: European League for Economic Co-operation, Institutional Convergence: A Prerequisite for Monetary Union, *Cahier Comte Boël*, No. 3, 7–22.

Eijffinger, S.C.W. (1996), *Future European Monetary Policy*, Inaugural Lecture, Humboldt University of Berlin, Berlin.

Eijffinger, S.C.W. and J.L. Gerards (eds.) (1993), *European Monetary Integration and the Financial Sector*, NIBE, Amsterdam.

Eijffinger, S.C.W., H.P. Huizinga and J.J.G. Lemmen (1997), 'Naar een Europese bronbelasting op rente', *Economisch Statistische Berichten*, November, **82** (4127), 40–2.

Eijffinger, S.C.W., H.P. Huizinga and J.J.G. Lemmen (1998), 'Short-term and Long-term Government Debt and Nonresident Interest Withholding Taxes', *Journal of Public Economics*, **68** (3), 309-34.

Eijffinger, S.C.W. and M. van Keulen (1995), 'Central Bank Independence in Another Eleven Countries', *Banca Nazionale del Lavoro Quarterly Review*, No. 192, 39–83.

Eijffinger, S.C.W. and J.J.G. Lemmen (1995), 'Money Market Integration in Europe', *Swiss Journal of Economics and Statistics*, **131** (1), 3–37.

Eijffinger, S.C.W. and E. Schaling (1993), 'Central Bank Independence in Twelve Countries', *Banca Nazionale del Lavoro Quarterly Review*, No. 184, 49–89.

Engle, R.F. (1982), 'Autoregressive Conditional Heteroskedasticity with Estimates of the Variance of United Kingdom Inflation', *Econometrica*, **50** (4), 987–1007.

Engle, R.F and C.W.J. Granger (1987), 'Co-integration and Error Correction: Representation, Estimation, and Testing', *Econometrica*, **55** (2), 251–76.

Epstein, G.A. and J.B. Schor (1992), 'Structural Determinants and Economic Effects of Capital Controls in OECD Countries', In: T. Banuri and J.B. Schor (eds.), *Financial Openness and National Autonomy, Opportunities and Constraints*, Clarendon, Oxford, 136–61.

European Commission (1996), *Taxation in the European Union*, Report on the Development of Tax Systems, Brussels, COM(96) 546 final.

Eurostat (1993), *Money and Finance*, Statistical Document, Statistical Office of the European Communities, No. 3, Luxemburg.

Fair, D.E. and R.J. Raymond (eds.) (1994), 'The Competitiveness of Financial Institutions and Centres in Europe', *Financial and Monetary Policy Studies*, No. 28, SUERF, Kluwer Academic Publishers, Dordrecht.

Feenberg, D.R. and J.M. Poterba (1991), 'Which Households Own Municipal Bonds? Evidence From Tax Returns', *National Tax Journal*, **54** (4–1), 93–103.

Feldman, R.A. (1986), *Japanese Financial Markets, Deficits, Dilemmas, and Deregulation*, MIT Press, Cambridge, Mass..

Feldstein, M. (1983), 'Domestic Saving and International Capital Movements in the Long Run and the Short Run', *European Economic Review*, **21**, 129–51.

Feldstein, M. and P. Bacchetta (1989), 'National Saving and International Investment', *NBER Working Paper*, No. 3164, Cambridge (also appeared in B.D. Bernheim and J.B. Shoven (eds.) (1991), *National Saving and Economic Performance*, University of Chicago Press, Chicago, 201–26).

Feldstein, M. and C. Horioka (1980), 'Domestic Savings and International Capital Flows', *Economic Journal*, **90** (2), 314–29.

Fieleke, N.S. (1982), 'National Saving and International Investment', In: Federal Reserve Bank of Boston, Saving and Government Policy, *Federal Reserve Bank of Boston Conference Series*, No. 25, 138–57.

Frankel, J.A. (1986), 'International Capital Mobility and Crowding-out in the U.S. Economy, Imperfect Integration of Financial Markets or of Goods Markets?', In: R.W. Hafer (ed.), *How Open is the U.S. Economy?*, Lexington, Mass., 33–67.

Frankel, J.A. (1988), 'International Capital Mobility and Exchange Rate Volatility', In: N.S. Fieleke (ed.), International Payments Imbalances in the 1980s, *Federal Reserve Bank of Boston Conference Series*, No. 32, 162–88.

Frankel, J.A. (1989), 'Quantifying International Capital Mobility in the 1980s', *NBER Working Paper*, No. 2856, Cambridge (also appeared in B.D. Bernheim and J.B. Shoven (eds.) (1991), *National Saving and Economic Performance*, University of Chicago Press, Chicago, 227–60).

Frankel, J.A. (1990), 'International Financial Integration, Relations among Interest Rates and Exchange Rates, and Monetary Indicators', In: C.A. Pigott (ed.), *International Financial Integration and U.S. Monetary Policy*, Federal Reserve Bank of New York, New York, 15–49.

Frankel, J.A. (1992), 'Measuring International Capital Mobility: A Review', *American Economic Review*, **82** (2), 197–202.

Frankel, J.A. and A.T. MacArthur (1988), 'Political vs. Currency Premia in International Real Interest Differentials, A Study of Forward Rates for 24 Countries', *European Economic Review*, **32**, 1083–118.

Frankel, J., S. Phillips and M. Chinn (1993), 'Financial and Currency Integration in the European Monetary System, The Statistical Record', In: F. Torres and F. Giavazzi (eds.), *Adjustment and Growth in the European Monetary Union*, Cambridge University Press, Cambridge, 270–306.

Fratianni, M. and L. MacDonald Wakeman (1982), 'The Law of One Price in the Eurocurrency Market', *Journal of International Money and Finance*, **1** (3), 307–23.

French, K.R. and J.M. Poterba (1991), 'Investor Diversification and International Equity Returns', *American Economic Review*, **81** (2), 222–6.

Frenkel, J.A. and R.M. Levich (1975), 'Covered Interest Arbitrage: Unexploited Profits?', *Journal of Political Economy*, **83** (2), 325–38.

Frenkel, J.A. and R.M. Levich (1977), 'Transaction Costs and Interest Arbitrage: Tranquil versus Turbulent Periods', *Journal of Political Economy*, **85** (6), 1209–26.

Fukao, M. and M. Hanazaki (1987), 'Internationalisation of Financial Markets and the Allocation of Capital', *OECD Economic Studies*, No. 8, 35–92.

Fuller, W.A. (1976), *Introduction to Statistical Time Series*, John Wiley & Sons, New York.

Gaab, W., M.J. Granziol and M. Horner (1986), 'On Some International Parity Conditions, An Empirical Investigation', *European Economic Review*, **30**, 683–713.

Garbade, K. (1982), *Securities Markets*, McGraw–Hill, New York.

Garber, P. and M.P. Taylor (1995), 'Sand in the Wheels of Foreign Exchange Markets: A Skeptical View', *The Economic Journal*, **105** (428), 173–80.

Gärtner, M. (1993), *Macroeconomics under Flexible Exchange Rates*, Harvester Wheatsheaf, New York.

Gemert, H.G. van and A.P.D. Gruijters (1994), 'Patterns of Financial Change in the OECD Area', *Banca Nazionale del Lavoro Quarterly Review*, No. 190, 271–94.

Giavazzi, F. and A. Giovannini (1989), *Limiting Exchange Rate Flexibility, The European Monetary System*, MIT Press, Cambridge, Mass.

Giavazzi, F. and M. Pagano (1988), 'The Advantage of Tying One's Hands, EMS Discipline and Central Bank Credibility', *European Economic Review*, **32**, 1055–82.

Goldsbrough, D. and R. Teja (1991), 'Globalization of Financial Markets and Implications for Pacific Basin Countries', *IMF Working Paper*, No. 34, Washington.

Goldstein, M., D.J. Mathieson and T. Lane (1991), 'Determinants and Systemic Consequences of International Capital Flows', In: International Monetary Fund, Determinants and Systemic Consequences of International Capital Flows, *IMF Occasional Paper*, No. 77, 1–45.

Goldstein, M. and M. Mussa (1993), 'The Integration of World Capital Markets', *IMF Working Paper*, No. 95, Washington.

Golub, S.S. (1990), 'International Capital Mobility: Net Versus Gross Stocks and Flows', *Journal of International Money and Finance*, **9** (4), 424–39.

Goodhart, C.A.E. (1990), 'International Considerations in the Formulation of Monetary Policy', In: C.A. Pigott (ed.), *International Financial Integration and U.S. Monetary Policy*, Federal Reserve Bank of New York, New York, 119–62.

Goodhart, C.A.E. (1992), 'We Should Distinguish between Financial Integration and Monetary Unification', In: G. Winckler (ed.), *Tax Harmonization and Financial Liberalization in Europe*, St. Martin's Press, New York, 121–5.

Goodhart, C.A.E. (1993), 'Can We Improve the Structure of Financial Systems?', *European Economic Review*, **37**, 269–91.

Goodhart, C.A.E., P.C. McMahon and Y. Lawan Ngama (1992), 'Does the Forward Premium/Discount Help to Predict the Future Change in the Exchange Rate', *Scottish Journal of Political Economy*, **39** (2), 129–40.

Gordon, R.H. and A.L. Bovenberg (1996), 'Why is Capital so Immobile Internationally? Possible Explanations and Implications for Capital Income Taxation', *American Economic Review*, **86** (5), 1057–94.

Goudswaard, K.P., J. de Haan, L. de Haan and R.M. Oort (1996), 'Schuldmanagement van de staat: Theorie en praktijk', *Financiële en Monetaire Studies*, **15** (1), Wolters–Noordhoff, Groningen.

Granger, C.W.J. and P. Newbold (1974), 'Spurious Regressions in Econometrics', *Journal of Econometrics*, **2**, 111–20.

Grauwe, P. de (1992), *The Economics of Monetary Integration*, Oxford University Press, Oxford.

Grilli, V. (1989), 'Financial Markets and 1992', *Brookings Papers on Economic Activity*, No. 2, 301–24.

Grilli, V., D. Masciandaro and G. Tabellini (1991), 'Political and Monetary Institutions and Public Financial Policies in the Industrial Countries', *Economic Policy*, No. 13, 341–492.

Grilli, V. and G.M. Milesi-Ferretti (1995), 'Economic Effects and Structural Determinants of Capital Controls', *IMF Staff Papers*, **42** (3), 517–51.

Groof, R. de and M. van Tuijl (1993), 'Financial Integration and Fiscal Policy in Interdependent Two-sector Economies with Real and Nominal Wage Rigidity', *European Journal of Political Economy*, **9** (2), 209–32.

Group of Ten (1993), *International Capital Movements and Foreign Exchange Markets*, A Report to the Ministers and Governors by the Group of Deputies, April, Rome.

Gruijters, A.P.D. (1995), *Financiële integratie en monetair beleid, Een empirisch onderzoek naar de mobiliteit van het kapitaalverkeer in de geïndustrialiseerde wereld sinds het einde van het Bretton Woods-stelsel*, NIBE-Publikatiereeks, No. 78, Amsterdam.

Gustavsson, C. (1990), 'Taxation of Personal Interest Income in 18 OECD Countries', *Bank of Finland Discussion Paper*, No. 8, Helsinki.

Haan, J. de, D. Pilat and D.-J. Zelhorst (1991), 'On the Relationship between Dutch and German Interest Rates', *De Economist*, **139** (4), 550–65.

Haan, J. de and C.L.J. Siermann (1994), 'Saving, Investment, and Capital Mobility: A Comment on Leachman', *Open Economies Review*, **5** (1), 5–17.

Haan, J. de and J.-E. Sturm (1994), 'Political and Institutional Determinants of Fiscal Policy in the European Community', *Public Choice*, **80** (1–2), 157–72.

Haan, J. de and G.J. van 't Hag (1995), 'Variation in Central Bank Independence Across Countries: Some Provisional Empirical Evidence', *Public Choice*, **85** (3–4), 335–52.

Hakkio, C.S. and M. Rush (1990), 'Cointegration: How Short is the Long Run?', *Federal Reserve Bank of Kansas City Research Working Paper*, No. 8.

Haldane, A.G. and M. Pradhan (1992a), 'Real Interest Parity, Dynamic Convergence and the European Monetary System', *Bank of England Working Paper Series*, No. 1, London.

Haldane, A.G. and M. Pradhan (1992b), 'Testing Real Interest Parity in the European Monetary System', *Bank of England Working Paper Series*, No. 2, London.

Hall, R.E. (1978), 'Stochastic Implications of the Life Cycle Permanent Income Hypothesis: Theory and Evidence', *Journal of Political Economy*, **86** (6), 971–87.

Hansen, L. and R. Hodrick (1980), 'Forward Exchange Rates as Optimal Predictors of Future Spot Rates: An Econometric Analysis', *Journal of Political Economy*, **88** (5), 829–53.

Harberger, A.C. (1980), 'Vignettes on the World Capital Market', *American Economic Review*, **70** (2), 331–7.

Hendry, D.F., A.R. Pagan and J.D. Sargan (1984), 'Dynamic Specification', In: Z. Griliches and M.D. Intriligator (eds.), *Handbook of Econometrics*, **II**, Elsevier Science Publishers, Amsterdam, 1023–100.

Herring, R.J. and R.E. Litan (1995), *Financial Regulation in the Global Economy*, The Brookings Institution, Washington.

Holmes, M.J. and E.J. Pentecost (1996), 'Changes in the Degree of Financial Integration within the European Community in the 1980s: Some Econometric Tests', *Journal of Economic Studies*, **23** (2), 4–17.

Huizinga, H.P. (1994), 'International Interest Withholding Taxation: Prospects for a Common European Policy', *International Tax and Public Finance*, **1**, 277–91.

Huizinga, H.P. (1996), 'The Incidence of Interest Withholding Taxes: Evidence from the LDC Loan Market', *Journal of Public Economics*, **59** (3), 435–51.

Hull, J. (1993), *Options, Futures, and Other Derivative Securities*, 2nd Edition, Prentice–Hall International Inc., Englewood Cliffs.

Interfisc, loose-leaf.

International Bureau of Fiscal Documentation (1989), *The Taxation of Savings when Capital Moves Freely: The Commission Proposes a Withholding Tax*, April, 121–2.

International Bureau of Fiscal Documentation, The Taxation of Private Investment Income, *Guides to European Taxation*, **3**, Amsterdam.

International Monetary Fund (1985), *International Financial Statistics, Supplement on Exchange Rates*, Washington.

International Monetary Fund (1994), *International Financial Statistics Yearbook 1994*, Washington.

International Monetary Fund (1995), *International Capital Markets, Developments, Prospects, and Policy Issues*, World Economic and Financial Surveys, Washington.

International Monetary Fund, *Exchange Arrangements and Exchange Restrictions*, Annual Report, 1979–1993 Issues, Washington.

International Monetary Fund, *Exchange Restrictions*, Annual Report, 1974–1978 Issues, Washington.

International Monetary Fund, *International Financial Statistics*, Various Issues, Washington.

Italianer, A. (1993), 'EMU and Macroeconomic Environment', In: S.C.W. Eijffinger and J.L. Gerards (eds.) (1993), *European Monetary Integration and the Financial Sector*, NIBE, Amsterdam, 21–45.

Ito, T. (1986), 'Capital Controls and Covered Interest Parity between the Yen and the Dollar', *Economics Studies Quarterly*, **37** (3), 223–41.

Jansen, W.J. (1995), *International Capital Mobility and Asset Demand: Six Empirical Studies*, Tinbergen Institute Research Series, No. 99, Thesis Publishers, Amsterdam.

Jarque, C.M. and A.K. Bera (1980), 'Efficient Tests for Normality, Homoscedasticity and Serial Independence of Regression Residuals', *Economic Letters*, **6**, 255–9.

Johansen, S. (1988), 'Statistical Analysis of Cointegration Vectors', *Journal of Economic Dynamics and Control*, **12** (4), 231–54.

Johansen, S. (1991), 'Estimation and Hypothesis Testing of Cointegration Vectors in Gaussian Vector Autoregressive Models', *Econometrica*, **59** (6), 1551–80.

Johansen, S. and K. Juselius (1990), 'Maximum Likelihood Estimation and Inference on Cointegration With Applications to the Demand for Money', *Oxford Bulletin of Economics and Statistics*, **52** (2), 169–209.

Johnson, D.R. (1992), 'International Interest Rate Linkages and the Exchange Rate Regime', *Journal of International Money and Finance*, **11** (4), 340–65.

Jorion, P. and E. Schwartz (1986), 'Integration vs. Segmentation in the Canadian Stock Market', *Journal of Finance*, **41** (3), 603–16.

Kasman, B. and C. Pigott (1988), 'Interest Rate Divergences among the Major Industrial Nations', *Federal Reserve Bank of New York Quarterly Review*, **13** (3), 28–44.

Kenen, P.B. (1995), 'Capital Controls, the EMS and EMU', *Economic Journal*, **105** (428), 181–92.

King, R.G. and R. Levine (1993), 'Finance and Growth: Schumpeter Might Be Right', *Quarterly Journal of Economics*, **108**, 716–37.

Kneeshaw, J.T. and P. van den Bergh (1985), 'International Interest Rate Relationships, Policy Choices and Constraints', *BIS Economic Papers*, No. 13, Basle.

Knot, K. (1996), *Fiscal Policy and Interest Rates in the European Union*, Edward Elgar, Cheltenham, Glos.

Knot, K. and J. de Haan (1995), 'Interest Rate Differentials and Exchange Rate Policies in Austria, The Netherlands, and Belgium', *Journal of Banking and Finance*, **19** (2), 363–86.

Koedijk, K.G. and D.J.C. Smant (1994), 'The Permanent Income Hypothesis, Business Cycles, and Regime Shifts: Evidence from Eight Countries', *De Economist*, **142** (3), 307–25.

Kollmann, R. (1995), 'Consumptions, Real Exchange Rates and the Structure of International Asset Markets', *Journal of International Money and Finance*, **14** (2), 191–211.

Kool, C.J.M. and K.G. Koedijk (1992), 'Uncovered Interest Parity and Economic Convergence in the EMS: An Evaluation', *Research Memorandum*, No. 92–026, Department of Economics, Limburg University, Maastricht.

Kopits, G. (ed.) (1992), 'Tax Harmonization in the European Community, Policy Issues and Analysis', *IMF Occasional Paper*, No. 94, Washington.

Kouri, P.J. and M.G. Porter, (1974), 'International Capital Flows and Portfolio Equilibrium', *Journal of Political Economy*, **82**, 443–67.

KPMG (1988), *Withholding Taxes on Interest*, July, 2nd Edition, Frankfurt.

Krasker, W.S. (1980), 'The Peso Problem in Testing the Efficiency of Forward Exchange Markets', *Journal of Monetary Economics*, **6**, 269–76.

Kremers, J.J.M., N.R. Ericsson and J.J. Dolado (1992), 'The Power of Cointegration Tests', *Board of Governors of the Federal Reserve System International Finance Discussion Papers*, No. 431, Washington.

Krugman, P.R. (1991), *Geography and Trade*, MIT Press, Cambridge, Mass.

Krugman, P.R. and M. Obstfeld (1994), *International Economics, Theory and Policy*, 3rd Edition, Harper Collins College Publishers, New York.

Lamfalussy, A. (1990), 'International Financial Integration: Policy Implications', *Lloyds Bank Annual Review*, **3**, In: C. Johnson (ed.), *Changing Exchange Rate Systems*, Pinter, London, 15–29.

Leachman, L.L. (1991), 'Saving, Investment, and Capital Mobility among OECD Countries', *Open Economies Review*, **2**, 137–63.

Lemmen, J.J.G. (1996), 'Financial Integration in the European Union: Measurement and Determination', *CentER Dissertation*, No. 22, Thesis Publishers, Amsterdam.

Lemmen, J.J.G. and S.C.W. Eijffinger (1993), 'The Degree of Financial Integration in the European Community', *De Economist*, **141** (2), 189–213.

Lemmen, J.J.G. and S.C.W. Eijffinger (1994), 'The Catching Up of European Money Markets: The Degree vs. the Speed of Integration', *CentER Discussion Paper*, No. 9466, Tilburg University, Tilburg.

Lemmen, J.J.G. and S.C.W. Eijffinger (1995a), 'The Quantity Approach to Financial Integration: The Feldstein–Horioka Criterion Revisited', *Open Economies Review*, **6** (2), 145–65.

Lemmen, J.J.G. and S.C.W. Eijffinger (1995b), 'Financial Market Structure and Institutional Development: A Comparative Study for the European Union', Tilburg University, Tilburg, January.

Lemmen, J.J.G. and S.C.W. Eijffinger (1995c), 'Financial Integration in Europe: Evidence from Euler Equation Tests', *CentER Discussion Paper*, No. 9532, Tilburg University, Tilburg.

Lemmen, J.J.G. and S.C.W. Eijffinger (1995d), 'The Trade-off Between the Degree and the Speed of Financial Integration: Empirical Evidence for the Old and New European Union Countries', In: B. Green (ed.), *Risk Behaviour and Risk Management*, Risk Research Group, School of Business, Stockholm University, Stockholm, 227–41.

Lemmen, J.J.G. and S.C.W. Eijffinger (1996a), 'The Price Approach to Financial Integration: Decomposing European Money Market Interest Rate Differentials', *Kredit und Kapital*, **2**, 189–223.

Lemmen, J.J.G. and S.C.W. Eijffinger (1996b), 'The Fundamental Determinants of Financial Integration in the European Union', *Weltwirtschaftliches Archiv*, **132** (3), 432–56.

Levich, R.M. (1989), 'The Euromarkets after 1992', *Salomon Brothers Center for the Study of Financial Institutions Working Paper Series*, No. 523, New York University, New York.

Lucas, R.E. (1978), 'Asset Prices in an Exchange Economy', *Econometrica*, **46** (6), 1429–45.

Lyon, A.B. and G. Silverstein (1995), 'The Alternative Minimum Tax and the Behavior of Multinational Corporations', In: M. Feldstein, J.R. Hines, Jr. and R. Glenn Hubbard (eds.), *The Effects of Taxation on Multinational Enterprises*, NBER Project Report, University of Chicago Press, Chicago, 153–77.

MacDonald, R. and M.P. Taylor (1992), 'Exchange Rate Economics, A Survey', *IMF Staff Papers*, **39** (1), 1–57.

MacKinnon, J.G. (1991), 'Critical Values for Cointegration Tests', In: R.F. Engle and C.W.J. Granger (eds.), *Long-run Economic Relationships, Readings in Cointegration*, Advanced Texts in Econometrics, Oxford University Press, Oxford, 267–76.

Mankiw, N.G. (1981), 'The Permanent Income Hypothesis and the Real Interest Rate', *Economic Letters*, 7, 307–11.

Mankiw, N.G. (1985), 'Consumer Durables and the Real Interest Rate', *Review of Economics and Statistics*, **67**, 353–62.

Marston, R.C. (1976), 'Interest Arbitrage in the Euro-currency Markets', *European Economic Review*, 7, 1–13.

Marston, R.C. (1995), *International Financial Integration: A Study of Interest Differentials Between the Major Industrial Countries*, Cambridge University Press, Cambridge.

Mathieson, D.J. and L. Rojas-Suarez (1993), 'Liberalization of the Capital Account, Experiences and Issues', *IMF Occasional Paper*, No. 103, Washington.

Mathieson, D.J. and L. Rojas-Suarez (1994), 'Capital Controls and Capital Account Liberalization in Industrial Countries', In: L. Leiderman, and A. Razin (eds.), *Capital Mobility: The Impact on Consumption, Investment and Growth*, Cambridge University Press, Cambridge, 329–47.

McCallum, B.T. (1993), 'Unit Roots in Macroeconomic Time Series: Some Critical Issues', *Federal Reserve Bank of Richmond Economic Quarterly*, **79** (2), 13–43.

McCulloch, J.H. (1975), 'Operational Aspects of the Siegel Paradox', *Quarterly Journal of Economics*, **89** (1), 170–72.

Milesi-Ferretti, G.M. (1995), 'Why Capital Controls?: Theory and Evidence', Paper Presented at the Conference Positive Political Economy: Theory and Evidence, Organized by the CentER for Economic Research of Tilburg University, Tilburg. Forthcoming in: S.C.W. Eijffinger and H.P. Huizinga (eds.), *Positive Political Economy: Theory and Evidence*, Cambridge University Press, Cambridge.

Mishkin, F.S. (1984), 'Are Real Interest Rates Equal Across Countries?, An Empirical Investigation of International Parity Conditions', *Journal of Finance*, **39** (5), 1345–57.

Mishkin, F.S. (1986), 'Comments', In: R.W. Hafer (ed.), *How Open is the U.S. Economy?* Lexington, Mass., 69–74.

Montiel, P.J. (1993), 'Capital Mobility in Developing Countries, Some Measurement Issues and Empirical Estimates', *The World Bank Debt and International Finance Policy Research Working Paper*, No. 1103, Washington.

Mooslechner, P. (1994), 'Institutional Patterns of Financial Systems: Do they make a Difference?', Paper Presented at the *CEEA Conference on Banking and Finance in a Changing World*, 27–29 April 1994, Gerzensee, Austrian Institute of Economic Research, Vienna.

Murphy, R.G. (1984), 'Capital Mobility and the Relationship between Saving and Investment Rates in OECD Countries', *Journal of International Money and Finance*, **3** (3), 327–42.

Neal, L. (1987), 'The Integration and Efficiency of the London and Amsterdam Stock Markets in the Eighteenth Century', *Journal of Economic History*, **57** (1), 97–115.

Neal, L. (1991), 'A Tale of Two Revolutions: International Capital Flows 1789–1819', *Bulletin of Economic Research*, **43** (1), 57–92.

Newey, W.K. and K.D. West (1987), 'A Simple, Positive Semi-definite, Heteroskedasticity and Autocorrelation Consistent Covariance Matrix', *Econometrica*, **55** (3), 703–8.

Nöhrbaß, K.-H. and M. Raab (1990), 'Tax Arbitrage and the German Withholding Tax Experiment', *University of Mannheim Discussion Paper*, No. 419, Mannheim.

Obstfeld, M. (1986), 'Capital Mobility in the World Economy, Theory and Measurement', In: K. Brunner and A. Meltzer (eds.), *The National Bureau Method, International Capital Mobility and Other Essays*, Carnegie-Rochester Conference Series on Public Policy, **24**, 55–104.

Obstfeld, M. (1989), 'How Integrated are World Capital Markets? Some New Tests', In: G. Calvo, R. Findlay, P. Kouri and J. Braga de Macedo (eds.), *Debt, Stabilization and Development*, Basil Blackwell, Oxford, 134–59.

Obstfeld, M. (1994a), 'International Capital Mobility in the 1990s', *CEPR Discussion Paper*, No. 902, London.

Obstfeld, M. (1994b), 'Are Industrial Country Consumption Risks Globally Diversified?', In: L. Leiderman and A. Razin (eds.), *Capital Mobility, The Impact on Consumption, Investment and Growth*, Cambridge University Press, Cambridge, 13–43.

OECD (1980), *Controls on International Capital Movements, Experiences with Controls on International Portfolio Operations in Shares and Bonds*, Paris.

OECD (1990a), *Code of liberalization of Capital Movements*, Paris.

OECD (1990b), *Liberalization of Capital Movements and Financial Services in the OECD Area*, Paris.

OECD (1990c), *Methodological Supplement, Part I, Interest Rates on Domestic and International Markets*, Paris.

OECD (1992), *Banks under Stress*, Paris.

OECD (1994a), *Economic Outlook*, No. 55, Statistics on Microcomputer Diskettes, Content Documentation, Paris.

OECD (1994b), *Economic Outlook*, No. 55, Paris.

OECD (1995a), *Economic Outlook*, No. 57, Paris.

OECD (1995b), *National Accounts of OECD Countries, Main Aggregates 1960–1993*, **I**, Paris.

OECD (1995c), *Quarterly National Accounts*, No. 1, Paris.

OECD (1996), *International Capital Markets Statistics 1950–1995*, Paris.

OECD, *Financial Accounts of OECD Countries*, Part II of OECD Financial Statistics Monthly, Data Diskettes, Paris.

OECD, *Interest Rates on International and Domestic Markets*, Historical issue, 1960–1989, Part I of OECD Financial Statistics Monthly, Data Diskettes, Paris and Part I of OECD Financial Statistics Monthly, Various Issues, 1990–1993, Paris.

OECD, *Main Economic Indicators*, Various Issues, Paris.

Officer, L.H. and T.D. Willett (1970), 'The Covered Arbitrage Schedule: A Critical Survey of Recent Developments', *Journal of Money, Credit and Banking*, **2**, 244–55.

Otani, I. and S. Tiwari (1981), 'Capital Controls and Interest Rate Parity: The Japanese Experience, 1978–1981', *IMF Staff Papers*, **28** (4), 793–815.

Penati, A. and M. Dooley (1983), 'Current Account Imbalances and Capital Formation in Industrial Countries, 1949–81', *IMF Staff Papers*, **31**, 1–24.

Penn World Table, *Mark 6*, Data Diskette.

Pigott, C. (1993), 'International Interest Rate Convergence: A Survey of the Issues and Evidence', *Federal Reserve Bank of New York Quarterly Review*, **18** (4), 24–37.

Popper, H. (1993), 'Long-term Covered Interest Parity: Evidence from Currency Swaps', *Journal of International Money and Finance*, **12** (4), 439–48.

Poterba, J.M. (1986), 'Explaining the Yield Spread between Taxable and Tax–exempt Bonds: The Role of Expected Tax Policy', In: H.S. Rosen (ed.), *Studies in State and Local Public Finance*, University of Chicago Press, Chicago, 5–49.

Reinhart, V. and K. Weiller (1987), 'Increasing Capital Mobility: Evidence from Short- and Long-term Markets', In: Federal Reserve Bank of New York, *Research Papers on International Integration of Financial Markets and U.S. Monetary Policy*, New York, December, 71–117.

Rogoff, K. (1985), 'Can Exchange Rate Predictability Be Achieved Without Monetary Convergence? Evidence from the EMS', *European Economic Review*, **28**, 93–115.

Sachs, J.D. (1981), 'The Current Account and Macroeconomic Adjustment in the 1970s', *Brookings Papers on Economic Activity*, No. 12, 201–68.

Santillán, J. (1991), 'The Adequacy and Allocation of World Savings', *Commission of the European Communities Economic Papers*, No. 88, Brussels.

Shepherd, W.F. (1994), *International Financial Integration: History, Theory and Applications in OECD Countries*, Avebury, Aldershot.

Siegel, J.J. (1972), 'Risk, Interest Rates and the Forward Exchange', *Quarterly Journal of Economics*, **86** (2), 303–9.

Siermann, C.L.J. (1996), *Politics, Institutions and the Economic Performance of Nations*, Rijksuniversiteit Groningen, Groningen.

Sijben, J.J. (1994), 'Financial Fragility and Macroeconomic Performance: An Overview', In: D.E. Fair and R.J. Raymond (eds.), *The Competitiveness of Financial Institutions and Centres in Europe*, Financial and Monetary Policy Studies, No. 28, SUERF, Kluwer Academic Publishers, Dordrecht, 353–402.

Sinn, S. (1992), 'Saving-Investment Correlations and Capital Mobility: On the Evidence from Annual Data', *Economic Journal*, **102** (414), 1162–70.

Smithson, C.W., C.W. Smith and D.S. Wilford (1995), *Managing Financial Risk, A Guide to Derivative Products, Financial Engineering, and Value Maximization*, Richard D. Irwin Inc., Burr Ridge.

Stulz, R.M. (1986), 'Capital Mobility in the World Economy: Theory and Measurement, A Comment', In: K. Brunner and A. Meltzer (eds.), 'The National Bureau Method, International Capital Mobility and Other Essays', *Carnegie-Rochester Conference Series on Public Policy*, **24**, 105–14.

Summers, L.H. (1988), 'Tax Policy and International Competitiveness', In: J.A. Frenkel (ed.), *International Aspects of Fiscal Policies*, University of Chicago Press, Chicago, 350–80.

Summers, R. and A. Heston (1991), 'The Penn World Table (Mark 5): An Expanded Set of International Comparisons, 1950–1988', *Quarterly Journal of Economics*, **106** (2), 327–68.

Taylor, M.P. (1987), 'Covered Interest Parity: A High-frequency, High-quality Data Study', *Economica*, **54**, 439–53.

Taylor, M.P. (1989), 'Covered Interest Arbitrage and Market Turbulence', *Economic Journal*, **99**, 376–91.

Tease, W., A. Dean, J. Elsmekov and P. Hoeller (1991), 'Real Interest Rate Trends, The Influence of Saving, Investment and Other Factors', *OECD Economic Studies*, No. 17, 107–44.

Tesar, L.L. (1991), 'Savings, Investment and International Capital Flows', *Journal of International Economics*, **31** (1/2), 55–78.

Tesar, L.L. and I.M. Werner (1992), 'Home Bias and the Globalization of Security Markets', *NBER Working Paper*, No. 4218, Cambridge.

Tobin, J. (1983), 'Comments on Domestic Savings and International Capital Movements in the Long Run and the Short Run', *European Economic Review*, **21**, 153–6.

Ubide, A.J. (1995), 'Is there Consumption Risk Sharing in the European Union?', *European University Institute Working Paper*, No. 37, Florence.

Ungerer, H. (1990), 'The EMS 1979–1990, Policies, Evolution, Outlook', *Konjunkturpolitik*, **36** (6), 329–62.

Vikøren, B. (1994), 'Interest Rate Differential, Exchange Rate Expectations and Capital Mobility: Norwegian Evidence', *Norges Bank Skrifserie*, No. 21, Oslo.

Westphal, U. (1983), 'Comments on Domestic Savings and International Capital Movements in the Long Run and the Short Run', *European Economic Review*, **21**, 153–6.

Wheatley, S. (1988), 'Some Tests of International Equity Market Integration', *Journal of Financial Economics*, **21**, 177–212.

White, H. (1980), 'A Heteroscedasticity-consistent Covariance Matrix and a Direct Test for Heteroscedasticity', *Econometrica*, **48** (4), 817–38.

White Paper (1985), *Completing the Internal Market*, White Paper from the Commission to the European Council, Commission of the European Communities, June.

Wong, D.Y. (1990), 'What Do Saving-Investment Relations Tell Us About Capital Mobility?', *Journal of International Money and Finance*, **9** (1), 60–74.

Wyplosz, C. (1988), 'Capital Flow Liberalization and the EMS: A French Perspective', In: Commission of the European Communities, 'Creation of a European Financial Area, Liberalization of Capital Movements and Financial Integration in the Community', *European Economy*, No. 36, 85–114.

# Index